*PHILIPPINES*
ARRIVAL #A132
NINOY AQUINO INT'L AIRPORT

FEB 17 2001

A132Flight Status/Stay

DEPARTMENT OF IMMIGRATION
PERMITTED TO ENTER
AUSTRALIA.
24 APR 1996
on
For stay of 12
SYDNEY AIRPORT 54

IMMIGRATION DIVISION BANGKOK THAILAND
A 72
DEPARTED
- 9 FEB 1998
SIGNED

T R A V E L E R ' S
# PHILIPPINES
C O M P A N I O N

IMMIGRATION & ETHNIC AFFAIRS
.........Person
30 OCT 1999
DEPARTED
AUSTRALIA
SYDNEY 32

上陸許可
ADMITTED
15. FEB. 1996
4
Status: 4-1-
Duration: 90 days
NARITA(N)
Immigration Inspector

U.S. IMMIGRATION
160-LOS C-4125

MAY 23 1998

ADMITTED
UNTIL _____ (CLASS)

ADMITTED
28 OCT. 1988
Status: 4-1-16
Duration (80 day
Port: HANEDA
Signature

USED
Narita Air Port

HONG KONG
(1038)
- 7 JUN 1997
IMMIGRATION
OFFICER

**The 2001–2002 Traveler's Companions**
ARGENTINA • AUSTRALIA • BALI • CALIFORNIA • CANADA •
CHILE • CHINA • COSTA RICA • CUBA • EASTERN CANADA • ECUADOR •
FLORIDA • HAWAII • HONG KONG • INDIA • INDONESIA • JAPAN • KENYA •
MALAYSIA & SINGAPORE • MEDITERRANEAN FRANCE • MEXICO • NEPAL •
NEW ENGLAND • NEW ZEALAND • PERU • PHILIPPINES • PORTUGAL • RUSSIA •
SOUTH AFRICA • SOUTHERN ENGLAND • SPAIN • THAILAND • TURKEY •
VENEZUELA • VIETNAM, LAOS AND CAMBODIA • WESTERN CANADA

**Traveler's PHILIPPINES Companion**

First published 1998
Second Edition 2001
The Globe Pequot Press
246 Goose Lane, PO Box 480
Guilford, CT 06437 USA
www.globe-pequot.com

© 2001 by The Globe Pequot Press, Guilford, CT, USA

**ISBN: 0-7627-0952-9**

Distributed in the European Union by
World Leisure Marketing Ltd, Unit 11
Newmarket Court, Newmarket Drive,
Derby, DE24 8NW, United Kingdom
www.map-guides.com

Created, edited and produced by
Allan Amsel Publishing, 53, rue Beaudouin
27700 Les Andelys, France.
E-mail: AAmsel@aol.com
Editor in Chief: Allan Amsel
Editor: Samantha Wauchope
Picture editor and book designer: Roberto Rossi
Original design concept: Hon Bing-wah

Printed by Samhwa Printing Co. Ltd., Seoul, South Korea

# TRAVELER'S PHILIPPINES COMPANION

by Kirsten Ellis

Photographed by Nik Wheeler and Robert Holmes

Second Edition

The Globe Pequot Press

GUILFORD
CONNECTICUT

# Contents

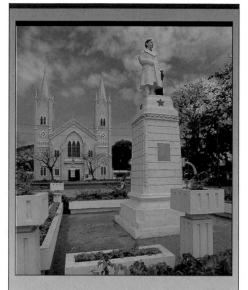

# TRAVELER'S
# PHILIPPINES
# COMPANION

## LEGEND

### Populations

◉ **MANILA**    Capital

○ Obando    Cities

○ Umiray    Towns

| 0 | 40 | 80 | 120 | 160 | 200 km |
|---|---|---|---|---|---|
| 0 | 30 | 60 | 90 | | 120 miles |

### Transportation

══[66]══    Major Highways

————    Main Routes

————    Minor Roads

▬ ▬ ▬    Railways

### Physical Features

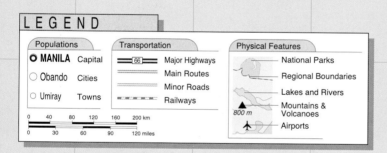

————    National Parks

————    Regional Boundaries

————    Lakes and Rivers

▲   Mountains &
800 m   Volcanoes

✈    Airports

N

CHINA

TAIWAN

HONG KONG

LAOS

VIETNAM

**PHILIPPINES**

BRUNEI

SINGAPORE   MALAYSIA
(BORNEO)

Ra
Mou
Matalin

B
I
Balaba
Island

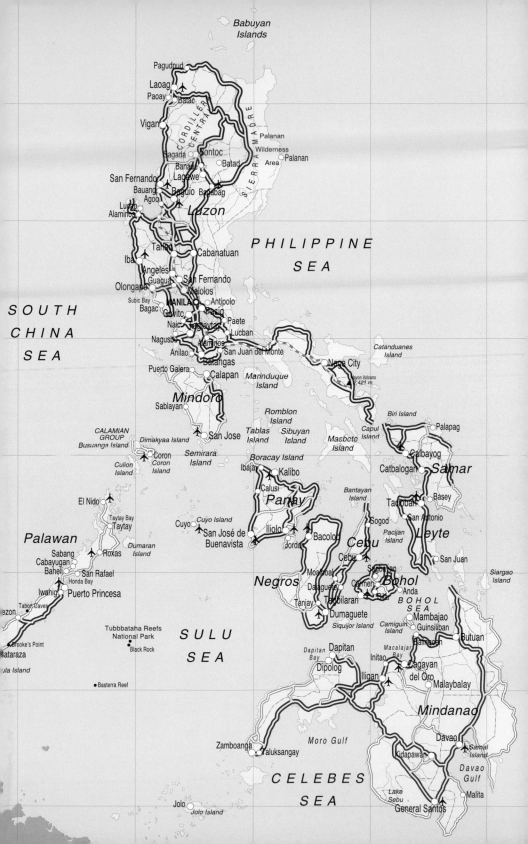

# TOP SPOTS

## Escape to El Nido

*EL NIDO EMBRACES SIMPLICITY.* Fishermen, like clockwork, make their daily trolls at sunrise, and the beaches are loitered with fishing lines and nets instead of bikinis and Speedos. It's a place where life is lived by the tides, and fresh tuna and lobster are as available as a hot dog on a Manhattan street corner.

*Time* essayist and traveler Pico Iyer once noted that "We flee certain resorts not just because they are touristed but more because they have begun to see themselves through tourists' eyes, to amend themselves to tourists' needs, to carry themselves in capital letters... they have simplified themselves into their sense of what a foreigner wants." There is little in El Nido that feels "amended." Even the luxury resorts

offer a simplicity — a seclusion and back-to-the earth feel that you won't find anywhere else. The traveler is here on Nature's terms — El Nido's terms — not the other way around.

Perched on the edge of the Bacuit archipelago marine reserve, El Nido — with its hidden lagoons enveloped by towering limestone formations, its sun-drenched beaches, vibrant reefs, and smiling residents — entices travelers with its isolation and sense of timelessness.

Yes, the locals make a good living from tourist revenue. But unlike other beach paradise destinations throughout Southeast Asia, the locals maintain a calm and relaxed attitude to their foreign guests. They smile as you pass by, are eager to help, but continue their daily rituals despite the onslaught of visitors.

Tourism has in fact increased over the last few years, but still remains relatively low compared to other beach resorts like Boracay or Cebu. Most come to the shores of El Nido to indulge in the many exotic resorts on private islands that punctuate the azure waters off its coast. Resorts including Miniloc, Malapacao, and the newer Lagen Island Resort are an ecotourism Eden, keeping in tune with the harmonious natural balance of El Nido and Palawan in general.

The reefs framing most of the islands in the area are excellent for divers and snorkelers of all skill levels. Most of the

OPPOSITE: The crystal-clear waters of El Nido give the illusion a *bancas* is floating on air. ABOVE: Local kids learn to swim almost as soon as they can walk.

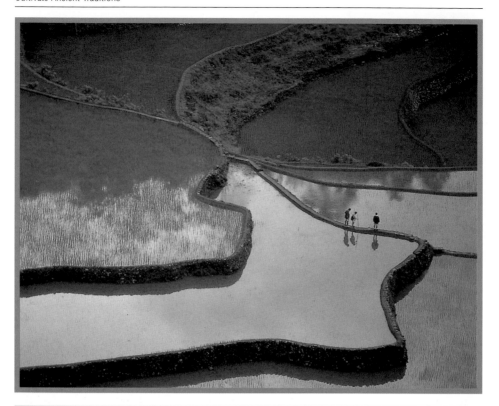

resorts here cater to divers, offering dive packages, and well-equipped diving facilities. Prices are a bit higher at the resorts than in El Nido town, however, where there are a handful of dive shops to choose from. For around US$25 you can take in two dives and they provide the equipment. More ambitious divers can opt for an excursion to the Philippines' most famed diving locale, Tubbataha Reefs National Marine Park, in the Sulu Sea east of Palawan. Most of the diving outfits can also arrange island hopping tours, which include lunch on a deserted isle along the way. It is the best way to spend an afternoon, and afterward either catch the sunset from your island resort, or head to the Blue Karrot Bar in El Nido town.

## Cultivate Ancient Traditions

*A PATCHWORK OF VARIEGATED COLORS AND GLITTERING POOLS THREADS ACROSS THE ACCORDION-LIKE LANDSCAPE.* Carved by hand out of the rugged mountainsides, dammed with stone and clay, Banaue's rice terraces rise like stairways to the sky.

Nowhere else in the world is rice cultivated on such a grand scale. Etched into the mountainsides of Northern Luzon up to 2,000 years ago, Banaue's terraces are as monumental as China's Great Wall or Egypt's Pyramids. They are a sight to behold, and a testament to the determination of the Ifugao tribespeople (literally, "eaters of rice"). The terraces represent a singular feat of engineering — an ingenious system of irrigation that holds water in the fields even during the dry season, achieved by people equipped only with primitive tools and undying dedication.

Although Banaue's pea-green rice terraces are still tended by descendants of the head-hunting Ifugao tribe who created them, there is some fear that, as more and more young Ifugao are lured away to look for jobs in nearby towns or cities, the terraces will be left untilled to dry out and crumble away. Another concern is increasing erosion, caused by

illegal logging of the surrounding forest. Worry that this might lead to irreversible damage has resulted in government efforts to protect the terraces, which have been declared a national park reserve.

With backpack in tow and plenty of water, a hike across the tiered and contoured hills to the mountain village of Batad is rewarded with breathtaking views of the terraces. Along the way, Cambulo is a relatively untouched Ilfugao village nestled amidst the rice terraces, with traditional thatched huts surrounded by small, enclosed vegetable patches. A jeepney can drop hikers at the trailhead, 12 km (seven miles) from Banaue. From there the walk is a strenuous three hours uphill, followed by a less-steep descent down about 2,000 steps that criss-cross the side of the mountain. Local children at the halfway point sell much-needed cool drinks to exhausted hikers. Farmers drag their huge caribou along the trail, often making progress slow to an inch-by-inch crawl for those not brave enough to overtake the hook-in-nostril bucking beast. Hikers can choose to stay overnight at the Hillside Inn in Batad, which overlooks the village, or trek back the way they came.

## Peek Into Vigan's Colonial Past

*LIKE GHOSTS OF THE DEPARTED SPANIARDS, GRAND BALUSTRADED HOUSES, ELEGANT PLAZAS AND STALWART CHURCHES ARE SCATTERED THROUGHOUT THE PHILIPPINE ARCHIPELAGO.* The historic city of Cebu and the old walled city of Intramuros in Manila have some beautiful examples, but nowhere is evidence of the nation's colonial past as strong as in Vigan.

The best-preserved Spanish town in the Philippines, Vigan is practically a seventeenth-century time capsule — a shrine to the era when Spanish

TOP: These Banaue rice terraces were made by hand over 2,000 years ago. BOTTOM: An old-fashioned *calesa* trots down a street in Vigan.

Although well known to Filipinos, Vigan is still relatively undiscovered by foreign tourists. Age-old street lamps light the path for *calesas*, horse-drawn carriages, which carry locals and tourists through the historical streets.

When the Spanish arrived in 1572, Vigan had already been an international maritime port for centuries. The Spanish made it the regional seat of political and religious administration, and for 300 years the galleon trade connecting Vigan to Europe via Acapulco made it the most prosperous city north of Manila. Permeated with languid charm, while at first glance Vigan's ancestral homes look Spanish, at closer inspection the infusion of different influences is obvious: Chinese, Filipino, and Mexican. Extending down the narrow avenues in long, solid rows, these mansions dominate your field of vision... and send you back in time.

To ensure Vigan's legacy, UNESCO has included it on its World Heritage List and money has been allocated for the redevelopment of the Heritage Village — the old town center.

conquistadors, merchants and friars roamed its cobblestone streets. Unlike Intramuros, this small city on Luzon's northwest coast was relatively unscathed by World War II, and is crammed with pleasantly dissolute antiquity. Its neat square plazas and rows of paint-peeling houses with their labyrinths of tiled courtyards are strongly reminiscent of faraway places — San Miguel de Allende in Mexico, perhaps, or Antigua in Guatemala.

Spanish conquistador Juan de Salcedo had his *encomienda* here, patterned after Intramuros, the city created by Salcedo's grandfather. Vigan's narrow streets are lined with old Castilan houses and baroque churches that have stood the ravages of time and modernization.

## A Hanging Tribute

*TUCKED AWAY AMONG OPALESCENT RICE TERRACES AND PATCHES OF FOREST HIGH IN THE CENTRAL CORDILLERAS OF NORTHERN LUZON,* Sagada's mountain air is fresh and cool, the villagers are friendly and laid-back, and coffins hang precariously along the honeycomb of steep cave-pocked limestone cliffs framing the town.

The Igorot people make up most of Sagada's population, a group including the Apayo, Benguet, Bontoc, Ifugao, Kalinga, and Tingguian tribespeople. According to Igorot tribal custom, coffins of the deceased are attached to pegs halfway down a cliff or positioned in the mouths of cliffside caves, in the belief that this will allow their spirits to roam free. Their unusual obsequial customs date back centuries and continued until about two decades ago. Guides can show you the way to the

Hanging Coffins View Point, where coffins can be seen hanging like bats against a sheltered section of limestone rock. The original inscription on the surface of the most recent addition is clearly visible from the ground below. The coffin contains the remains of a tribal woman whose great-nephew is one of today's Sagada villagers. Finding smaller groups of coffins on your own can be a fascinating experience in itself.

Probably the most dramatic cave open to tourists is the beautiful Matangkib Cave, with coffins up to 600 years old. Most of the coffins are weathered and aged, adding to their mystique. The bodies are still intact in many of the cave's coffins, and the old, thin wooden coffin lids are not bolted on — sadly, though, many of the skulls have been removed, apparently the work of decades of tourists wanting to claim souvenirs.

The underbelly of Sagada is as amazing as its hanging relics. Below the village streets, a network of limestone caves filters rainwater through to the water-hungry rice terraces. Like the rocky cliff tops up above, these caves once served as final resting places for the local Igorots in pre-Christian Sagada.

The deceased were enclosed in pine coffins and placed in the fetal position — a simulation of the maternal womb.

Sumaging (Big Cave) is considered the most exciting for adventure spelunking — a dizzying maze of winding paths, water pools, narrow passages and huge limestone formations. It's a 40-minute walk from Sagada on the Suyo Road; a dirt path that winds its way through cozy villages and above beautiful rice terraces and rivers. Curious limestone sculptures inside the cave have been given creative names like Pig Pen, Giant's Food, Pregnant Woman, Romeo and Juliette, and King's Curtains.

Entering the cave is slippery business, partly due to the limestone, but also from the droppings of the squealing bats overhead. Be prepared to get grimy. The second part of the exploration is done barefoot, mostly over sandpaper-like calcium formations. Spelunkers have the chance to wash the dung off their clothes in the cave's ponds and brooks. Toward the end, you navigate a confined, narrow

OPPOSITE TOP: The Ifugao tribespeople, Banaue, are known for their brilliant tribal wear. BOTTOM: Tribal ornament from Bukidnon, Mindanao. ABOVE: The cliffside burial site of the Igorot tribespeople at Sagada.

space appropriately called "the tunnel," using a rope and lots of upper body strength. The claustrophobic should simply take a deep breath; the tunnel doesn't last longer than two minutes or so, and then you're back in the huge dome-like space.

## An Underwater Wonderland

*FLOATING ALONG THE CORAL WALL IN THE DEEP BLUE OCEAN,* the only sound is the rhythmic hissing of packaged air being sucked into my compressed lungs and then expelled — a derby of bubbles racing to the surface, tickling my face on their way. Pulled by the current as if on some underwater moving sidewalk, there is a sense of weightlessness. I'm complete, self-contained, underwater and breathing — a Scuba-Doo of sorts — snooping around each mushroom of coral for signs of colorful life.

And off the islands of the Philippines, there is much to snoop around. Practically every island in the archipelago is framed by coral reefs teeming with diverse marine life. From batfish to puffer fish, angel fish, lion fish, moray eels, turtles, and yes, even sharks — they are all represented in underwater Philippines. Fish and coral, though, aren't the only attractions beneath the water. Coron, a small island northeast of Palawan, is home to dozens of Japanese shipwrecks. They are in surprisingly good condition and are not very deep.

The king of all dives is Tubbataha Reefs, found in the Sulu Sea, 322 km (200 miles) off the east coast of Palawan, and reached by live-aboard boat only. Here, a wall dive plunges hundreds of feet. The suspense of what might pass by — from circling hammerheads to whalesharks — always makes the dive exciting. But if the commitment of a live-aboard boat and a week at sea is too much for your time or skill level, choose the calm waters off Boracay. Even closer to Manila, Puerto Galera on the island of Mindoro is a favorite diving and beach getaway with urban dwellers from Manila and expatriates.

enormous mushroom rising off a sea bottom rich in hard and soft corals, is praised by divers as one of the best sites in Southeast Asia.

Much of the coral reefs have been destroyed and badly injured. Measures to prevent such destructive behavior as continued dynamite and cyanide fishing by local fisherman have been introduced, and some of the sites, particularly off the coast of Palawan, are on their way toward rejuvenation. Another culprit has been Mother Nature. El Nina's unusually warm temperatures have increased the temperature of the water, resulting in coral bleaching.

## Trek a Volcano

*RED-HOT OOZE DEEP WITHIN THE MOUNTAIN SENDS SMOKE SIGNALS SEEPING OUT OF THE CRACKS AND CREVICES ON ITS SURFACE.* Trekking towards the cone-shaped peak we try to ignore the volcano's furious potential.

The beaches of the Philippines get most of the attention from visitors, but mountaineering is becoming an increasingly popular pursuit, particularly scaling the country's many active volcanoes and mountain peaks. You don't have to go far from the country's capital either. On Luzon, only a two-hour drive from Manila, Mount Pinatubo, the volcano that erupted in the early 1990s, is a popular trak. The hike isn't very difficult, but the devastation left after it blew its top is quite a sight to behold. The lahar fields are expansive and the ethereal lunar-like landscape is spotted with quicksand, smoking cracks, and sulfuric ravines. The 1,780-m-high (5,840-foot) volcano is said to be stirring for another eruption, probably within the next 10 years. Tours are arranged in Angeles or in Manila and can be done in a day, or you can choose to stay overnight, camping at the crater rim.

Another volcano within a day's reach of Manila is Taal Volcano — the

An introductory dive is an unforgettable experience. Both PADI and NAUI, globally recognized diving organizations, are present throughout the Philippines and take the uninitiated on Discovery Dives —'where no certification is needed. Test the waters and see if scuba is something you like. Dive Centers come a dime a dozen here and provide all equipment. Standard fees for the usual three- to five-day certification program are cheaper than anywhere in the West — and you won't train in any pool. It's probably one of the best places for certification. You'll find your training quite challenging, as trigger fish and moray eels come peeking at you while you try to perfect your underwater signals.

Once you have achieved an Open Water Certification, test your skill and work toward an Advanced Open Water Certification. Moalboal, a sleepy fishing village on the southwest coast of Cebu is a popular place for divers from all over the world to rest their hats and invest the time toward an advanced course. Moalboal's Pescador Island, with its

*TOP SPOTS*

Looking across Lake Taal from Tagaytay Ridge.

volcano within a lake within a volcano! Lake Taal is an enormous and ancient crater lake an hour's drive south of Manila, and little Taal Volcano is a smaller volcanic cone that has more recently appeared in the center of the lake: there's a small lake within its crater too. Trekkers can walk along the rim of Lake Taal at Tagaytay Ridge, and take a dip after a hot hike up the slopes. An hour's drive further, at 2,177 m (7,142 feet), Mount Banahaw in Laguna can be difficult if trekking isn't something you are used to. But it is well worth the effort. Much folklore and legend surround the mountain.

Further south, near Legazpi in South Luzon, is the quintessential volcano — perfectly cone-shaped, but formidable. When it's not erupting, Mayon Volcano (2,462 m, or 8,060 feet) is one of the favorites with seasoned volcano climbers. The volcano demonstrated its temper as recently as March 2000. Sometimes the mountain is off-limits for climbing due to activity within the volcano, so it's best to check with the Department of Tourism office in Legazpi on conditions, as well as to arrange guides and porters for the climb. Not far from Mayon, Mount

Bulusan (1,551 m, or 5,079 feet) is another popular active volcano trek; partly because of the beautiful and varied surrounding landscape, including Lake Bulusan. The summit of Mount Bulusan can be reached in a day.

There are several mountains in Mindanao worthy of trekking, including Mount Kitanglad and Mount Hibok-Hibok, but none so much as Mount Apo in Davao, the country's highest peak. The diversity of flora and fauna along the mountain's many trails makes this trek quite extraordinary. Whether you prefer the shade of a forest or the refreshing splash of waterfalls, bird-watching or insect-spotting, you will find Mount Apo one of the more interesting and challenging climbs.

If trekking the country's many mountain peaks is on the agenda, standard equipment should include sturdy hiking books, water bottle, sunglasses, sunscreen, insect repellent, and a waterproof sandal like Tevas. Temperatures can be quite deceptive. At lower elevations the heat can be stifling, but as you climb, temperatures can decrease to an almost uncomfortable chill. A fleece or warm sweater is a must.

# Visit "The Rock"

*"I SHALL RETURN" WERE THE FAMOUS WORDS UTTERED BY GENERAL DOUGLAS MACARTHUR* at Lorcha Dock ruins on Corregidor Island before he boarded a boat for Australia in April 1942.

The Americans had utilized the strategic importance of this small island at the mouth of Manila Bay by building a full-scale fortification on Corregidor and equipping it with long-range and tractor-drawn guns, minefields and anti-aircraft guns. In January 1942, as the Japanese forces overwhelmed the combined American and Filipino troops in much of Luzon, MacArthur declared Manila an "Open City" to protect it from further bombardment and, with a contingent of troops, retreated to set up his headquarters at Corregidor, with the majority of his forces dispatched to the nearby Bataan Peninsula. MacArthur was accompanied by his family, Philippine President Manuel Quezon and United States High Commissioner Francis Sayle.

For those into World War II relics and memorabilia, a trip to Corregidor, the largest of the five islands lying across the entrance to Manila Bay, is definitely in order. Corregidor — or "The Rock" — was the scene of some of the most grueling and bloody battles ever fought against the Japanese, and the island is braced and buffeted by history. As you wander about, exploring the extant tunnels and fortifications and examining documentary footage in the island's museum, you gain a strong sense of each stage of the unfolding drama.

A highlight of a visit is the light-and-sound show in the Malinta Tunnel. Completed in 1922, the tunnel, which is almost a kilometer long and has side tunnels adding up to nearly another four kilometers (two and a half miles), operated during the World War II as an arsenal, underground hospital and bomb-proof headquarters for MacArthur; it also served as home to the resistance forces and the seat of the Philippine Government under President Quezon. Visitors walk through the dark

Corregidor Island — OPPOSITE: Beating the heat, a trolley bus ride takes visitors on a guided tour around the island's main sites. ABOVE: Heavy artillery still stands sentinel, a legacy of the days when General MacArthur made a last stand against the Japanese.

tunnel accompanied by the sounds of bombs exploding and gunfire; with realistic figurines, recreated rooms and World War II photographs adding to the atmosphere.

Toward the west end of the island sit the huge cannons of Battery Hearn and Battery Way, and visitors can wander through the nearby ruins of Topside Barracks. The island's name is derived from *corregir*, meaning *to correct* or *to check*, as it served as a checkpoint for vessels entering Manila Bay during the Spanish occupation. Bonfires were lit here to announce homecoming galleons. An interesting Spanish Museum opened on the island in November 2000, but the only testament to the Spanish presence is Corregidor's lighthouse, although even this had to be rebuilt after being destroyed in World War II.

Sun Cruises ( (2) 831-8140 runs daily Corregidor ferry trips from Manila. It is also possible to stay overnight on the island — in a hotel with a dramatic sea view — a tranquil alternative to Manila.

Roughly the size of Manhattan, for more than three months MacArthur commanded the 76,000 malaria-plagued American and Filipino forces on Corregidor Island and the Bataan Peninsula from this island base, defending their ever-shrinking territory against the numerically superior Japanese invasion. Finally, Roosevelt ordered MacArthur off the Philippines,

marking the end of wartime hostilities in the Philippines and the beginning of its Japanese occupation. Until MacArthur fulfilled his promise, recapturing The Rock, after an 11-day battle, in January 1945. (Manila was liberated a month later.)

## Lazing in Paradise

*BELOVED BY OLD ASIA HANDS, BORACAY IS ONE OF THE ARCHIPELAGO'S LOVELIEST BEACH SANCTUARIES.* Its stretch of white sugar-like sand has been called the most beautiful beach in the world. Take to the hills on a motor scooter, jet-ski along the calm surf, dive the reefs, or just put your hat on your head and prop yourself up against a palm tree with a Kerouac book — priorities tend to shift in Boracay.

The island's festive mood, topped with quintessential island scenes — talcum powder-white beaches, crystal-clear, warm shallow waters, brilliant sunsets, swaying palm trees, tropical sunshine, peerless blue skies and

colorful fruits and flowers, make it one of the most visited and loved island getaways in the Philippines. Unlike its rugged neighbor Palawan, getting around is easy — simply comb the two-mile stretch of White Beach, backed by a string of resorts, restaurants, bars, and shops. Vendors walk the beach selling shells, jewelry, fruit, and sunglasses, or giving evening massages that will have you feeling better than the Tin Man after a lube job.

Tourists discovered the tiny island after it became a backpacker's Mecca in the late 1970s. In those days, travelers slept on its legendary soft white sands or rented out tiny native huts. There were no hotels, electricity, roads, discos or hot water. Today Boracay's resorts vary from native nipa-style cottages with cold water and fan to stylishly hip art-deco rooms with luxurious amenities. Motorized tricycles zip tourists to and fro along the central White Beach, lined with a buzzing, active path of shops, restaurants and open-air bars where you're never too far

from a refreshing mango shake. White Beach is the widest, longest and most sheltered beach on the island, with safe swimming in clear, calm water of the Sulu Sea. At the northern tip, Yapak and Puka beaches are both beautiful, with sheltered sandy coves and inviting water with a deep ocean floor, good for scuba diving and snorkeling close to shore. At the opposite end of the island, on the northwest, are the more secluded coves of Diniwid, Balinghai and Punta Bunga.

The island is active, festive, yet feels foreign enough to give it that deserted isle seclusion. From the time we step off the *banca* and wade through the shallows to the beach — luggage in tow and dungarees rolled up to their knees — civilization as we know it is peeled away layer by layer.

That is the magic of this place.

OPPOSITE: Outrigged *bancas* are the usual form of sea transport around the islands. ABOVE: Boracay beaches are usually voted the best in the archipelago.

# YOUR CHOICE

## The Great Outdoors

Adventure can be found in the Philippines anywhere from 130 m (420 feet) below sea level to 2,954 m (9,691 feet) above. Take your pick: explore Technicolor coral reefs, follow paved hiking trails through scenic rainforests in its national parks, or go where the air is thin — by climbing the country's high peaks and volcanoes. Whatever appeals, be assured that, away from the cities or beaches, the Philippines is more likely to suit rugged individualists than those who expect brochure travel — and this is one of its greatest attractions.

The Philippine national boundary extends 1,900 km (1,178 miles) from north to south; from east to west it stretches 1,110 km (688 miles). Three main islands or island groups — the Luzon group (which includes Palawan and Mindanao), the Visayas, and Mindanao — divide the country into north, central, and southern regions respectively. Within these three main island groups there are more than 15 national parks, and with 7,107 islands (give or take a few in high and low tides) you'll never be too far from the beach or ocean.

**TREKKING AND MOUNTAINEERING**
Visitors to the many mountainous and wilderness regions of the Philippines will quickly find themselves enamored of the land's untamed beauty. High mountains, active volcanoes, green and lush valleys — with its variety of high terrain, low-lying jungles, swamps and rivers, and indigenous flora and fauna there is much to instill a wondrous sense of discovery.

It is important to be aware that — like its coral reefs — the nation's forests are endangered. Before 1900, most of the land in the Philippines was densely forested. A mere century later, half of this forest is gone. Of the remaining forest, around 33 percent has genuine forest cover. As the forests disappear, the country's exceptionally rich wildlife is increasingly threatened. Many of its tens

OPPOSITE: Remote and beautiful, El Nido attracts water-sports enthusiasts. ABOVE: From dawn to dusk the mood, and the hue, of the extraordinary Chocolate Hills of Bohol changes.

of thousands of species of flora and fauna are found nowhere else — and their habitat is disappearing rapidly. Nevertheless, the possibilities for ecotourism in the Philippine Archipelago are promising, and there are dozens of trekking and mountaineering clubs and associations to help you organize and carry out your trip.

There are 18 major mountain peaks in the Philippines, all offering challenging climbs for experienced trekkers — although it is possible to organize less demanding treks around the foothills and mountain slopes. Guides and porters can be hired at most base camps. Standard equipment should include strong and comfortable boots, warm clothing, a large water canteen, sleeping bag, flashlight, adequate food and water, a sturdy tent, insect repellent, and water purifying tablets. You must carry all your non-biodegradable refuse down to the base camp for disposal.

In Mindanao, **Mount Apo** — *apo* means "grandfather" — is the nation's highest peak, at 2,953 m (9,745 feet). Straddling the provinces of Davao and North Cotabato, Mount Apo is part of the largest national park in the Philippines. The four-day-return climb to the peak is regarded by most as grueling yet rewarding, passing mud pools, waterfalls, lakes, sulfur springs and thick forest. You may even get a glimpse of the rare monkey-eating eagle, and will almost certainly see the waling-

waling orchid. The forest is the home of the endangered Philippine eagle, which is being bred in captivity at the Philippine Eagle Research and Nature Center on the mountain's slopes. The Department of Tourism in Davao ( (82) 221-6798 FAX (82) 221-0070, Magsaysay Park Complex, Santa Ana District, Davao City, can help organize your trip and will be up to date on weather conditions and local insurgencies, which are not uncommon. Additional information is available from the Mount Apo Climber Association. They can be contacted through the Davao Department of Tourism (see above).

The active **Mayon Volcano**, at 2,432 m (7,979 feet), near Legazpi in Southern Luzon, is a popular climb when it's not erupting. The volcano is much admired for its near-perfect cone shape and dramatic views. Much closer to Manila is **Mount Banahaw** (2,177 m, or 7,142 feet), which dominates the landscape in Laguna and Quezon, an hour and a half's drive southwest of Manila. This is a challenging climb — and local legend says Banahaw has mystical powers.

Other mountain peaks include **Mount Pulog** near Baguio in North Luzon, **Mount Halcon** in Mindoro Oriental, **Canlaon Volcano** in Negros Occidental, **Mount Makiling** in Laguna, and **Mount Kitanglad**, west of Impasugong in Bukidnon, Mindanao.

Walking the trails through the mountainous regions around **Banaue**, **Sagada**, and **Bontoc** in North Luzon is an excellent way to learn about the culture of the architects of Banaue's giant rice terraces; the Igorot tribespeople. The burial caves and hanging coffins at Sagada provide an added, if somewhat macabre, attraction. Local tribes positioned their dead above ground in caves, or hung them halfway down a cliff face, believing this allowed the spirits of the dead to roam free.

Less than two hour's drive from Manila, **Tagaytay Ridge** offers a fascinating walk around the rim of massive Lake Taal. By a freak of nature, the lake — which is contained within the crater of an ancient dormant volcano — has another smaller active volcano within it.

In turn, this smaller volcanic island, known as **Taal**, has its own lake. Contact the Mountaineering Federation of the Philippines ( (2) 810-2422, Room 407, Citiland III Building, Esteban Street, Legaspi Village, Makati, Metro Manila, or the Philippine National Mountaineering Association ( (2) 832-2964, 1500 Roxas Boulevard, Makati, Manila. If you are concerned about the safety of climbing in the vicinity of potentially dangerous volcanoes, contact the Institute of Volcanology and Seismology ( (2) 426-1468 FAX (2) 926-3225, C.P. Garcia Avenue, UP-Diliman, Quezon City. They can brief you on the current state of a volcano's temper and whether it's safe to plan a trek.

**NATURE TOURS AND BIRD WATCHING**

Nature tourism and ecotourism may be the wave of the future for the Philippines. A string of wildlife sanctuaries, conservation areas, game and bird refuges and national park reserves — both at sea and on land — have been established in recent years by the Department of Environment and Natural Resources. Conservation programs are doing their best to save the endangered Philippine eagle (the national bird), eastern sarus crane, tamaraw (a dwarf variety of water buffalo), Philippine crocodile, dugong, marine turtles, and a variety of rare deer species.

OPPOSITE: An active Mayon Volcano attracts plenty of hikers. ABOVE: Banaue's rice terraces. Both of these wonders are in Luzon.

The protection of the country's habitat is frequently at odds with government plans for rural development. Yet there does seem to be a growing awareness of ecological matters, reflected in efforts made by various nongovernmental organizations, such as the Haribon Foundation, and the Central Visayas Regional Project, to promote sustainable practices within rural communities.

**Caluit Island Wildlife Sanctuary**, on a tiny island that is part of the Calamian Group north of Palawan, is home to both indigenous wildlife and a number of African animals; it's a fascinating place to visit and probably the only island in Southeast Asia where you can expect to see giraffes, zebras, elands, and gazelles grazing in an "open zoo" tropical setting.

These animals were given a home here when the Philippines responded to an appeal by the International Union of Conservation of Nature to save endangered species. Equally at home are some of the archipelago's endangered animals, such as the Philippine mouse deer, Calamian deer, Palawan bear cat, tarsier, scaly anteater, monitor lizard, and the Philippine man-eating crocodile.

Elsewhere in the Philippines, indigenous animals include nocturnal flying lemurs, rare cloud rats (found in the mountains of northern Luzon, Mindoro and Marinduque), clawless otters, and leopard cats. Reptiles and lizards abound in remote areas, including iguanas and monitors, king cobra and pythons.

The Philippines will delight bird lovers, yet many of its more than 500 species are endangered. Among them, the impressive Philippine eagle — the world's second largest, after the American happy eagle — can be seen in captivity in Davao at the **Philippine Eagle Research and Nature Center** ( (82) 229-3021 FAX (82) 224-3022, Farnet Diamond Street, Amarfori Heights, Davao City. The Center is open daily from 8 AM to 5 PM, and the fee for adults is P12, teens P7, and children P3. Not long ago, there was an estimated population of some 10,000 of these magnificent birds — but the destruction of their habitat through slash-and-burn agriculture has reduced this number to fewer than 300.

In Laguna, Mount Makiling's forested cover provides shelter to many endemic species, such as the Philippine serpent eagle, the Luzon bleeding heart (so named because of the splash of red on its chest) and the shiny drongo, which is easily identified by its long, fish-like tail. The **Olango Island Migratory Bird Sanctuary** in Cebu is also the seasonal home to several endangered birds, among them the Asiatic dowager and Chinese egret, while farther south in Mindanao.

### NATIONAL PARKS
The largest protected area in North Luzon is the **Palanan Wilderness Area,** which is home to 10 percent of the

remaining primary forest. **Mount Isarog National Park** on Bicol is a dormant volcano, while **Mount Iglit-Baco National Park** on Mindoro is one of the last remaining habitats for the endangered tamaraw. The remote **Mount Guiting-Guiting Natural Park** in Romblon is a living testament to the ice age: its geology and geography stand as evidence of the big freeze, with ancient teak trees and unique species of birds and monkeys. It is biodiversity at its best here. On **Palawan**, Coron Island, El Nido Marine Reserve, and Malampaya Sound are all fishbowls for the country's rare marine life and coral reefs.

## Sporting Spree

With its multitude of islands, beautiful beaches and reefs — with innumerable diving and snorkeling locations throughout — the Philippines can be considered among the best water-sports destinations in the world. Scuba diving, game fishing, sailing, surfing and windsurfing enthusiasts all have an organized presence in the Philippines.

**SCUBA DIVING AND SNORKELING**
As a scuba-diving and snorkeling destination, the Philippines has been steadily growing in popularity, and the scuba-diving industry is particularly well-established, as reflected in a growing number of resorts and on-site dive shops that cater to serious divers as well as novices.

The warm, crystalline waters that lap the archipelago's coastlines host a vast world of colorful corals, sea grass, algae, and fish species — not to mention sunken galleons — while the clarity of the water allows visibility of up to 60 m (200 feet). With currents flowing in from Japan, the South China Sea, the Indian Ocean and the Celebes Sea, it is no wonder that Philippine waters are rich in species of underwater flora and fauna. Like undersea rainforests, coral reefs are one of the nation's most precious — and threatened — natural resources. They span 40,000 sq km (15,444 sq miles)

*YOUR CHOICE*

and teem with no fewer than 2,000 identified species of fish and 800 species of soft and hard coral.

It is important to be aware that the coral reefs in the Philippines have become significantly threatened. A range of illegal fishing practices are the cause of most of the coral damage. Fishermen using dynamite, cyanide and spears, as well as foreign vessels using trawling nets, contribute the destruction. Collectively, these practices have had a devastating effect on the underwater environment, depopulating fish colonies and obliterating coral reefs, which have taken centuries — sometimes even thousands of years — to build up. It is also staggering to consider that some 80 percent of the world's aquarium fish come from the Philippines.

More recently however, the Philippine government and international and local environmental agencies have made strides in stamping out harmful practices and have tried to promote sustainable fishing as well as ecologically sound

OPPOSITE TOP: A tarsier monkey, the world's smallest primate, spotted in Bohol. BOTTOM: Protected eagles at Mount Talomo National Park. ABOVE: Gentle Mactan breezes provide benign conditions for new windsurfers.

management for local communities. The resorts in El Nido, Palawan, are the nation's most successful models of ecotourism, with their coral reef and marine life conservation programs.

Your priority when making travel arrangements is to decide whether you wish to base yourself aboard a specialized boat or at a diving resort. Diving in the Philippines is generally markedly cheaper than in other parts of the world. Sharing the expense of hiring a boat and divemaster with a group of other divers is sensible, and dive shops should be able to help you organize a group for the adventure.

**Diving resorts** — such as Anilao in Batangas province (Southern Luzon) and Moalboal in Cebu (Visayas) — provide comprehensive diving facilities and may offer packages that include diving trips, accommodation, and meals. Major resorts have experienced diving instructors and guides, as well as all necessary equipment. While packages range from expensive and luxurious to cheap and Spartan, the underwater experience will be pretty much the same. Nonetheless, it is wise to be very attentive to the quality and state of repair of equipment. If you are diving on a budget, bringing your own familiar and trustworthy equipment is preferable to renting second-rate equipment on the cheap. While the quality of gear should never be compromised, accommodation and transport can be. On the other end of the scale, if you are intent on diving in style, most of the more exclusive resorts within the Philippines can provide a luxurious backdrop to your diving experience.

Another possibility is to **hire a dive boat**. The MV *Nautika*, based in Manila, is a well-equipped, extremely comfortable dive boat which visits otherwise difficult to reach dive spots in the Sulu Sea, including Tubbataha Reefs east of central Palawan, the Visayas, and wreck sites around Coron and Busuanga islands in the Calamian group. Depending on the time of year and the requirements of the charter, the *Nautika* caters for up to 18 people. It has eight air-conditioned cabins with private bath, excellent diving equipment and a ratio of one instructor

and dive master to every six people. Prices vary seasonally, ranging from US$155 to US$190 per person per night. For *Nautika* reservations, contact Eagle Trek Adventures ( (2) 521-9168 FAX (2) 521-7358.

The best time of year for diving is during the dry season from February to June, when the weather is calm and plankton bloom is minimal. (Plankton bloom can make the water cloudy.) Visibility differs from place to place, however, in some areas the water can be clear even during typhoon season. Local divers divide the season into two parts — the southwest monsoon, *habagat*, from June to October, and the northeast monsoon, *amihan*, from November to March.

You wouldn't think that some of the best diving in the country could be found only a few hours from Manila. But Luzon's Batangas province and nearby Mindoro provide excellent quick diving excursions from the big city. The main diving locations in Batangas are **Balayan Bay** and **Nasugbu** and the man-made **Cathedral Rock Marine Sanctuary**. Other locations which merit exploration include **Sombrero Island**, **Layaglang Point**, **Sepok Point** and **Mapating Rock**; these spots are more suitable for experienced divers and are good for observing sharks (called locally *pating*) and numerous large pelagic fish. **Culebra Island**, also called Bonito, and **Malahibong Manok Island**, both of which are marine sanctuaries, are also excellent diving locations.

Best known of Mindoro's diving locations is the **Apo Reef National Marine Park** — an atoll-like reef which lies 32 km (20 miles) off Mindoro's west coast. Split into two large lagoons, the area is flush with coral species, large colorful fish, sharks, manta rays, crevice-dwelling morays, and smaller tropical-aquarium fish. **Puerto Galera** is the diving epicenter of Mindoro, with its bevy of bays, islands and lagoons all located within a 10-km (six-mile) radius of the town. Hundreds of years ago Spanish galleons sheltered here — today

El Nido is known for its extraordinary limestone formations, which prove a haven for snorkelers and divers.

the bays harbor many diving operators and beach resorts, eager to cater to tourist demands.

Bohol is a good destination for all types of divers, with diving centers around nearby **Cabilao Island**, **Panglao Island**, and **Balicasag Island**.

Experienced divers will enjoy the challenges offered by the remote, largely undeveloped islands of Palawan, which earned superlatives from the late diving guru, Jacques Cousteau. In the El Nido region, the **Miniloc** and **Lagan** island resorts provide ideal accommodation in this isolated region and offer basic diving instruction as well as advanced tours into deeper waters where the truly incredible lies unseen and unspoiled. The Palawan islands are a sanctuary for many rare and endangered species, such as giant sea turtles, manta rays and *dugongs*, or sea cows. White-tipped and gray reef sharks can be seen on most dives. Both the **Tubbataha Reefs National Marine Park** and the **Basterra Reef** in this region are acknowledged as premier diving destinations.

**Shipwreck diving** has become an exciting new addition to the adventures being offered in the Philippines. Ancient Chinese junks, Spanish galleons and American and Japanese World War II vessels can all be found, coral-encrusted, on the ocean floor. Many treasure hunters operate in the Philippines, where the promise of lifting gold from an ancient galleon is probably more likely than anywhere else in the world. For 250 years, Spanish galleons laden with gold, ivory, coins, pearls, and precious stones traveled between Manila and Acapulco in Mexico, and many did not survive the journey.

Of the many wrecks that have been located, quite a number are used for diving. The two main areas of interest are Coron Bay, off Palawan, and Subic Bay, Luzon. In Coron Bay, a 24-strong convoy of Japanese warships and freighters was sunk by an American bombing attack during World War II. In Subic Bay, which was originally a Spanish naval base, some 19 ships — including a wooden gunboat scuttled in 1898 — have been located and are divable. A number of live-aboard vessels and charter dive boats make trips to Coron, while in Subic Bay the only dive operation exploring wrecks is Subic Bay Aqua Sports ( (47) 252-6097 FAX (47) 252-6084.

Treasure hunters in the Philippines are treated quite generously. If you find something of importance, you are obliged to notify the National Museum in Manila, but you are usually allowed to keep a share of your findings.

The Australian-based group MV *Discovery* Charters (/FAX (61-47) 586220 offers punters a chance to take part in **treasure-hunting missions** led by Brian Homan, one of the most famous treasure hunters in the Philippines. You'll be given the chance to use proton magnometers (metal detectors), to dive and photograph wrecks and, perhaps, to discover treasure. The company that conducts these explorations, Archipelago Search and Recovery, has in the past undertaken projects in cooperation with the National Museum of the Philippines and has successfully located and excavated many wrecks, including Chinese junks and Spanish galleons. Only four passengers can be accepted on each 10-day charter trip. The voyage takes the form of a working cruise, with basic living conditions onboard the 15-m (50-foot) Filipino parau survey boat, although the ship's cots are reportedly comfortable, and the diving equipment is first-class.

Don't dive without certification, unless you're taking a lesson with a qualified instructor. Dive operators are legally required to check the qualifications of anyone renting equipment or hiring guides. Scuba-diving instruction courses — through both the Professional Association of Dive Instructors (PADI) and the National Association of Underwater Instructors (NAUI) — are offered throughout the archipelago. Costs for these courses vary from US$200 to US$400.

It is not wise to attempt drift dives on your own. This method, which exploits underwater currents and allows you to move effortlessly through canyons, ravines and along walls, is regarded, along with wreck diving, as one of the

most dangerous underwater situations, with a high potential for fatalities.

If you are snorkeling, strong currents will be your main concern. Avoid touching coral without gloves, as any cuts or scrapes can easily become infected. Also, make sure your feet are protected against stonefish, sea urchins, and stingrays — if you aren't wearing flippers, sneakers are better than nothing. Walking on coral will contribute to the reef's destruction and should be avoided. It is a good idea to go snorkeling with a hired *banca*, since many of the coral reefs are too far from the shore to make them easily accessible by swimming.

The Department of Tourism has useful brochures, booklets and a diving map of the Philippines. You can also contact the **Philippine Commission on Sports Scuba Diving (PCSSD)** ( (2) 599031, Department of Tourism Building, T.M. Kalaw Street, Rizal Park, Manila, the organization responsible for developing and regulating all diving-related activities in the Philippines. A good source of detailed information is the excellent *Diver's Guide to the Philippines* by David Smith, Michael Westlake and Portfirio Castaneda (Unicorn Books Limited, Hong Kong, 1982). It's available in Manila bookstores, although it is probably due for an update.

Underwater, the Philippines are a photographer's dream. OPPOSITE: Divers adjust flash units of a camera before taking the plunge in Moalboal, Cebu. ABOVE: Little Lagoon, El Nido.

Action Asia magazine is also useful, with current information on resorts, dive shops and charter operators. The free Philippine Diver magazine is another good reference, with a listing of registered dive establishments and recommendations.

## GAME FISHING

With so many islands and so much coastline, the tropical Philippine waters provide the perfect breeding ground for game fish. Of the 2,400 species of fish in the Philippines, many are ideal for game fishing. Anglers can expect to encounter fish such as giant yellowfin tuna, king mackerel, great barracuda, marlin, Pacific sailfish, and snapper. The cost of sport fishing in the Philippines is inexpensive by international standards.

Fishing expeditions are usually made with outrigger bancas up to five meters (16 feet) long, powered by outboard motors, although increasingly a larger vessel, known as the superbanca, which offers greater speed and maneuverability, is being used as well as specialized sport-fishing boats outfitted with diesel engines, depth finders, outriggers, and fighting chairs.

Well-known starting points for sport fishing include **Naic** in Cavite, **San José** in Mindoro, **Puerto Princesa** in Palawan and **Bagac** in Bataan.

Given the large number of professional fishermen around the Philippines, it should be easy to find a friendly fishing partner with a good boat at an agreeable price. Bringing or buying your own fishing rod and tackle is wise; once you are equipped with these, fishing opportunities should be plentiful. You can contact the **Philippine Game Fishing Foundation (** (2) 373-0743 or (2) 415-5540 FAX (2) 373-2838, at 1320 Quezon Avenue, Quezon, Manila, for advice and information.

## SURFING

The Philippine surfing scene is starting to gain momentum. There are two world-class surfing locations in the Philippine Archipelago: **Catanduanes Island**, off southeast Luzon, and **Siargao Island**, off the northern tip of Mindanao. Being on the eastern coast of the Philippines, these islands get hit by large surfable swells during the typhoon season. Since surfing is relatively new to the Philippines, not many tourist guide maps feature wave-riding locations on them. But generally speaking, the whole of the exposed east coast offers good surf and clean large swells between July and December.

Siargao Island has come into vogue as a surfing destination in the last decade, and held its first trial Cloud Nine Surfing Competition in 1995, an impromptu, now annual event, in which competitors brave the massive swells, some breaking their boards in the process. Images of snapped boards, broken leg rope, and coral scrapes might deter some, but serious surfers have not been discouraged. Surf photographer John Callahan took a team of hot American surfers to Siargao Island in 1993 and his fantastic photographs have lured many more. Somewhere on the island there will be a break suited to your style of surfing, whether you are a wave guru or a tea bag. For a non-surfing holiday, as well, the island is idyllic, with dozens of excellent beaches.

A number of beach resorts around Siargao Island cater primarily to surfers. The Australian tour company **Surf Express (** (02) 262-3355 FAX (02) 262-3210 organizes specialized vacation tours to the Philippines out of Australia.

## GOLF

When ex-President Ramos (an enthusiastic golfer) had guests to dinner, he was known to give out autographed golf balls as mementos. Increasingly, it seems, Filipinos regard the sport as a symbol of the good life.

The Philippines' major international-standard golf courses are all in Manila, where golfing was introduced by colonizing Americans a century ago. With its dozens of courses, Manila qualifies as the golfing capital of Asia, a fact that gives it considerable merit in Japanese eyes. Aspiring Japanese golfers travel to Manila to play their first-ever game on an 18-hole course. It isn't only the Japanese

who find playing golf in the Philippines appealing and inexpensive. The average greens fee is about US$50, compared with over US$100 in other Asian cities. Caddies are generally paid around US$6.

Manila's most popular course is the aptly named **Wack Wack Golf and Country Club** ( (2) 878-4021, which frequently hosts the Philippine Open. Other courses include the **Villamor** ( (2) 833-8630, a long and flat layout located close to the airport, which has also hosted the Open. There are two military courses, the **Fort Bonifacio Golf Club** ( (2) 885-8323 or (2) 885-8464 and the **Navy Golf Club** ( (2) 887-3732. The exclusive **Manila Golf and Country Club** ( (2) 817-4948 — whose early exclusion of Filipino players led to the creation of the Wack Wack Club — has as an impressive backdrop the Makati skyline.

New courses have sprung up outside Manila, including the **Alabang Golf and Country Club** ( (2) 842-3530, **Canlubang Golf and Country Club** ( (2) 890-9321, **Valley Golf Club** ( (2) 665-8565, and **Capitol Hills Golf Club** ( (2) 931-3050, all within an hour's drive of Manila. There are now more than 50 courses throughout the archipelago.

Robert Trent Jones Jr. designed the **Calatagan Golf Club** ( (2) 813-2636 in Batangas, as well as the aforementioned Canalubang Golf and Country Club. Also on the list of celebrity-designed courses, the recently opened Legends Course in Manila was created by Jack Nicklaus, transforming what had previously been a simple mango orchard. The course has hosted the Philippine Open in 1994, 1996, and 1999.

Full service golf resorts have also been sprouting up. **The Everest Golf and Country Club** ( (2) 712-9293, at Banyan Tree Nasugbu Resort, close to Tagaytay in Luzon, is considered the nation's ultimate golf resort. Its 18-hole "masterpiece" golf course was designed by Arnold Palmer. Banyan Tree has an appealing list of other facilities including a swimming pool, a kid's club and a health center.

On the island of Boracay, one golf resort, including a 600-room condominium complex, has recently been completed. **Fairways and Bluewater** is a world-class golf course created by champion golfer and master designer Graham Marsh.

Camp John Hay in Baguio, north Luzon, has one of the most popular golf links in the country.

The **Philippines Golf Association** ( (2) 588845 FAX (2)521-1587, 209 Administration Building, Rizal Memorial Sports Complex, Vito Cruz, Manila, can answer all your golf-vacation questions and provide broad-based information on golfing in the Philippines. The Philippines Department of Tourism has published a comprehensive and useful brochure, *Golfing in the Philippines*, which includes information and contact numbers for the nation's major golf clubs and courses. Philippine Airlines offers special golf vacation packages as well.

# The Open Road

It's called the **Halsema Highway** — and what a hair-raising road it is. The span between Baguio and Banaue provides one of the most scenic nail-biting experiences on the Philippines' open road. The "highway" twists and turns its way through Central Cordillera's best vistas — thousand foot drop-offs are only inches away from the bus tires that are struggling to get traction on the dusty or muddy unpaved roads. Waterfalls that are escaping their massive cliff confines shower you as you pass by — which is especially refreshing if you are sitting on top of a crowded public jeepney. Sitting on the right side of any vehicle will have you saying your prayers and practicing the famous "left lean."

The Philippines' roads, with a unique set of road rules (or lack thereof), are chock-full of memorable experiences, and the scenery found along many of them makes for excellent day or weekend excursions. These are good options if your trip to the Philippines requires you to base yourself in Manila and you don't have time to travel to more far-flung parts of the archipelago. A word on Manila traffic here is in order. The thought of getting out of the stand-still traffic en route to a destination elsewhere might seem quite daunting, considering a trip from Ermita to Makati, which is only a few miles, could take as much as two hours. In an effort to limit the number of cars on the road, locally owned vehicles are registered to be on the roads on certain days of the week only (a similar policy is used in Milan, Italy). Interesting concept, however the traffic remains horrendous, so be prepared for frighteningly long trips through the city center.

The most convenient scenic day-trip destinations from Manila are within the five provinces spreading west, east and south of the capital: Cavite, Laguna, Batangas, Rizal and Quezon. These provinces are known collectively by locals as "**Calabarzon**."

Calabarzon is rich in tribal culture, lushly endowed with lakes, rivers, mineral springs, waterfalls, caves and subterranean rivers. It is the market garden of the Manila area, with a brisk trade in fish from its seas and lakes and fresh produce and flowers from its orchards and fields. Stalls and markets reveal a long tradition of artisan work, especially in silverware, embroidery and carved furniture, much of which is exported. Rizal province in particular is notable for its many artists' villages and workshops.

Good day-trip options include the dramatic **Tagaytay Ridge**, **Lake Taal** and **Taal Volcano**, reached after passing through some historic towns in Rizal and Cavite provinces; the hot mineral springs at **Los Baños** and **Hidden Valley Springs Resort**; the working

plantation and hacienda museum at **Villa Escudero**, in Laguna province; and the artist villages of **Angono** and **Antipolo** in Rizal province.

Since hiring a car and driver is relatively cheap in the Philippines, there is little to be recommended in trying to negotiate the roads alone, especially as you may find yourself confronted with obstacles like water buffaloes (*carabao*) and kamikaze jeepney drivers. Manila is the most convenient place to find a reliable car and driver, and they are familiar with the roads, driving conditions, and road rules. However, if you are determined to be self-propelled, automobile rentals are available in Luzon at Olongapo, Angeles, and Baguio. All of these areas are favorable destinations from which to make day trips. Vehicles drive on the right side of the road — by all indications. It's often hard to tell; as Filipino drivers are in the habit of overtaking as many as five or six vehicles at one time. As a result, defensive driving is in order. The outside lane is the safest — although eager overtakers dominate both sides if there's a gap in traffic. Be extra careful in the evenings, as many trucks and cars cruise at high speeds with no headlights.

OPPOSITE: Highly individualized and brightly-decorated jeepneys are labors of love for their driver-owners. ABOVE: The highest point of central Luzon.

# Backpacking

The strong backpacking culture so familiar in neighboring Thailand and Indonesia has certainly found footing in the Philippines as well. Each era of backpackers has staked their claim on discovering a piece of the paradise pie.

The country is certainly a backpackers' Mecca. The Asian financial crisis has opened the door even more to those free spirits short on cash but well-endowed with a sense of adventure. Prices are cheap — for US$20 a day or less you can board a bus, arrive on an island, find a simple guesthouse or bungalow (no air-conditioning and either private or shared bathrooms), eat a simple meal (but arguably more authentic than resort offerings), and have some left over for a cool San Miguel at the local bar. There are plenty of **budget accommodations** — some which are downright dirty and crawling, while others are equivalent to some of the top island resorts. Generally dirty hotels are the exception.

**Camping** is widely acceptable as well. For a few pesos you can hire a *banca* to take you to a nearby unpopulated island (there are 7,107 of them after all) where there is a small stretch of beach, and you can pitch your tent for a night or two. Don't forget to arrange a pick-up. Having your own island for a night has become a popular option, however you should ask beforehand about tides and whether or not you will wake up floating at sea.

**Boracay** in the 1960s was a little known backpacking getaway, but it has since exploded into one of Southeast Asia's most mainstream destinations. The increasingly popular backpacker destination is **Palawan**. Its rough and rugged nature is the appeal, and it has yet to be overrun with large resorts, allowing the shoestring budget to stretch a bit further. It also has some of the best diving in Southeast Asia for about US$20–$30 per dive, including equipment rental.

In fact, most of the country's adventures that raise the adrenaline won't drain the

purse. Local guide hire and porters for hiking any of the active volcanoes — like **Mount Pinatubo** in northern Luzon and **Mount Mayon** in southern Luzon — are quite affordable. And getting to any of these destinations is cheap as well. For true backpackers, spending US$5 for the 48-hour bus trip from Manila to points north or south is the only option.

Hiring a **private *banca*** for long journeys on the sea, particularly in Palawan, from Puerto Princesa to Sabang and El Nido further north, can be very expensive. Having a group to split the inflated rate is your best option. Local fishermen know they have you between a rock and hard place with the lack of

transportation options, as it really is your only way to some destinations. Rates can be as high as US$100 one way, but if you have a group of four or five it is less costly. If you are a solo backpacker then choosing these less expensive transport options will certainly put you amongst the best of the backpacking crowd.

**Flights** to some of the major hubs like Cebu or Mindanao are pretty reasonable as well. Hiring a charter flight to Coron for instance, where famed Japanese wrecks are luring droves of backpackers, will cost substantially more.

Renting your own **motorcycle** is the trend on islands like Bohol and Mindoro, where the unpaved roads and tribal cultures make for an unforgettable adventure. It's easy to rent a bike — just check with the local tourist office or ask any of the dive shops. You probably won't have to show an international driver's license, though legally it is required. Wherever an expensive option seems to stand in the way, there is always a cheaper, although much more time-consuming way of getting to a destination. You just need flexibility; and of course bag locks!

**Eating cheaply** in the Philippines is no problem, either. If you find yourself on the road a lot, the food stalls that line

Celebrating Ati-Atihan on Sikogon.

many routes in the country offer some of the best, most authentic local cuisine around. Even simple local restaurants won't break the bank — you can eat a hearty local meal including rice and beef or a whole tuna for less than P200. The local brews and rum are very cheap too. At many popular restaurants on Palawan, backpackers place their dinner order in the morning, and by evening it has been caught or bought and prepared just for you.

The islands are generally safe for backpackers. However, anytime you are attempting such unprotected travel — the nature of backpacking — you leave yourself open to the expected and the unexpected. Hold onto your shoes! Thefts of shoes have been reported among the backpacking community. Ferries and beaches are hot spots for shoe hoists. Money, passports and other valuables should be kept with you in a hidden money belt, not in your bag.

## Living It Up

### EXCEPTIONAL HOTELS AND RESORTS

"Have you ever seen heaven?" my masseuse asked me as I rolled my blood-rushed face off my beach towel and looked up. Without talking she simply nodded to the sky. While sipping my mango shake and receiving a full body massage on the cool white sands of Boracay, all things, including myself, seemed to bow down in awe of the sky's evening portrait. Should I have the lobster or shrimp for dinner?

You won't have to look too far in the Philippines to be pampered. For some it's simply watching the almost electric sunsets. For others, it's coming back to their hotel room with chocolates and rose petals on the turned-down sheets. It's all here.

Manila, like most other Southeast Asian capitals, offers palatial comfort at its raft of five-star hotels. To top it off, Manila's room rates have yet to soar to the excessive heights of Hong Kong, or

even those of Singapore and Bangkok. In Makati — Manila's wealthy financial and shopping district — you can take your pick of opulent hotels, including the **Peninsula Manila** and **Mandarin Oriental Manila**. Ostentatious chic is most in evidence at the **Shangri-La Hotel Manila**, the hotel of the moment, with its three-story atrium entrance, multitude of restaurants, shopping arcades, and lounges. Their butler service is popular with business travelers. The most fascinating hotel in the capital, however, will always be the **Manila Hotel**, which personifies the charms of the city's past. Since its opening in 1912, the hotel, nestled between the walled city of Intramuros and Manila Bay, has hosted everyone from Ernest Hemingway to John F. Kennedy to Michael Jackson to the Beatles. General MacArthur lived here for six years, and you can stay in his re-created suite, although priority for this museum-like room goes to diplomats and presidents. If traffic's got you down, the hotel's heliport might come in handy.

Away from the bright lights of Manila and the recognized hotel chains that have also begun to proliferate in the beach resort zone of Mactan in Cebu, the Philippines offers scores of resorts designed for siesta-style relaxation. Many small, locally-owned beach and island

ABOVE: Luxury at the Manila Hotel. OPPOSITE: On Samil Island, Mindanao, the Pearl Farm Resort has a deserved reputation as a luxurious hideaway.

resorts and popular scuba-dive centers are renowned for having the most competitive room rates in Asia.

The most elite of all the resorts is **Amanpulo**, which means "peaceful island," on the tiny private island of Pamalican, one of the cluster known as the Cuyo islands in the Sulu Sea. It can be reached only by charter plane. One of the more recent additions to the exclusive Amanresorts chain, which includes some of the most luxurious and expensive resort hotels in the world, Amanpulo has 40 splendid casitas decorated with exquisite furnishings and gallery-quality artifacts. You don't even have to walk — each casita is equipped with its very own golf cart at your disposal to tour the island.

Exotic, faraway Palawan has twin resorts, located in the El Nido region, which offer both pampering and adventure. Both resorts promote themselves as ecotourism destinations: **Miniloc Island Resort**, which is designed to resemble a small fishing village, with hillside rooms and stilt casitas, is popular with serious scuba-divers; **Lagan Island Resort** also attracts divers and couples. Both are set in stupendously beautiful, pristine and remote locations — Miniloc Island is more sheltered, with a tiny cove and pebbly beach; Lagan has a spacious stretch of sandy beach.

The **Pearl Farm Beach Resort** on Samal Island, off Davao in southern Mindanao, has become one of the more popular, out of the way, resorts in the Philippines. The beautiful island surroundings can be enjoyed from the comfortable privacy of stilt cottages and longhouse rooms with interiors featuring colorful crafts by Mindanao's tribes. Owned by a Filipina, (Miss Universe 1973), the management's attention to detail makes this among the country's better resorts.

Situated on the dramatic north coast of Mindanao, the **Dakak Beach Resort** is another lush hideaway alongside a forested hillside in which 80 air-conditioned, marble-floor cottages rest amid carefully landscaped surroundings.

The sheltered 700-m (765-yd) white sand beach is nothing less than spectacular, and plenty of water sports are offered. The resort has become very popular with wealthy Manileños, partly because it is owned by a flamboyant Filipino television producer.

Although the resort island of **Boracay** is a bit too touristy for many, it nonetheless provides a unique set of offerings. With seafood barbecues on the beach, inexpensive back massages, and a lively and eclectic crowd — and including resorts such as Friday's, with its private beach cottages — Boracay is a one-stop shop for adventure, cultural touchdowns, and luxury.

EXCEPTIONAL RESTAURANTS
The choices for international fine dining are numerous in Manila. Put on your best threads and head to **Prince Albert Rotisserie** in the Inter-Continental hotel. The French food is exquisite and includes such items as grilled lobster *feuillantine* (between thin, leaflike layers of pastry), veal mignon with sage butter, chicken breast with truffles, and Black Angus beef. Another French restaurant tops the list of the best restaurants in Manila — **Le Soufflé Restaurant and Wine Bar**, also in Makati. The atmosphere is casual yet sophisticated and the chef's motto is, as long as they have the ingredients they can customize any dish you might want that isn't on the menu. For refined dining on local cuisine, **Maynila**, in the Manila Hotel, is the place to go. One of the most unique dining experiences in Manila is the **Aviary Restaurant, Iguana Bar, Pet Museum Café and Pet Park**. This place is virtual zoo. While you dip your beef fondue or enjoy a drink at the bar, resident lizards and Australian cockatoos, not to mention a three-meter (nine-foot) boa constrictor, are free to roam, slither, and fly around the restaurant.

Cebu is a great location for wining and dining on seafood. **Lantaw Gardens** is one of the best around with its well-priced buffet in an open-air, garden setting. The restaurant also hosts a folk dance show and has scenic views of the city.

The winner of the most diverse dining options is Boracay. Boracay is packed with over a hundred restaurants serving Filipino, Japanese, Korean, Thai, German, Italian, French, Swiss, Indian, and Continental cuisine all within a seven-kilometer-wide (four-and-a-half-mile-wide) island.

## Family Fun

The Philippines is not the first place most people think of as a family vacation spot. Not exactly Disneyland, the country can be adventurous even for hardy adult travelers, let alone small children. Nevertheless, recent years have seen much development in the tourism infrastructure. Hotels and resorts — especially the international chains in such places as Manila, Cebu and Boracay — are now set up to cater to the tastes of and needs of young visitors, with swimming pools, playgrounds and children's menus. When you journey off the beaten track, however, be prepared to forego child-friendly services and amenities. It is always worth calling ahead to request more room space or extra beds and to alert resort owners of your needs. In general, Filipino society is very much attuned to children and their needs.

Easter is a prime time for family fun. Don't miss the Moriones Festival, in Marinduque, if you're in the country over Holy Week. It is one of *the* great festivals.

If your child is enthralled by exotic travel, you should all be able to enjoy the sort of pleasures that make the country special, whether this means visiting a deserted island by *banca*, spotting wildlife in nature reserves, climbing mountains, or simply fishing, lazing, and swimming at the beach.

Most children will love the adventure of visiting natural wonders like **Saint Paul Subterranean National Park**, the thrilling seascapes in places such as **Palawan**, and the layered rice terraces and caves of **Banaue** and **Sagada**. Still, before heading off, you should feel confidant that your child is ready and willing to endure long bus or jeepney rides through rugged countryside.

In Manila, the **Aviary Restaurant and Iguana Bar**, **Pet Museum Café and Pet Park (** (2) 726-4618, 233 Jose Abad Santos Street, is a zoo on any night! The food is excellent and the kids will get a kick out of the birds, snakes, lizards and such that are free to wander the restaurant. The albino boa constrictor hanging from the bar is only the owner's pet snake!

Places that are tailor-made for young children include **Paskuhan Christmas Village**, in Pampanga, Luzon, where Christmas is played out all year round. Jingling and tinkling with endless Christmas decorations, special Filipino snacks and sweets, with Christmas corals sung by people as well as mechanical toys, Paskuhan is worth a day visit.

The best time to visit is Christmas time, when nearby San Fernando stages a beautiful **Lantern Festival**.

The Philippines' version of Disneyland is **Enchanted Kingdom (** MANILA (2) 635-5099 in Santa Rosa, Laguna, the country's only world-class theme park. From the jungle outpost to Brooklyn Place, the seven theme zones have rides and attractions that will hold the attention of the kids every second. **Splash Island (** MANILA (2) 633-5265 or (2) 633-5261, also in Laguna, is the country's largest water park. It's the perfect escape if the kids are finding the heat hard to handle.

With great frivolity, fun and much dressing up, festivals and fiestas are a Filipino specialty especially likely to appeal to children (see FESTIVE FLINGS, page 51). Some of the best are the **Ati-Atihan Festival** held during January (Kalibo, Panay), the **Moriones Festival** during Holy Week (Marinduque), and the **Gigantes Festival** held during August (Lucban, Quezon).

And for complete rest and recreation for all the family, the expensive **Shangri-La Mactan Island Resort** in Cebu, with its all-day child care program, is clearly the best that the Philippines has to offer.

# Cultural Kicks

Some say the Philippines' cultural identity has been lost among the infusions of outside influences from Malaysia, Indonesia, Japan, Spain, and the United States. They fail to realize however, that it is that very fact — the potpourri of cultural traditions — that separates the country from its Southeast Asian neighbors. You needn't go any further than Manila to get a dose of what it is culturally that makes this nation and the people tick.

In Manila, the ancient walled city of **Intramuros**, built by the Spaniards in the sixteenth century, is still formidable, with cannon emplacements atop the nine-meter-thick (30-foot) walls and a strategic location facing the bay. From its foundation in 1571, Intramuros was the exclusive preserve of the ruling classes. The walled fortress is a welcome reprieve from the hectic pace of the surrounding tourist belt, and offers one of the most authentic glimpses into Spanish colonial occupation.

One of the biggest cultural kicks for many tourists used to be the collection of Imelda Marcos' shoe that was displayed at **Malacañang Palace**. The shoes have since been replaced with showcases of positive achievements of each Philippine president. The palace is also a wonderful showcase of colonial Spanish architecture and interior décor — the three chandeliers in the reception hall are remarkable, as are the beautiful hardwoods used for the grand staircase. The opulence of the Spanish ruling classes is certainly evident here.

If contemporary art is your way of witnessing the heritage of a people, then you can't do much better than the **Metropolitan Museum of Art**. It is the best museum in Manila for contemporary fine arts, pre-Columbian pottery, and exquisite pre-Hispanic gold jewelry. A rather off-beat place to visit is the **Chinese Cemetery**, where you can pay your respects to the dead in their air-conditioned tombs.

Further north in Central Luzon, the hills of Baguio, Bontoc, Sagada, and Banaue hold much of the rich and active tribal culture of the Igorot. The Igorot group, including such tribes as the Apayo, Benguet, Bontoc, Ifugao, Kalinga, and Tingguian, retain their deeply ingrained culture, and their farming skills — as epitomized by the Ifugao-built rice terraces in Banaue — are incredibly well developed. Before heading to **Banaue's rice terraces**, a stop at the **Baguio public market** is sure to prepare you for some of the more surprising cultural experiences further north in Sagada.

Market scenes have always held a place in travelers' hearts as a sure way to get a dose of local flavor and people, and Baguio's market is one of the best and most colorful in the country. The local people are more than happy to explain

---

A strong Chinese element, such as this bright temple in Cebu, is present in many Philippine cities.

traditional preparations for some of the more popular dishes — including *aso*, or dog. The market also sells local handicrafts and antiques.

Hikers and spelunkers head to the sleepy town of **Sagada** for adventures in the labyrinth of caves that snake beneath the town. The caves aren't the only attraction however. Traditionally, the Ifugao tribespeople hang the coffins of the recently deceased onto the limestone cliffs that frame the town, as well as along the inside of many of caves that are open for exploration. The bodies are still intact also, so observe and handle with caution. It's an all-together eerie yet awe-inspiring sight. In fact, Sagada is a great launching point to delve into the tribal traditions of the Ifugao — the most popular and well known of the country's tribes. The Masferre Inn in town showcases famed photographer Eduardo Masferre's photographs. He spent his life documenting the mountain life of the Ifugao tribespeople. Not widely publicized, but possible if you network with the right guides in Sagada, is hiking the rugged and long trek deep into the mountains where the Kalinga, a once head-hunting tribe, still live.

If you happen to be in Luzon during Easter, the most interesting festival to witness takes place in **Pampanga**, a short drive from Manila. The Crucifixion Re-enactment attracts flocks to San Fernando to see loyal, and arguably fanatical, Christians offering themselves up for crucifixion. At noon on Good Friday, a number of volunteers are physically nailed to wooden crosses, paraded through the streets, and whipped by gangs of flagellants until they bleed. It is quite a gory spectacle.

Made famous by Francis Ford Coppola's film *Apocalypse Now,* **Baler** in the province of Aurora on Northern Luzon, is home to the Moro-Moro Zarsuela performance. Shown on February 19 annually, it combines drama and dance that takes three days to complete. The form of "Zarsuela," as it is called, is a combination of several acts that revolve around the main theme

of Moro-Moro, or Muslim-Christian conflict. What makes this performance worthy of seeing is that real knives and bolos are used. Often, in the heat of the presentation, miscalculations result in knife and bolo gashes. Both actors and actresses participate in this particularly sensitive and dangerous sword-play.

Visitors interested in history will appreciate the town of **Butuan**. The city has been a major port to a greater or lesser extent since at least the fourth century AD. Butuan is widely recognized as the earliest known place of settlement and sea trade in the Philippines. In 1976 the oldest boat in the Philippines — a carefully crafted *bulangay* (sea-going outrigger) — was discovered here; it been carbon-dated to AD 320. This find, along with finds of extensive wooden coffins of tribal peoples who practiced skull deformation, has made Butuan a center of archaeological and ethnographical importance.

No mention of culture would be complete without including Philippine pop culture on wheels — the ubiquitous jeepney. When I ask people to describe the jeepney, I get many interesting replies. "A tin can meets a disco ball," one tourist said. "It's Elvis reincarnated," a proud driver boasted. Created out of surplus United States army jeeps, no two jeepneys are ever alike. They're longer than the usual four-person American jeep they are modeled after, seating up to 15 comfortably in the elongated metal cab. It's hip-to-hip on the long benches that face each other, and the comfortable 15 can turn into a very uncomfortable 30 passengers, especially in rural areas, where jeepneys are less frequent.

## Shop till You Drop

The Philippines offers extraordinary opportunities for serious shoppers. Fussy antique collectors, furniture hunters and aficionados of ethnic fabrics will find that the archipelago has some of the best buys in Asia. Naturally, you can expect to see a lot of mass-produced junk around, but in general the quality of handcrafted goods is high. If you have the chance to immerse yourself in the search, it is fascinating to see native artisans in their own environment.

While you are in Manila, it is well worth browsing in some arts and crafts emporia, either to make purchases or to give you a glimpse of what to look for — at a cheaper price, with more variety and perhaps better quality — out in the provinces. The best place to begin is Silahi's Arts and Artifacts, Calle Real in Intramuros. With its abundance of artifacts, crafts, fabrics, and antiques as well as contemporary wares, it provides shoppers with an excellent overview of regional artistry. Narda's Handwoven Arts and Crafts, 578 Félipe Street, Makati, specializes in tribal fabrics with a contemporary twist.

The Philippines has a still-thriving tradition of indigenous carving, weaving, pottery and metalworking, much of it undertaken by tribes working in the manner of their ancestors.

### WOODCARVING

Once in the provinces, check with the regional Department of Tourism offices

for suggestions about artists workshops, village markets or factory tours that may help you find extraordinary bargains, whether you are looking for fabrics or furniture. Cebu, for example, teams with manufacturers based in its Mactan export zone, and many sell directly. Other towns, such as Angono and Antipolo (Rizal), Baguio and Paete (Laguna), all on Luzon, survive largely from selling wares such as paintings, fabrics, and carvings.

Carved wares are offered in many different media, ranging from mass-produced geegaws to luminous art objects imbued with much significance by their makers. In northern Luzon, you can look for statues of the Ifugao rice god, the *buhul*, who is believed to bring a good harvest and create peace within a household or community. With tourism changing some of their priorities, the Ifugao now carve bowls, platters and giant utensils and have begun to incorporate some of their sacred images into these items.

Ancestral figures and images of deities, called *latches*, are much sought

OPPOSITE: A guitar-maker (and young helper). ABOVE: Local markets are an ideal source for inexpensive but intricate baskets and woven goods.

after. *Latches* can be seen throughout the Philippines, adorning churches and houses. In Palawan, the Tagbanua tribe uses soft wood to carve quirky images of birds, lizards, turtles, and other animals; the images are used in rituals or given to children. In Muslim-dominated Mindanao, carved fragments of beams used in traditional noblemen's houses are sold as curiosity pieces. They are admired for their beauty and their distinctive linear patterns, called *okir*. The Maranao people are especially well-known for their fine workmanship, as are the woodcarvers of Paete, in Laguna, Luzon.

In your travels throughout the Philippines, you are sure to see many *santos*. These are carved wooden or ivory images of saints. *Santos* date back to the Spanish period. The earliest and finest examples are greatly valued by collectors. Genuine *santos* often have ivory faces, hands and feet. Some show signs of defacement, apparently because, during colonial times, Filipino revolutionaries identified the *santos* as images of their oppressors. Be aware that clever fakes, especially of antique *likhas*, or tribal carvings, and *santos* abound.

Lastly, handcrafted antique furniture — made in the style popular with the early Spaniards, and later appropriated by the Filipino elite — is a great find if you do not mind having to go to the trouble of exporting it out of the country. Craftspeople in the town of Betis, in Pampanga province, Luzon, still make Spanish-style furniture by hand, in small quantities.

## BASKETRY, MATS AND WEAVING

The making of baskets and mats is a highly evolved craft in the Philippines, and there is a wonderful range of form and function, using fiber from plants and reeds, including nipa, pandanus and coconut. Distinctive designs tend to indicate the region of origin. There is a basket for almost everything you could imagine (including catching locusts), and many of them have great decorative potential. In Manila, you are bound to see ox-drawn carts filled with baskets of all shapes and sizes, from which wares are sold directly.

Probably the most inventive and eye-catching baskets come from Mindanao tribespeople: Bagaboo baskets festooned with horse hair, beads, and bells; T'boli

geometric-patterned square baskets; and over-plaited Hanunoo baskets, to name a few. The most sophisticated baskets are made by the Ifugao in northern Luzon. These finely woven, dark-hued creations have an almost sculptural quality, and are usually blackened by the smoke-filled interiors of the Ifugao's mountain huts.

Mats from Samar and Leyte in the Visayas are altogether another story, dyed in primary colors and woven to depict scenes of bright flowers, birds and rustic landscapes; they're irresistibly cheerful. The mats woven from elaborate geometric patterns and bold colors by the Samal and Badjao tribes in the outreaches of the Sulu Archipelago are exceptional enough to stand alone as works of art in themselves.

The Philippines has a lively tradition of weaving and creating intricate fabrics with many regional styles. For several centuries, Filipinos have been adept cultivators and weavers of cotton and *abaca* (Manila hemp), often using ancient Malay-style looms. Though less commonly found, some fabrics are woven from *piña* and *jusi*, pineapple and banana fibers, resulting in a semi-translucent cloth. These fabrics are used

for, among other things, the national Filipino dress: the long-sleeved shirt, *barong tagalog*, as well as the short-sleeved version, the *polo barong*.

It is worth looking for variations on the barong theme fashioned by Filipino designers, some embellishing the basic model and experimenting with tie-dyed silk and dressed-up versions for women.

Luzon and Mindanao are both producers of exceptionally fine fabrics, usually created by tribeswomen and carrying motifs that have been handed down over many generations. In Luzon's central and northern mountain settlements of Banaue, Bontoc, Sagada and Baguio, you can see workshops devoted to the production of intricate cotton *lepanto* cloth, which incorporates Igorot motifs in its designs. In the southern Philippines, Mindanao's Muslim and minority ethnic tribes are renowned for their richly decorative cloths, as well as for the commonly worn *malong*, a sarong-like garment. T'boli tribeswomen have created a unique style of tie-dying, called *t'nalak* and the clothes and coverings

OPPOSITE: Bohol and Cebu are great for handicrafts. ABOVE: The vivid colors and patterns of Zamboangan woven fabric.

made from this are traditionally believed to attract good spirits to guard over pregnant mothers and marriages.

Across the archipelago, there are innumerable varieties of wares made from woven materials. It is possible to find dozens of varieties of leaves, fibers, grasses and vines shaped into mats, hats, purses, shoes and handbags. In addition, Philippine bamboo cane and rattan furniture is considered to be among the highest quality in the world. Large-scale production of rattan furniture is centered on Cebu in the Visayas islands.

## METALWORK

In Mindanao, Muslim tribes are the creators of the fine bronze and brasswares sold throughout the Philippines, especially the Maranao artisans of Lanao del Sur province. Whether authentic antiques or contemporary renditions, these pieces range from ceremonial urns (often taller than a human) to platters and betel-nut containers to shields and scimitars, usually engraved with swirling Islamic okir motifs and patterns, and cast through the ancient lost-wax method. In other parts of Mindanao, the T'boli tribespeople use the same method to produce small figurines, usually depicted in scenes of village life. The T'boli also cast buttons, musical instruments and jewelry in brass.

Unusual items to look for are silver *exvotos*, ecclesiastical offerings shaped into eyes, noses, lips, limbs, and hearts

for people who have been cured of their afflictions by divine intervention. Betel-nut containers in silver and brass are also curious *objet d'arts*; most are rectangular in shape, but some are fashioned into animals, birds or butterflies.

## JEWELRY

If you are set on finding unusual pieces of Filipino jewelry, perhaps the most distinctive items to look for are the antique and contemporary *tamborin*, a gold-filigreed necklace, and the imposing silver disc necklaces worn by the Mandaya women in Mindanao, which are etched with geometric motifs. These designs are also used in earrings, bracelets, and combs.

Pearls cultivated in Philippine waters are another unique feature of the region, and it is hard not to covet these lustrous jewels. Perfect conditions for the cultivation of *pinctada maximus*, the large pearl oyster, are found throughout the Philippines. This species produces the most beautiful varieties of pearls, ranging from 10 to 16 mm (two fifths of an inch to two thirds of an inch) in diameter and, on occasion, reaching a staggering 40 mm (1.6 inches), in the form of the baroque pearl. The pinctada maximus comes in a dazzling array of colors — ranging from white and gold to silver and gray. There are some 20 large and medium-size pearl farms throughout the archipelago, making the Philippines one of the world's largest pearl producers.

The Philippines has a long tradition of pearl cultivation, dating back to 1420 when Paduka Suli, a Suli *datu* (chieftain) is said to have offered the Chinese imperial court a gift of a pearl weighing nearly 200 grams (seven ounces). Badjao folk legends recount tales of datus who demanded their daughters' suitors prove their devotion by diving for pearls.

The Philippines produced the world's largest pearl, the "Pearl of Allah" — referred to as the "Pearl of Lao-Tze" in the *Guinness Book of Records*. Found in Palawan in 1934, it weighs almost six and a half kilograms (more than 14 lbs).

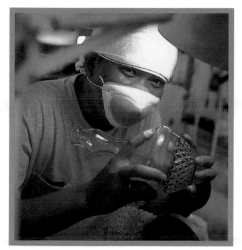

techniques used by mountain tribes, including the Ifugao in the Baguio and Banaue region of Luzon. Located in Makati and Baguio City, her shops showcase an interesting fusion of styles, translated into items as different as textured women's clothes and table linen.

Shell craft is another modern ware unique to the Philippines. This often takes the form of picture frames and small laminated boxes adorned with stones and shells. There are also capiz lampshades and shell-covered handbags, *papier mâché* toys, handcrafted guitars from Cebu, and Filipino Christmas decorations from Pampanga in Luzon.

It was given by the *datu* of Palawan to a group of Americans after their intervention saved his son from dying of malaria. Since then, it has been valued at over US$42 million and displayed at the Smithsonian Institute in Washington, DC.

## POTTERY

The ancient routes that brought early Asian settlers to the Philippines also resulted in a widespread appreciation for trade porcelain from China, Thailand, and Indochina. Excavated pottery points to an early tradition of shaping implements from clay, and the closest contemporary examples of ethnic pottery are made today in Vigan, Luzon, where the solid storage pots, *burnays*, are still being produced as they were when they were introduced by Fukienese settlers at the turn of the last century.

In most of the major cities, and especially in the artisan villages of Antipolo and Angono in Rizal province near Manila, you will find craft shops selling the wares of contemporary potters and ceramists.

## CONTEMPORARY CRAFTS

Many modern handicraft manufacturers are reviving traditional processes, or adapting them to their own designs. For example, Filipina weaver Narda Capuyan — whose fabrics are used by Issey Miyake among other international designers — has integrated weaving

# Short Breaks

To truly appreciate what the country has to offer, you need at least two or three weeks, given the variety of activities and their distances from each other. But the world isn't an ideal place for many of us, and the opportunity to explore the Philippines might come down to a few days.

With such little time, your best bet would be to concentrate on **Manila** and sites close to the city. A day or two should be sufficient time to explore sights such as Intramuros, Malacañang Palace, Rizal Park, and the Metropolitan Museum of Art. Popular destinations for day trips are **Pagsanjan Falls**, a two-hour drive from the city, or **Tagaytay Ridge** to view **Taal Volcano** (a volcano within a lake within a volcano). A drive to Mount Pinatubo is possible within a day as well — although if you decide to trek its fascinating lahar fields up to the crater rim, you will need to stay overnight in neighboring Angeles.

From Manila, the easiest beach destination packed with nightlife, resorts, and world-class diving is **Puerto Galera**. A taxi or bus can take you the two-hour trip to the Batangas port, where ferries

OPPOSITE : In the more remote regions, women still weave with the traditional backstrap loom.
ABOVE: Craftspeople at the Crystal Corporation Glass Factory in Angeles, Clarkfield, Luzon, turn out a variety of glassware.

shuttle beach-going expats and locals across the strait to Mindoro. A real time-saver is to take the day-trip that leaves from the Centrepoint Hotel in Manila. If you really want a concentrated paradise haven, then try **Boracay**. There are direct flights from Manila and Cebu, and after hopping off the transport *banca*, you won't have to go much further than the small stretch of White Beach for fun, sun, and R&R.

If you have a week, you can spend two days exploring Manila, then either join a tour or head on your own to **Baguio**, **Banaue**, and **Sagada** in Northern Luzon. This would be an excellent circuit if you like outdoor adventure with a mingling of cultural sights. You can either hire your own tour, or bus it on your own. There are also flights to Banaue, which would save time, and you could work your way south by bus, taking in the vertigo inducing, but beautiful Halsema Highway toward Baguio. Plan an overnight stay in Banaue to visit the magnificent rice terraces, built more than two millennia ago. From there, Sagada is a quick ride. Get your flashlights ready and explore the

honeycomb of caves that maze beneath the town. There are innumerable hiking opportunities as well where you can come up close to the limestone caves used by the Ifugao to hang the wooden coffins of their deceased.

From Sagada, proceed to Baguio to investigate faith healers or take in one of the most fascinating market scenes in the country. Two days is sufficient time to spend here before heading back to Manila.

Of course, if your plan is to avoid Manila altogether, then flying into **Cebu**, the main hub for islands in the Visayas region, is your best bet. From there you might choose to relax the days away at an all-inclusive resort on nearby **Mactan Island**, like the Shangri-La Mactan Island Resort. It is also less than two hours by ferry from Cebu to **Bohol**. Here you can take in a day of diving on Panglao Island or Balicasag Island, or hire a car to visit Bohol Museum, Hinagdanan Cave, Baclayon Church (the oldest stone church in the country), the tarsier monkey, and finally the mysterious Chocolate Hills. This circuit of sights is quite easy to organize. The ferries from Cebu leave quite regularly

throughout the day for Bohol, and drop you right in Tagbilaran, where you can hire a car from the port to take you to the sights, or you can rent a motorbike and brave the bumpy roads yourself.

## Festive Flings

One salient aspect of Filipino culture is the almost daily occurrence of various festivals and holidays: Filipinos love lavish processions and spectacular displays of gaudiness. For reasons ranging from the venerable to the eccentric, and for periods of a few hours to nine days to even a month, each festival or holiday is zealously celebrated in commemoration of a specific event (whether religious, political or rite of nature) or in honor of a religious or national icon.

### JANUARY
The **Feast of the Black Nazarene** is held in Quiapo, Manila, on January 9. A life-size black wooden Christ is carried through town by barefoot men yelling, "*Viva Señor*," while a huge crowd tries to touch the effigy in the hope of having their sins forgiven. A week later, from January 16–22, **Ati-Atihan** is held in Kalibo, Panay. Kalibo runs joyfully amok for three days and nights in celebration of the Atis selling a portion of Panay in the mid-thirteenth century to 10 families fleeing from Borneo. The descendants of these Bornean families have been grateful ever since, holding the Ati-Atihan festival to glorify peace and camaraderie among peoples. The term "Atihan" means to "make like the Atis," thus the revelers blacken their faces to look like the Ati, who were among the Philippines' Negrito people. They march and brandish their spears, chanting, "*Hala bira!*" (Come on and join!). Participants and thousands of spectators dance and sing around the clock until the final night, when a procession of the participants closes the festival. Ironically, although the festival celebrates hospitality and good will, in the sixteenth century the Spanish used the props of the festival — the black skin dye and the warlike clothing — to repel hostile Muslims who sought to

OPPOSITE: An enthusiastic band at the Quiapo Fiesta, Manila. ABOVE: Young Muslim girls, from Mindanao, participating in the National Day Parade.

convert the recently Christianized Kalibo to Islam. The Spanish were successful against the Muslims and attributed their victory to Jesus Christ. This has lent the festival a layer of religious significance in addition to its original purely historical import. It is the oldest and most spectacular festival in the Philippines. A slightly smaller and less touristed Ati-Atihan occurs in Ibajay, Panay, the weekend after the Kalibo festival. Ibajayans claim theirs is the original and authentic celebration of Panay's barter by the Atis. An even smaller and less chaotic version is held in Iloilo City, Panay — where they call it **Dinagyang**.

Prized bulls from San Joaquin, Iloilo and neighboring areas fight amid wild cheering from spectators on the hillsides of San Joaquin for **Pasungay**, on the second Saturday of January. In Cebu City, during the third week of January, **Sinulog**, or **Santo Niño de Cebu**, commemorates the Christianization of Cebu and, specifically, of Cebu City's patron saint, Santo Niño. Costumed, soot-covered crowds dance and march through town to the beating of drums. The dance rhythm derives from the *sulog* (river current).

## FEBRUARY

The **Feast of Our Lady of Candelaria** is the biggest religious event in the western Visayas island group. Held in Jaro, Iloilo City, on February 2, it honors the patron saint of Jaro with parades and the blessing of candles, which people take to their houses for protection against danger. The three days from February 22 to 25 are the Philippines' **People Power Days**, when celebrants give thanks for the demise of the Marcos regime and commemorate the return of democracy borne by the People Power revolution. February 25 is an official national holiday to recognize this political milestone.

## MARCH/APRIL

The island of Marinduque metamorphoses into a colossal Roman theater for the **Moriones Festival**, the most colorful Lenten festival in the Philippines. Every island citizen is a cast member in this week-long drama, wearing tunics, painted masks and helmets of flowers, and dramatizing the conversion of the Roman soldier Longinus. In the play, Longinus pierces the side of the crucified Jesus with his sword, regains his sight when Jesus's blood splashes on his eye, sees Jesus ascend to heaven and, as the result of telling his fellow Romans what he saw, is forced to flee for his life. The play culminates in the Romans' capture and execution of Longinus on Easter Sunday.

**Maundy Thursday** and **Good Friday** are national and official holidays. The most intensively celebrated day of the holy week is Good Friday, where in almost every Philippine town religious plays and processions fill the day with solemnity and pageantry. These are not for the fainthearted — widespread crucifixion re-enactments can involve actual nailings on the cross. Some of the biggest celebrations are those in San Fernando (Pampanga province, Luzon), Antipolo (Rizal province, Luzon), Jordan (on Guimaras Island, Western Visayas) and in Manila. Throughout the country, hundreds of flagellants beat their backs to a bloody pulp with bamboo whips in processions that can become increasingly frenzied and gory. In some cases, barefoot men wearing thorn crowns stop and ask helpers to cut their skin with shards of broken glass to make the penitential rite still bloodier. On **Easter Sunday**, church bells chime throughout the country at dawn while mothers and sons march in separate processions to honor Jesus's meeting with his mother after his resurrection. Otherwise, this holiday is celebrated in traditional Catholic fashion.

The 1942 World War II battle against the Japanese is remembered on **Bataan Day**, April 9, an official national holiday. At Mount Samat Shrine on the Bataan Peninsula, boy scouts re-enact the "Death March," when the Japanese army forced American and Filipino soldiers captured on Corregidor Island to march 184 km (114 miles) through Bataan to Capas, Tarlac, where they remained imprisoned throughout the war. Nearly 10,000 men died on the march; many more died as prisoners.

## MAY

May means flowers in the Philippines, and the **Flores de Mayo** festival is

observed nationwide. In Ermita, Manila, little girls dressed in white present flowers at the altar to the Virgin Mary every day in May. In Ermita and across the country, a procession of *sagalas* (the most beautiful girls of the town) marks the end of the festival on May 31.

The patron saint of Filipino farmers, San Isidro de Labrador, is celebrated at the **Pulilan Carabao Festival** at Pulilan, Bulacan province, Luzon, on May 15. The festival honors the saint with a presentation of the farmers' best friend,

OPPOSITE: A young reveler flags after three exhausting days of Ati-Atihan celebrations.
ABOVE: Ride a buffalo? The annual Water Buffalo Festival, in Pulilan Town, Bulacan, is the place to do it.

the *carabao*, or water buffalo, to the parish priest. The splendor which accompanies this presentation is perhaps unsurpassed anywhere in the Philippines: brass bands, contests, games, displays of harvest produce, and comedic stage shows, herds of carabao dressed to the nines in flowers and ribbons — culminating in the carabao race, which finishes with the carabao all kneeling before the priest to be blessed. A similar festival is held the same day in Lucban and Sariaya in Quezon province, Luzon, where every house is lavishly decorated with all manner of agricultural products and chandelier-like floral designs made from rainbow-colored rice wafers known as *kiping*. Parades and processions for the saint are held in mid-afternoon, with homeowners throwing the fruit and other produce decorating their homes to the passing crowd. This festival is called *Pahiyas*, which means "precious offering."

**Obando**, in Bulacan province, Luzon, holds a three-day celebration from May 17 to 19 in honor of the town's three patron saints — Santa Clara, patron saint of the childless; San Pascual Baylon, model of religious virtue; and Our Lady of Salambao, to whom fisherman pray for a bountiful harvest. For Santa Clara, the childless dance, praying for children, and the unmarried dance in the hope of finding a spouse (women and men dance on separate days). Parents dance in thanksgiving and to bless their children. Fishermen and farmers dance to pray for a good harvest. All of the Obando dances and processions are based on pre-Christian fertility rites.

## JUNE TO AUGUST
June 12 is the Philippino **Independence Day**, a national holiday commemorating the beginning of the First Philippine Republic (1895). It is celebrated throughout the nation with parades, firework displays, concerts and pealing church bells. A giant military parade is staged through Rizal Park, in Manila.

All towns and suburbs named San Juan celebrate the **Feast of Saint John the Baptist** on June 24 with a playful "baptism" with ilang-ilang scented water. Meant to be a coy flirtation between the sexes, it can degenerate into a free-for-all water fight with much drenching and laughter. Balayan, in Batangas province, Luzon, celebrates the day too, with its **Parada Ng Lechon**. Early in the morning, people assemble at the patio of the town church dressed in zany clothing (whatever amuses them) and present their golden-red roast pigs. Water is thrown over pigs and people, and the parade begins, all culminating in a *lechon* (roast pork) feast. June 24 is also **Manila Day**, the anniversary of Manila's proclamation as capital in 1571. It is celebrated with a parade, film festival and concerts in Manila, as well as a proliferation of "I love Manila" T-shirts.

Legend has it that two hostile ancestral tribes were unified and then rent asunder by the marriage of Bilawin, daughter of a Muslim chief, to Bagani, a Manobo warrior, in Misamis Oriental province, Mindanao. The community suffered shame (*kagayhaan*) as the result of this reversal of their optimism about peaceful tribal coexistence. A reason to party lurks somewhere in this event: the **Kagayhaan Festival** in Cagayan de Oro City celebrates solidarity in the midst of tribal cultural diversity with a week of street dances and lyrical melodies performed by members of Cagayan de Oro's schools in the last week of August.

## SEPTEMBER AND OCTOBER

Catholic rituals and ancient tribal practices combine in the **Lem-Lunay T'Boli Festival** in Lake Sebu, South Cotabato province, Mindanao during the third week in September. Six South Cotabato tribes partake in a commemorative mass, horse fighting, games and dances, all in an endeavor to remember their promise to work toward the Christian paradise, Eden. In the same week, and featuring a boat parade carrying the Blessed Virgin of Penafrancia, set on a floating pagoda, hundreds of devotees occupy boats and line the riverbank in Naga City, Camarines Sur, Luzon for the **Penafrancia Festival**, also known as Feast of Nuestra Señora de Penafrancia. The **Zamboanga Hermosa Festival** in the second week of October in Zamboanga City, Zamboanga del Sur province, Mindanao also celebrates the Virgin Mary, towards whom the people of this province hold a special devotion

as a unifying cultural and historical symbol of the land. There are fireworks, parades, a regatta, variety shows, games, a carnival and the Miss Zamboanga Pageant.

The **Masskara Festival** is held in mid-October in Bacolod City, Negros Occidental province, Negros. No event of religious or cultural history, no saint or divine spirit serves to justify this big blowout. What we have here is fun for fun's sake. In this city, on these days, it's time to party, masked, costumed, and in the streets. Even if you don't feel like dancing and singing, the pig-catching and pole-climbing competitions are musts. The contest for the best mask is also exciting. Of course it's not as purposeless as it may appear: the festival is meant to lift people's spirit and to attract tourists, who flock here to join the merrymaking and to buy the orchids and ornate handicrafts on sale.

Also called the Feast of San Clemente, **Gigantes** is a festival held in late October in Angono, Rizal province, Luzon, in honor of the town's patron

OPPOSITE: Harking back to days of Spanish rule, these elegant dresses are paraded in Zamboanga.
ABOVE: A fire eater on Mindanao island.

saint, San Clemente. The party centers around *papier mâché* giants, colorfully garbed and painted, surrounded by much dancing, singing and feasting. These *gigantes* (giants) lead the procession, mounted on stilts or carried by members of the community. Puppets, trailed by dolls that portray the occupation of their creators, follow as part of the entourage. At the end of the procession are small puppet children and a brightly painted *papier mâché* bull, whose body sparks with fireworks.

## NOVEMBER AND DECEMBER

**All Saints' Day** on November 1 is an official holiday nationwide. In the evening, families gather in cemeteries with candles and flowers and do not leave until the break of dawn — an impressive spectacle. From November 10 to 30, the **Baguio Arts Festival** exhibits works by local, national and international artists; from paintings and sculpture to photography, drawing and mixed media. There are also workshops and lectures on local tribal arts. The **Baguio Christmas Festival** then begins, on December 1, and the partying continues for over a month, as various Christmas activities — dances, fireworks, agricultural exhibitions, contests, and craft demonstrations — dominate this mountain resort town. **Paskuhan** is the collective term for the fiestas celebrated throughout the Philippines during December.

A **Giant Lantern Festival** is held in San Fernando in Pampanga, Luzon on December 24 and 25 (the *parol*, a star-shaped lantern, is the Philippine symbol of Christmas). Lanterns representing the ultimate in *parol* art are indisputably unique in design and grandiosity. *Parols* are displayed in all shapes, colors and sizes — some so huge they must be mounted on flat-bed trucks for the festival procession and competition. Once launched, the kaleidoscopic pattern of lights sways to the music of accompanying bands. The procession begins at around 11 PM, and the most magnificent lantern is selected after midnight mass.

In San José de Buena Vista, Antique province, Panay, the year ends with **Binirayan**, a celebration of the barter of Panay on December 28–30, re-enacted most graphically here. This barter is commemorated with a mass followed by nonstop dancing until dawn, feasting and carousing. Festivals honoring this inaugural barter of Panay continue through January.

# Galloping Gourmet

Standing in the shadow of more popular and distinctive cuisine from neighboring Thailand and Malaysia, the Philippines' unique blend of Asian and Spanish flavors has never received the fanfare it deserves.

Philippine cuisine starts with the same ingredients used in much of Southeast Asia — coconut and other native produce, meat, and fish. But added to these indigenous basics are layers of influences from several cultures — Chinese, Spanish, Mexican, Indonesian, Japanese, and American. The result is a cuisine that reflects the country's history, and one that succeeds in concocting mixtures of unique flavors found nowhere else.

In general, emphasis is placed on fresh ingredients and light seasonings, with minimal preparation, rather than a reliance on elaborate sauces, spices, or intensive cooking. Rice — served on a plate or a banana leaf — coconuts, vegetables, and fish constitute the main staples. Filipinos tend to prefer serving an array of dipping sauces, or *sawsawan*, so dishes can be seasoned to individual taste. These vary from vinegar with minced garlic, soy sauce, ketchup, chili sauce, and *patis* (mustard). Other accompaniments include *bagoong* (chopped green mangos mixed with shrimp) and *achara* (pickled papaya). Usually, Filipinos like to serve all the dishes at once, rather than having several courses and, especially in the rural provinces, people eat in the traditional way — with their hands.

Many of the classic Filipino dishes are derived from Spain, with some Mexican influences too, but most are mixed with Asian flair. This means that *lengua con champignon* (marinated ox tongue in cream-of-mushroom gravy) crosses paths with crispy *pata* (deep-fried pig's knuckles in garlic and soy sauce) and *laing* (taro leaves in spicy fresh coconut milk, flavored with shrimp paste) in what may seem somewhat surreal combinations.

Probably the most popular staple dish is *adobo*, a casserole which combines pork or chicken stewed in a mixture of vinegar, bay leaves, peppercorns and garlic over a slow fire.

The Spanish influence is also evident in such dishes as *paella Valenciana* (rice cooked with meat and seafood) and the popular pork stews, *cocido* and *puchero*.

*Lechon* (oven-baked or charcoal-broiled roast pork) is typically served at special occasions or fiestas. Depending on the restaurant, you can usually order single portions or an entire whole roast pig, if your party is large enough.

Many dishes are Chinese in origin, but have evolved a distinctly Filipino twist. Noodle dishes and soups can be found everywhere; street cafés and restaurants devoted to them are called *panciterias*, named after the classic noodle dish, *pancit*. There are many regional varieties, including *pancit malabon*, made with seafood, or *pancit molo*, an adaptation of wonton soup. Dining at panciterias is a good way of experiencing Filipino life — they are always busy, with rickety little tables and chairs on the street — and usually good. Many *panciterias* and *carinderias* (the Filipino version of a fast-food stall) serve an array of Filipino morsels, which are fun to sample.

It is always useful to remember that carinderias operate on a *turo-turo* (literally, "point-point") system, allowing you point to whatever looks good. *Ihaw-ihaw* (grilled or barbecued meat or seafood), *morisqueta tostada* (Yangzhou fried rice), *camaron rebozado* (shrimp fried

Fresh vegetables on display in a Laoag market, Ilocos Norte (Luzon).

in batter), and *siopo* (a steamed bun filled with meat) are all tasty examples of what you will encounter. The Chinese staple of rice congee has found its way into the national diet, renamed *arroz caldo*: rice porridge with slices of meat or tripe topped with spring onions. Another Chinese addition is the popular *hopia*, lightly sweet pastries filled with lotus or mashed bean paste. Once you are familiar with a few Filipino terms, you will soon find your way around a menu. The name of each dish usually describes how it has been prepared. *Sinigang* is a hot, sour broth and can be made with fish, prawns, or meat, cooked with vegetables. *Prito* means fried, while *gisa*, *gisado* and *ginisa* mean sautéed. *Pakisaw* indicates the dish has been stewed in vinegar; *ginataan* is a dish that has been cooked with coconut; and *ihaw-ihaw* means broiled or barbecued.

In a classic Filipino restaurant, you will generally find *adobo karekare* (beef and vegetables stewed in peanut sauce), *sinigang*, *rellenong bangus* (milkfish, deboned and stuffed with chopped meat and vegetables), crispy *pata*, fresh or fried *lumpia* (spring rolls), *tinola* (chicken stew), and *bistek* (Filipino beefsteak).

Seafood is abundant and rarely disappoints. *Lapu Lapu* (garoupa), *tanguigue* (a local species) and blue marlin are Filipino staples, while *bangus* (milkfish), lobsters, prawns, shrimps, and crabs are plentiful. If you come across *tatus* (coconut crab), try it for its unusual, rich flavor.

Filipinos are great devotees of their afternoon ritual of *merienda*, a break to savor a few snacks, typically sweet and full of calories. Whether served in a humble roadside stall or in a five-star hotel lobby, they are usually delicious. Merienda usually comprises such sweets as *bibingkas* (sweet coconut cakes), *ginataan* (glutinous, sugary concoctions), and *halo-halo* — a dessert made from crushed ice mixed with diced flavored gelatin, candied sweets and fruit, with sweetened condensed milk poured over it. Another popular way to snack is to indulge in a local delicacy — slurping up *balut* — semi-raw fertilized duck and chicken eggs.

Fruits are superb in the Philippines, almost always perfectly fresh and, no matter where you go, beautifully presented. Tropical fruits include mango, jackfruit, star apple, and dozens of banana varieties, as well as pomelos, custard apples, rambutan, lanzones, and the infamous Durian — specialties of Mindanao.

As for drinks, there are many fruit concoctions which are good thirst quenchers, either on their own or mixed with water. Fresh *calamansi* (a small fruit which is a cross between an orange and lemon), mango and pineapple juices are especially good. Delicious and healthy coconut milk is served everywhere by roadside or beachside sellers, who lop off the coconut's top with a flourish. Otherwise, the national drink is San Miguel, the best known and only locally brewed beer. You may encounter various fermented creations on your travels: *tuba*, made with coconut sap, or *buri* from nipa palms are both distilled into the powerfully inebriating *lambanog*.

## Special Interests

With world-class sites like Tubbataha Reefs and Pamalican Island, its no wonder so many divers from all over the world come to the Philippines. **Diving tours** can be organized once in the country or from abroad, taking in the best reefs of the country, as well as some of the best wreck-diving in the world, thanks to the American-Japanese war.

Some tours choose to resort-hop. Many resorts offer good-value dive and accommodation packages, which are probably the best and most affordable way to dive in the Philippines. Packages include transport between resorts and in most cases include equipment rental. Still other tours involve a live-aboard boat that takes divers to the harder to reach destinations like the famed Tubbataha Reefs. These boats are quite luxurious, serving three meals a day usually, and offering private cabins. Often you can customize the route by taking in major sites like those found off the coast of Mindoro, then proceeding to Moalboal and Olango Island, and then onto Bohol for the marine Meccas of Balicasag, Pamalacan, and Cabilao Islands. After taking in the Visayas, Palawan is the next

step. El Nido and Coron are magnificent. Coron is the main jumping-off point for wreck dives on the devastated Japanese support fleet. From here the long journey, 182 km (113 miles) into the Sulu Sea, takes you to Tubbataha Reefs, the best site in the country, and one of the best in Southeast Asia. Dive operators are everywhere in the country. You can inquire with any of them regarding dive tours or live-aboard options; Scuba World Dive Shop in Manila ( (2) 895-3551 is a particularly good resource for information on diving tours.

Many specialized tours can be arranged once you are in the country. Those with a passion for **arts and crafts** can take an organized visit to the artist village of Angono, the woodcarvers' village of Paete, the barong-weavers of Lumban in Laguna, the furniture-makers in Pampanga, the gold jewelers in Bulacan, the silversmiths of Baguio, or the tribal woodcarvers in Banaue.

The Philippines is also home to more than 500 species of birds. The protected forests on mountains and island coves are interesting destinations for ornithologists and **bird watchers**. Tours can be arranged through Manila's travel agencies to top destinations including Mount Apo, Mount Makiling, Mount Canlaon, Palawan Islands, and Butuan Marsh.

A **sailing** vacation strengthens the arms and makes the most of the Philippines endless islands and inlets. A restored Vietnamese sailing junk, the *Mariposa* cruises from Boracay through the islands of the Visayas. The *Mariposa* junk tour is your opportunity to sail through tropical waters and leave your footprints on the Semirara group of islands, some 30 km (19 miles) west of Boracay and 25 km (16 miles) south of the large island of Mindoro. The creaking rigging and furling red sails are reminiscent of another era, and daily stops on lonely islands allow you time to beachcomb, snorkel, explore caves, and even mountain bike. Scuba diving and

LEFT: Food stalls everywhere will serve up dishes of spit-roasted suckling pig or chicken. RIGHT: The myriad tropical fruits, available year round, lend themselves to exotic cocktails.

equipment can also be provided. Dinner is taken onshore, where friendly locals might be persuaded to share stories, drinks and a meal around the bonfire. For reservations, contact Andy Haberl at Aquarius Diving (/FAX (36) 288-3132, in Boracay. Standard cruises include day trips for up to 20 people, or seven-day expeditions for up to six people.

For the active adventurer, **spelunking** as well as **mountain climbing**, **trekking**, and **paddling** tours can be arranged — taking in the best of the honeycombs, high peaks, and whitewater that the country has to offer.

## Taking a Tour

Those who want to explore as much as possible within the time available, but are wary of having to organize it all themselves, could find that a tour may provide the solution. The many "**Rediscovery**" or "**Islands Magic**" tour packages offer particularly good value, and are recommended for their compact and well-managed approach — plus, they always stay at reputable hotels. Tours include a six-day trip taking in Baguio, Mount Data, Sagada, Bontoc and Banaue; and a five-day trip combining a trek to Mount Mayon and a beach holiday in and the Catanduanes. Other excursions take in Vigan, Villa Escudero, Bohol, Iloilo and Isla Naburot. On Bohol, you have a choice of either renting your own motorbike or hiring a day tour to take you through the sites easily and comfortably. The tour takes in all the important sites. It starts out at the Bohol Museum, once the home of the fourth president of the Philippines, and continues north to the Blood Compact Site, stopping at Hinagdanan Cave, an eerie underworld of stalactites and stalagmites that form sculptures in the underground pool. You can go caving and swimming here before heading on to a quick stop at Baclayon Church, one of the oldest stone churches in the country. Not far from Baclayon, you have the remarkable opportunity to

interact with the tarsier monkey, the world's smallest primate. From there you can stop at Magasa Falls, Loboc River where there is a bamboo hanging bridge, and on to Chocolate Hills, your final destination. All trips offer a good cross-section of places and the option to be on your own for some of the journey. Contact any of the following participating agencies: Danfil Express ( (2) 525-3578, GF units D, E, and F, Isidro Building, Malate, Manila; Marsman Tours and Travel Corporation ( (2) 892-9731 to 9750 FAX (2) 813-3329, 2246 Chino Roces Avenue, Makati, Manila; or Rajah Tours Philippines ( (2) 522-0541 to 0548, Third Floor, Physicians' Tower Building, 533 United Nations Avenue, Ermita.

Those with limited time can investigate the seven-day "flight-seeing" tour offered by **Philippine Air Safari**. An island hop around the country's major attractions, it visits parts of the archipelago that would take months to see if traveling by land, flying across active volcanoes, mountains and coral reefs. Flights usually last 90 minutes or less, and nights are spent in comfortable selected hotels or resorts with excellent food. The package includes such activities as paddling in outrigger canoes, sampling coconut wine, visiting tribal villages and riding water buffalo.

**Blue Horizons** ( (2) 848-3901 FAX (2) 848-3909, 20th Floor, Trafalgar Plaza, Makati, Manila, also offers a popular air safari.

**Around-the-World tickets** have become increasingly cheaper over the last couple of years, and these tickets have really taken off in Asia. Australia's national airline, Qantas, offers a multi-Asia ticket for less than US$2,000, and allows a maximum of five stops in eastern Asia, including Manila. The **Circle Pacific ticket** from North America has you departing San Francisco to any or all of the following cities: Hong Kong, Guangzhou, Bangkok, Manila, and Honolulu; then back to San Francisco.

It's always a good idea to check with the Philippine Department of Tourism in Manila for new tours or excursion packages.

Fort Ilocandia Resort, along Suba Beach, near Laoag.

# Welcome
# to the
# Philippines

AN ARCHIPELAGO NATION SPRINKLED LIKE EMERALD confetti on the ocean, the Philippines is the envy of many of its regional rivals for its innumerable beaches, fabled coral reefs, and remarkably rich patchwork of tribal cultures. Reaching up to China at one tip and to Borneo and Malaysia on the other, its clustered islands number, at last count, 7,107 at low tide — most of them uninhabited.

For many years, the Philippines seemed the lost heart of Southeast Asia. While its neighbors, Indonesia, Taiwan, Malaysia, and Thailand surged forward to become the regional economic "tigers," the Philippines remained mired in economic chaos and turbulent politics. When, each Easter, devout Filipinos struggled to carry huge wooden crosses on their bare backs, it was difficult not to think of their efforts as a metaphor for the nation's burdens. Yet appearances, often at their most deceptive in Asia, can be especially misleading in the Philippines.

Unlike any other Asian nation, the Philippines is a unique mingling of Western and Eastern influences, for both Spain and America have left indelible traces of former domination, ranging from a stepping-stone array of baroque churches, staunch Roman Catholicism and the Spanish *mañana* attitude to an American-styled legislative system — as well as an openness to Western mores.

It may well be that, long before encountering the Philippines, you have glimpsed something of the optimistic Filipino spirit, for not many other countries have so many of its citizens working abroad, while remaining so dedicated to their mother country. A huge percentage of the Philippine gross national product comes from remittances from Filipinos abroad. Within the Philippines, that spirit is all-embracing: from the high-voltage Makati restaurants and pleasure dens of urban Manila to the most remote outposts of undeveloped Palawan and the populous barrios and barangays in the provinces. "*Bahala na*," (What will be, will be) the Filipinos say and, somehow, this philosophy is all-pervasive.

After two decades of dictatorship under Ferdinand and Imelda Marcos (credited with robbing the national treasury and crippling the country's economic growth) and a sudden incandescent expression of "People Power" under the yellow-clad presidency of Corazon Aquino (and, more recently with the rejection of playboy president Joseph Estrada) the Philippines has been working hard to transform itself into Asia's latest economic miracle and tourist playground. These days, foreign investment is evident everywhere, with a bouquet of idyllic resorts sprouting on far-flung islands. Meanwhile, Manila appears to be making a much needed rejuvenation, with new buildings rising on every street corner of Makati, the capital's business and entertainment magnet.

With its dizzying abundance of islands, the Philippines can seem overwhelming when it comes to planning your travels. There are great wilderness areas and lush forests, island clusters and resorts to match those in the Caribbean, and awe-inspiring seascapes to explore; but remember, this is also a land where insurgent armies and kidnappings occasionally make the news, along with reports of unsafe airports and ferries.

While it is tempting to venture off the beaten track, you may also wish to ensure that your vacation doesn't turn out to be more of an adventure than you expect. Although menaces do exist, few involve visitors. And, while an adventurous spirit is required to enjoy traveling in the Philippines, be warned: the rewards can be so spectacular and the beauty so soulful, that you may soon find that you have the country under your skin. As they say in the Philippines,"*Mabuhay!*" Welcome!

OPPOSITE: Soot and revelry at the Ati-Atihan festival in Kalibo. ABOVE: Elaborate weaving characterizes the dress of the T'boli tribespeople of Mindanao.

# The Country and Its People

HISTORY CASTS LONG AND VARIED SHADOWS across the Philippines. Given that the nation encompasses an archipelago made up of 7,107 islands — some concentrated in highly populated clusters, others far-flung and remote — this is hardly surprising. Of these many islands, however, some 2,500 are not named, only 1,000 are inhabited, and a mere 11 of them constitute 94 percent of the Philippines' total landmass. The 11 are, in order of size: Luzon, Mindanao, Palawan, Panay, Mindoro, Samar, Negros, Leyte, Cebu, Bohol and Masbate.

Any portrait of the many indigenous people of the Philippines also becomes an account of two of its most influential conquerors, the Spanish and the Americans, who both profoundly shaped the politics, religion, economy and culture of the Philippines. Significantly, unlike any other nation in Asia, the Philippines is a Christian nation: 85 percent of the population is Catholic; an additional eight percent is Catholic-based and Protestant.

From this perspective, the history of the Philippines is dominated by that of a manageable 11 islands, two peoples, and one religion. Some even subscribe to the boiled-down version of Philippine history as stated in the oft-quoted phrase, "three centuries in a Catholic convent and 50 years in Hollywood," which refers to the country's subjugation under Spanish rule from the late sixteenth to the late nineteenth centuries, and to the nearly half-century of American governance from 1898 to 1946.

## EARLY HISTORY

Human migration to the Philippines began at least 35,000 years ago. It is unknown whether people came in large waves or in a steady trickle, but scholars are reasonably certain they settled as families, who evolved into clans or tribes. During the period from about 35,000 BC until Spain laid uncontested claim to the Philippines in the late sixteenth century, this sprawling archipelago became home to numerous disparate languages and cultures without any semblance of national unity. Those who came by sea developed trading relations with their countries of origin and other countries.

Those who came earlier, by land, remained land-bound nomadic hunters: the Negrito.

Approximately 65 native tribes survived Spanish and American subjugation. They are scattered throughout the archipelago, comprising six million of the nation's 68 million inhabitants. Only about 10 percent of these surviving tribes maintain their prehistoric belief systems and behavior and speak their own dialects — in all, some 111 dialects are known to exist. They range from the Badjao sea gypsies of the Sulu Archipelago to the only recently reformed

headhunting Kalinga tribe in the mountains of northern Luzon.

In a discovery that amazed anthropologists worldwide, in 1978 the Tau't Batu tribe of Palawan was found living as they did 20,000 years ago, dwelling exclusively in limestone caves and subsisting on birds, bats, and snails. Tourism to the region where they live is not permitted.

The first people to reach the Philippines were the Australoid Negrito from Borneo. Over a 25,000 year period, roughly from 35,000 BC to 10,000 BC, they followed the

OPPOSITE: Vibrant color plays an important part in the dress of the T'boli tribe from South Cotabato Province, Mindanao, one of the most prestigious tribes in the Philippines. ABOVE : A traditional Ifugao stilted house in Kiangan, North Luzon.

migrations of animals over the land bridges which then connected the Philippines with the rest of Southeast Asia; until melting ice and rising sea levels submerged them 7,000 to 10,000 years ago. The Negrito were nomadic hunters armed with bows, arrows and blow guns, who migrated to Luzon, Palawan, Mindoro and Mindanao. At least 15,000 Negrito survive today, principally in eastern Luzon. These tribal people are governed only by family leaders — still clad in bark and living in huts built from branches and grass, still hunting with blow

to as Late Neolithic or Indonesian-B. Their houses, sheltered by pyramidal roofs and raised on stilts, were protected against rains and flooding, unlike those of their predecessors, whose houses were covered with rounded roofs and were built directly on the bare ground or even inside meter-deep pits.

The third group of migrating mariners, who came between 800 BC and 500 BC, were from southern China and Indochina. They made many invaluable contributions to human advancement on the Philippines,

guns and bows and arrows. Descendants of the early Negritos are found in tribes throughout the Philippines, but they are concentrated in the Aeta, Agta, Ati, Baluga, Batak, and Mamanuwa tribes in Luzon and the Visayas (the main island group of the Philippines).

Immigrants who came after the Negritos arrived by sea. The first group of these seafaring immigrants sailed from Indonesia 5,000 to 6,000 years ago. Anthropologists refer to them as people of the Early New Stone Age, or the Indonesian-A. They were expert builders of boats, carpenters of wood-framed houses, and skilled in dry (non-irrigated) agriculture. The second group arrived between 1,500 BC and 500 BC, and are referred

including the introduction of copper and bronze tools, copper mining and smelting technologies, and irrigated rice culture using landscaped terraces. These immigrants are the direct ancestors of the present-day tribes of northern Luzon and Mindanao.

The Malay Peninsula produced subsequent immigrants, who are believed to have arrived in three waves: between 300 BC and 100 BC, between AD 200 and AD 1200, and during the fourteenth and fifteenth centuries. The first wave took two different ocean routes — from west Borneo via Palawan and Mindoro to Luzon, and from east Borneo via the Celebes Strait to Mindanao and the Visayas — and eventually settled in the mountains of Luzon,

Mindanao, and the Visayas (the islands of Panay, Samar, Negros, Leyte, Cebu, and Bohol). Their contributions were many and of enormous significance: the discovery and use of iron for tools, weapons, and utensils, as well as for forging and smelting; the introduction of the back loom and spindle for making woven textiles for mats, baskets and clothing, which supplanted bark cloth; the further development of agriculture with their introduction of the horse and *carabao*, or water buffalo, and of improved irrigation methods; finally, their sophisticated techniques for making pottery and personal ornaments. In the mountains of Luzon and Mindanao today, tribes descended from these Malays still practice the same methods of iron forging and back-loom weaving.

The second wave of Malays were even more advanced in that they possessed an alphabet. Unlike their mountain-dwelling Malay predecessors, they chose to settle in lowlands, especially along coasts and rivers, which proved a natural training ground for their development into skilled sailors and traders. They also became rice farmers and devised superior irrigation methods, which increased their food supply, allowing rapid population growth. Thus the Malays proliferated across the flatlands of the entire archipelago and overwhelmed the interior tribes in number.

Surrounded by open space and water, the Malays, like rivers flowing to the sea, were naturally bound to connect with the outside world — unlike their predecessors who had settled and remained secluded in mountainous and backwater habitats. The Malays' literacy endowed them with intellectual curiosity, and their involvement in trade with India, China and Indochinese states taught them acceptance of foreign peoples and customs. No wonder then that it was these outward-gazing lowland Malays, spreading their population across the Philippines for over a millennium beginning in about AD 200, who succumbed (on the whole, peaceably) to the exploitative Spanish, and became the forefathers of modern-day Filipino Christians.

The final wave of Malays settled mainly in Mindanao and in nearby Sulu during the

fourteenth and fifteenth centuries. They are believed to be the ancestors of the current population of Mindanao's Muslims. The Philippines' Muslims, forming around seven percent of the nation's population, are still concentrated in Mindanao today.

## FOREIGN INFLUENCES AND THE RISE OF ISLAM

Straddling ancient sea trading routes, it was inevitable that the archipelago become a landing place and transfer station

for early seafarers — Chinese, Indian, Arab, Japanese, and Siamese among them. It is not known exactly when the first contact with China began, but it is certain that by the early part of China's Zhou Dynasty (1066 to 221 BC), trade links had been established with the Philippines, which were strengthened in the period leading up to the Ming Dynasty (1368 to 1644).

Chinese traders bartered their exquisite silk textiles, porcelain, bronze, fans and beads — as well as lead sinkers for fishnets — while the Philippines offered such wares as gold, pearls, rough cotton, betel nut,

OPPOSITE: Descendants of some of the islands' earliest settlers, the Negritos. ABOVE: A Muslim girl from Zamboanga, a stronghold of Philippine Islam.

hemp and tortoiseshell — and encouraged the Chinese craze for birds' nest soup. Another more subtle trade and cultural influence came from India, beginning in the late seventh century and permeating as far as Java and Sumatra.

By the thirteenth century, Arab merchants and missionaries were regularly trading with the inhabitants of Jolo, the capital of Sulu province, and converting them to Islam. By then, Islam's sphere of influence in the region spanned throughout Southeast Asia including Sumatra and

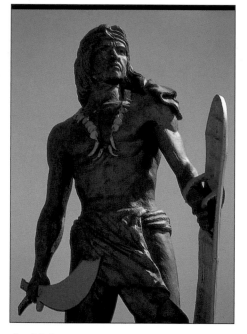

the Malay Peninsula. Islam became the dominant creed in the Sulu islands by the late fifteenth century. A generation later, the first sultanate was established in Mindanao under Sharif Mohammed Kabungsuwan. His followers and other Muslim immigrants propagated Islam in Southern Luzon, Mindoro, and Manila. Islam began to impart to converts a collective sense of identity and pride, which no doubt explains the success of their resistance to the Spanish invaders, as distinct from the passive reception by non-Muslim lowlanders. If it wasn't for the Spanish incursion in the mid-sixteenth century, the Philippines today might well be an Islamic nation.

# THE SPANISH INVADE

To many sixteenth-century Roman Catholic Europeans, life's most important duty and responsibility was Catholic worship and observance, and the loftiest accomplishment was converting the ignorant to Catholicism. In 1519, Ferdinand Magellan set sail with his men and a large wooden cross on a mission for the glory of God and Spain. Their mission was to find new routes to the Orient and its spices and to convert those encountered there to Catholicism. Two years later, Magellan reached Samar in the Visayas and soon after erected his cross on nearby soil on the auspicious date of Easter Sunday, 1521. He was to make a blood pact with the island's leader, Rajah Humabon, followed by a mass baptism and conversion to Christianity.

No one knows exactly why Magellan lost his life a few weeks later on neighboring Mactan Island. He had a clear foe in Lapu Lapu, the chieftain of a nearby island who confronted the Spanish adventurer on the beaches of Mactan. It is only known that he was killed in a skirmish with natives and that of his five ships only one, loaded with spices, returned to Spain. Those spices more than paid for Magellan's expedition and justified the dispatch by Spain of another four galleons between 1525 and 1542. Ironically, the Philippines probably did not produce these spices, as was discovered by later Spanish explorers who found the Philippines without export-quality spices, its only native spice being an inferior type of cinnamon. No matter, though, as these explorers saw future wealth for Spain and themselves in the porcelains, silks, velvets, pearls, lacquer, and other sumptuous goods pouring into the islands, as they had for centuries, from China — which at that time barred all foreign merchants except the Portuguese in Macao. Confident of Spain's eventual ownership of the islands, the captain of the last of these expeditions re-christened Samar and Leyte *Islas Felipinas*, after

ABOVE: A statue of Chieftain Lapu Lapu, in Mactan, Cebu. Lapu Lapu slew Magellan in 1521 for reasons still largely unclear. RIGHT: Many Baroque churches, such as this in Bohol, in the Visayas, remain from the days of Spanish rule.

King Charles I's son, Felipe, who became King Felipe II in 1556. Spain eventually draped this imperial pendant on the entire archipelago.

Anticipating fortunes born of the re-export of Chinese products from Manila to Mexico (a Spanish colony known then as New Spain), the Spanish began rapid colonization of the Philippines in 1565 and completed their occupation a mere decade later — a feat of conquest perhaps not entirely astonishing, given that the people of the archipelago were so divided amongst

themselves. At the helm of the Spanish occupation was Miguel Lopez de Legaspi, who became the colony's governor-general and founded Manila in 1571, only to die of a heart attack a year later.

During the Spanish conquest of the Philippine islands, the conquistadors brutalized the *Indios*, as the natives were called. Their armed troops would enter villages and rob, rape, raze, and kill indiscriminately, as the priest Francisco de Ortega described: "They first send in an interpreter, not with gifts or to speak of God, but to demand tribute. The people, never having been subjects of a king or a lord, are puzzled and shocked when forced to hand over their necklaces or bracelets, their only

property. Some refuse, others submit reluctantly and still others flee to the hills, terrified by this strange new race of armed men. The Spaniards pursue them, firing their arquebuses and killing without mercy, then return to the village to slaughter all the pigs and poultry, carry off all the rice and burn all the houses." In 1570, a prelate, Diego de Herrera, wrote that the Spaniards were committing "acts of violence against people in their homes and against their wives, daughters and property."

In 1583, King Felipe II, supporting the Catholic clergy, wrote, "the natives have conceived such great hatred of the Christian name, looking upon the Spaniards as deceivers who do not practice what they preach, that whatever they do is only out of compulsion." In reforms decreed that same year, the king protected native villages against officers and troops by closing them to all Spaniards except tax collectors, inspectors and friars. He confined officials and soldiers to towns, permitting them to stay only temporarily on rotating tours of duty.

These reforms enabled the Catholic monastic orders to rule the country absolutely. There were five such orders, each of which answered to a separate leadership in Rome and each of which controlled its own zone of territory: the Augustinian, Franciscan and Dominican orders were dominant in Luzon; the Jesuit and Recollects orders occupied the Visayas and Mindanao. In Spain's campaign to subjugate the Philippines, the friars were now the troops, armed not with swords but with a knowledge of local languages and customs, which they used to ingratiate themselves to the natives, and with Catholic education and rituals, which they manipulated to keep the natives servile and placated.

One of the friars' first items of business was the relocation of natives from their autonomous, scattered villages into consolidated settlements. This was not difficult: under the friars, the natives learned Catholicism and, in God's name and honor, built churches and townships. Today almost every Philippine town is dominated by a florid baroque church. As a seventeenth-century Spanish official wrote,

"Travel around the provinces and you will see populations of 5, 10 or 20,000 Indios ruled in peace by one old man who, with his doors open at all hours, sleeps secure in his dwelling." The religious orders founded colleges and universities, hospitals, museums, and libraries, established printing presses, studied and documented indigenous flora and fauna, and sought to introduce the principles of European learning and culture.

For 300 years, the education offered by the friars was limited to memorizing the

nothing except the preservation of their material comfort, colonial privileges, and absolute authority over the Indios.

## THE ADMINISTRATION UNDER THE SPANISH

Between 1565 and 1813, the colony's direct command came from the Viceroy of Mexico. Meanwhile, the real business of the Spanish presence in the Philippines was taking place in Manila, where Spain, the monastic orders and individual traders and merchants were

catechism and the lives of the saints. They also refused to teach natives the Spanish language or to allow the ordination of Filipino priests. A 1903 survey by United States missionaries found most of the Filipino population to be illiterate. To maintain the natives' passivity, the friars did not alter their indigenous tribal structure or its values; indeed, the friars combined pagan practices and paraphernalia with Catholic rituals to sustain their complacency. The friars also did nothing to improve the natives' subsistence economy of rice cultivation, livestock raising and fishing in local waters. It would seem that the friars — who had previously protested the more obvious rapaciousness of the Spanish conquistadors — cared for

all cashing in on the trade of precious Oriental goods, bought with silver Mexican pesos. The pesos were loaded onto a galleon in Acapulco, which made the four-to five-month journey to Manila, where it was unloaded and filled with goods for reshipment to Mexico. Only one galleon a year was permitted to make the trip, with the Manila-bound pesos always exceeding in value that of the returning Mexico-bound goods (this surplus constituting a subsidy). The galleon trade swelled the coffers of both church and crown, and supported the colonial govern-

OPPOSITE: Altar in the walls of Fort Pilar, Zamboanga, Mindanao. ABOVE LEFT: The Santacruzan Festival in Lucban Town, Quezon. ABOVE RIGHT: Ceiling fresco depicting the Goddess of Fertility, in a Bulacan church.

ment in Manila (consisting of a joint post of governor and military commander and his subordinate officials, officers and troops, all of whom answered to the king's viceroy in Mexico). Just as the friars who controlled the Indios of the countryside conferred nothing to them of value, so too, the bureaucrats of Manila shared nothing of their lucrative trade with the provinces.

In the early eighteenth century, a Jesuit priest, Pedro Murillo Velarde, criticized the galleon trade and said the Spanish in Manila were like "visitors to an inn," leaving

captured the capital city. The British occupied Manila for nearly two years following this, during which they stopped the galleon trade and confiscated every Spanish ship in the harbor, an act which destroyed Manila's economy. The city reverted to Spain under the Treaty of Paris in 1763.

Spain's display of weakness triggered revolts and conspiracies by Filipinos and Chinese alike in Luzon, and by Filipino Muslims in Mindanao and Sulu. These rebellions were quickly crushed, but the seeds of revolt were sown.

nothing of value behind. Of Manila's population of 90,000 in 1780, only three or four thousand were Spaniards — living along the spacious boulevards and plazas of the walled city of Intramuros. The rest were natives, living packed into bamboo shacks along streams and swamps.

Late in the eighteenth century, Spain's exploitative dominion over the largely passive Filipinos began to crack. Earlier, the Portuguese, the Dutch and a Chinese warlord had all made attempts to wrest away possession of the islands. This time, fragmentation began with Spain's defeat by the British in 1762. Britain — as part of its Seven Years' War against Spain and France — sailed its ships into Manila Bay and

## REBELLION AND REVOLUTION

To revive Manila's economy, Spain's King Charles III sent a new governor to Manila in 1778: José de Basco y Vargas. In a public speech condemning Spain's abuse of the archipelago, Basco announced, "The sun will rise over our islands after more than 200 years of darkness." With the galleon trade now on the decline and the Asian and Mexican markets no longer Manila's exclusive domain — Europe now traded directly with Asia, while Spain permitted foreign exporters to compete in the Mexican market — Basco demanded that commerce shift from the harbor to the countryside, where money, in the form of tobacco, could be pulled from the ground. Soon native Filipinos were forced to convert rice fields into tobacco plantations. They toiled in conditions of semi-slavery; growing increasingly resentful, while the newly formed Royal Company of the Philippines exported tobacco at an immense profit for Spain.

Mexico's gain of independence in 1821 was Spain's loss. To maintain its profit margin from its Philippine operations, Spain introduced sugar, copra, indigo and hemp as cash crops. Native Filipinos suffered, as rice fields disappeared, food shortages grew and supplies replenished at the natives' expense with costly imported staples.

Filipino hardship only grew worse with the advent of the Industrial Revolution in the early 1830s. As factories spread throughout Europe and America and foreign firms opened offices in Manila, Cebu and other towns, the need for raw materials accelerated — Filipinos labored all the harder. Collective Filipino suffering found comfort in Christian rituals, especially the Easter celebrations that re-enacted the suffering, death and resurrection of Jesus Christ. Ironically, Catholicism itself, which had been used as a tool to subjugate and pacify the natives, evolved into the source of their insurrection. They identified with the persecuted Christ. They championed insurgent leaders who, emulating Christ, promised salvation. One of the earliest examples of these heroic figures was Apolinario de la Cruz, who, in 1841 was executed along with 200 of his disciples by the Spanish for instigating rebellion in Luzon; he and his disciples had dedicated themselves to spreading the gospel and healing the sick.

Spain's eventual downfall was all but guaranteed by its educational reforms in 1863, which established a public school system making higher learning available to Filipinos. The opening of the Suez Canal in 1869 enabled children of wealthy families to study in Madrid, where they picked up many modern European ideas — including nationalism — as well as the history of Mexico's revolutions against Spain. Known as the *ilustrados*, these members of the Filipino intelligentsia — a racial mixture of Spanish, Indio, Chinese, Malay, and even Japanese — grew to oppose Spanish domination. Their influence ignited the first major uprising in 1872 in Cavite province, Luzon, when 200 Filipino soldiers mutinied and murdered their Spanish officers. The government executed three Filipino priests who had joined this revolt — the friars Burgos, Gomez and Zamora — who had dared to challenge the power of the Spanish officers. They were publicly garroted, an act which by itself galvanized demands for reform.

## AN ERA OF NATIONAL HEROES

From 1889 to 1895, a nationalist magazine called *La Solidaridad* was published in Spain by the Propaganda Movement, led by Filipino reformers José Rizal, the Luna brothers, Marcelo H. del Pilar and Graciano Lopez Jaena. The luminary of the group was Rizal, a medical doctor and nationalist writer, who was the well-educated son of an upper-class *ilustrado* Filipino family. Through his writings as an expatriate — *Noli Me Tangere* and *El Filibusterismo* — now both compulsory reading at Philippine schools, he depicted the abuses of the friars and the government. Rizal's vision was to see the Philippines represented in Madrid — not as a colony but as a province.

In 1892, Rizal returned to the Philippines and founded an organization seeking peaceful reform, La Liga Filipina, which promptly saw him deported to Mindanao. Four years later, in 1896, Rizal was executed in Manila on a conviction of "rebellion, sedition and illicit association." Today, more than just martyred hero, Rizal is a national messiah, worshipped in his home town of Calamba, south of Manila, as the reincarnation of Christ.

In late 1896, General Emilio Aguinaldo emerged as the nation's next revolutionary leader. He fought that year against the Spanish in Luzon, as part of an eight-province-wide revolt instigated by Andres Bonifacio, a warehouse clerk from Tondo (now a slum suburb of Manila), and his secret

San Agustin's Monastery Museum in Intramuros — offering rich pickings from the days of Spanish colonial rule.

society, the Katipunan. Soon, revolutionary fever spread across the island provinces. A year later, Bonifacio and his Katipunan, considered seditious, were ousted by Aguinaldo's new revolutionary government, which then tried, convicted and executed Bonifacio. In late 1897, the Spanish and Aguinaldo negotiated a truce, whose terms included amnesty for the rebels in exchange for payment to Aguinaldo to procure his exile to Hong Kong.

Despite the agreed peace, in early 1898, battles erupted anew. Filipinos might have

finally recaptured their own country but for unfortunate timing: America was then warring with Spain over Cuba. One side-effect of this Spanish-American War involved America's attack on the Spanish navy in Manila Harbor. On May 1, 1898, United States Commodore George Dewey and his sailors demolished the Spaniards. Unlike Britain's belligerent visit to Manila Harbor nearly 125 years earlier in the Seven Years' War, the Americans stayed not a mere 20 months, but 48 years. And they did not confine themselves strictly to Manila as had the British; the Americans made the entire archipelago theirs. Another momentous chapter in Filipino history was about to begin.

## THE ARRIVAL OF THE AMERICANS

"Have captured the Philippines; what shall we do with them?" cabled Commodore Dewey to President William McKinley. Fearing the loss of his job to a politically powerful expansionist such as Theodore Roosevelt, Henry Cabot Lodge or Alfred Thayer Mahan, the isolationist McKinley decided colonization was unavoidable. Not wishing to cite "job security" as the reason for seizing 300,439 sq km (116,000 sq miles) of land supporting a foreign population of seven million at a distance of 20,000 km (12,000 miles) from the White House, McKinley instead took the Spanish approach: "We'll Christianize them! It's our duty!" The problem was, the Spanish had already taken the same approach 300 years earlier.

No matter, most Americans exulted hysterically over Dewey's victory — they, like their president, knew nothing about the history of the Philippines — and felt intoxicated by the prospect of making the Philippines another part of their "manifest destiny" (a phrase coined in 1845 to promote the annexation of Texas).

The Americans established a military government in Manila and, despite the ending of the Spanish-American War on December 10, 1898 under the Treaty of Paris, in which Spain ceded the Philippines, Guam and Puerto Rico to the United States, they did not disband it. Less than a month later, Emilio Aguinaldo proclaimed the establishment of the First Philippine Republic, nominating himself as president. Only a few weeks after that event, an American shot a Filipino soldier and Aguinaldo declared war. Nearly three years, many battles and 200,000 Filipino fatalities later, Aguinaldo was captured and the First Philippine Republic fell. In 1902, President Roosevelt declared the Philippines "pacified." William Howard Taft, who became president of the United States and later Chief Justice of the Supreme Court, served as the first governor of the Philippines.

By World War I, anti-imperialists had gained considerable clout in America. Both Roosevelt and Lodge, for example, had disavowed their original expansionist views. The winds of American politics had shifted to favor self-government for the Filipinos, as reflected by the Jones Act of 1916, which was intended to provide Filipinos substantial autonomy over internal affairs. Meanwhile, in the Philippines, the Filipinos who wielded the political power to enforce the Jones Act were the native economic elite, those who were educated in Spain and in Manila in the late nineteenth century. They served on the American-created Philippine Assembly, elected because they could afford the time

## ADOPTING A "MOTHER CULTURE"

In the 1920s, overt American imperialism ended and Filipino autonomy began, yet, paradoxically, it was in that decade that Filipinos "lost free will," according to the most revered Filipino writer, Nick Joaquin (who was educated in Spanish but writes only in English). The Filipino lost his sense of self, Joaquin notes, when he ceased to identify the American as alien, enemy, Yanqui or Gringo and embraced him instead as

and money to campaign. They were also favored by the Americans, as their complacency was assured by America's redistribution to them of church-owned land; the United States had purchased these lands from the Vatican for US$7.2 million.

Like the friars of old whose clamoring for reforms in the 1560s and 1570s led the king to quiet them with a grant of the entire Philippine countryside, elite Filipinos who sought reforms in the late nineteenth century forgot about reforms after they acquired that very same land. Like the friars, they did not want their positions of comfort and privilege disturbed and had no real desire to better the lot of their Filipino brethren.

*The Country and Its People*

benefactor and America as "the mother culture." The old culture, whose heroes were Rizal, Bonifacio and Aguinaldo, began to look alien. "For in discarding the old culture we discarded as well the sense of identity it had achieved during its fight for freedom," Joaquin claimed.

Identifying with America made the Filipino provincial, according to Joaquin: "The cultured Filipino of the 1880s was intellectually at home in several worlds: Europe, Spanish America, the Orient (there was a special interest in Japan), not to mention the classic world of the hexameter; and his OPPOSITE: Supporting the team from distant Philippines, basketball player Dennis Rodman's father in Angeles, Luzon. ABOVE: The ruins of United States Barracks on Corregidor Island.

frame of reference had a latitude unthinkable in the 'educated' Filipino of the 1920s and 1930s, for whom culture had been reduced to 'knowing about the world contained between Hollywood and Manhattan.'" Writer Ian Buruma adds: "One could say that the legacy of Spanish Catholicism and secondhand Americana are the two things most Filipinos have in common. Even NPA guerrillas wear UCLA T-shirts. America is like a birthmark on the Filipino identity — no matter how hard you rub, it won't come off."

Following World War I, Americans patterned the Philippines after their own country. Church was separated from state, the legal system was modified to include courts of original and appellate jurisdiction, the country's infrastructure was dramatically improved with American dollars and technology and the market economy featured modern products used by most Americans. United States investors and businessmen flocked to the Philippines to exploit its raw materials and cheap labor market for manufactured goods. Quickly, Filipinos adapted to the American way of exploiting land and labor purely for the economic gain of the owners and their corporations.

There was a tug-of-war in the United States between those who favored overseas trade and holdings and those who urged that American workers must be protected against foreign competition. With the onset of the Great Depression, American farm and labor groups successfully fought for legislation authorizing Philippine independence. In 1935, a Philippine Commonwealth was established which, in 1946, would become fully independent of the United States. Significantly, it was Americans and not Filipinos who pushed for and won Philippine independence.

The first president of the Commonwealth government, inaugurated in 1935, was Manuel Quezon. At that time most Filipinos were impoverished, buut heirs of the wealthy, landowning old culture clamored for reassurance that America's "letting go" would not mean the demise of their comfortable lifestyles. Quezon instituted social programs to ameliorate the problems of the masses but at the same time promised the landed gentry, of which he (and all subsequent Filipino leaders) was a member, that their lives would not be affected.

## WORLD WAR II AND THE RETURN OF THE AMERICANS

World War II hit the Philippines on December 8, 1941, when the Japanese bombed United States aircraft based at Clark Field in Central Luzon. The Japanese quickly invaded nearby Lingayen Gulf and Lamon Bay and marched toward Manila. Although the Filipino forces had been incorporated into the United States Army under General Douglas MacArthur in 1941, they were poorly trained and ill-equipped to defend the country against the Japanese. On January 2, 1942, MacArthur declared Manila an "Open City," and with his American and Filipino forces, he withdrew to the narrow Bataan Peninsula and Corregidor Island.

President Quezon implored President Roosevelt to grant immediate independence to the Philippines so that it could declare neutrality. Roosevelt, not wishing to surrender the Philippines to the Japanese, rejected Quezon's demands and promised to defend the Philippines to the end. For the next three months, the American and Filipino forces fought the Japanese on Bataan. Finally, Roosevelt ordered MacArthur off the Philippines, prompting MacArthur to make his famous "I shall return" pledge. One month later, on April 9, 1942, the 76,000 men on Bataan surrendered to the Japanese. Starving and rife with malaria and dysentery, these men were forced to begin marching up the peninsula to boxcars in San Fernando in Pampanga, which took them to an internment camp at Capas in Tarlac province. That march is known as the "Death March"; it took 10 days and 10,000 lives were lost to exhaustion or to the horrific conditions imposed by their captors.

Japan's military ruled the Philippines from May 1942 until Japan officially surrendered on September 3, 1945. In 1944,

---

The Japanese ended 48 years of American rule with their long, bloody siege of Bataan and Corregidor Island, Luzon. OPPOSITE: General MacArthur's GM Cabriolet on Corregidor Island.

MacArthur fulfilled his promise and returned to the Philippines, landing along the Leyte coastline — to wade ashore with his trademark pipe clenched in his jaw — with 174,000 servicemen and 700 vessels. The American forces dwarfed and decimated those of the Japanese (who defended the islands with an obstinacy bordering on the insane) with feats that quite easily overshadowed D Day, although they were never portrayed as such by the official wartime publicity machine. In two months, Leyte was totally cleared of the Japanese

occupation. Luzon lay five hundred kilometers (310 miles) to the north, toward which the Americans, well supported by 250,000 Filipino guerrillas, began to march in late 1944. In January 1945, they landed at Lingayen Gulf, recaptured Corregidor in an 11-day battle and stormed Manila the following month. After a two-week bloodbath in Manila, the Japanese made their last stand at Intramuros, where American and Filipino forces fought them hand-to-hand, street-to-street.

Manila was finally liberated on February 23, 1945. Mopping up operations lasted until September 3, 1945, when the last remaining Japanese forces, near Kiangan, in Ifugao province, Luzon, were routed.

## THE POSTWAR PERIOD AND PHILIPPINE INDEPENDENCE

World War II claimed approximately one million Filipino lives. Property damage throughout the archipelago was vast. After the war Manila was in ruins, second only to Warsaw in the damage it sustained. The Commonwealth government was not ready for independence in 1946, for it was without a president — Quezon had died in 1944 — and without the resources or facilities to reconstruct a country in shambles. In these circumstances, it was probably no accident that Filipinos, economically and psychologically dependent on America, elected a strongly pro-United States president, Manuel Roxas, to lead the Commonwealth, which in 1946 became the Philippine Republic. Under Roxas, American dollars were used to rebuild the war-ravaged Philippines — and to construct on Luzon America's two largest military bases outside the United States: Clark Air Force Base in the mountainous Pampanga province, and Subic Bay Naval Base on the Bataan Peninsula west of Manila.

The Philippine economy rebounded quickly, growing during the 1950s at a fast yearly clip of five to six percent. Its economy also grew increasingly diverse during this period. Filipinos now not only grew rice, corn, sugarcane, copra and coconuts; they had begun to build factories (which made textiles, shoes and cement), dig mines (for gold and copper) and clear forests (for mahogany and other hardwoods). There was a familiar problem, however: the production of such wealth neither bettered the lives of nor decreased the ranks of the impoverished masses, but rather benefited the Philippine elite, the government (which in all practicality represented solely its own interests) and American business.

Rather than a giving-back to the Filipino people, there was a giving-to the Americans (just as there had been for centuries with the Spanish). The Laurel-Langley Treaty of 1955 gave Americans equal rights with Filipinos to exploit local resources in the operation of general public utilities and in numerous other businesses. As a Philippine biographer of Imelda Marcos, Carmen Navarro Pedrosa, wrote: "The small number of families who had once enjoyed the patronage of the Spanish crown had formed economic alliances with American business and divided the spoils as if the poor, or indeed the rest of the nation, did not exist."

Economically impoverished, yet politically free, the people expressed their will by never electing to a second term any of

feudal landlord-tenant system with its militia of armed guerrillas. In 1953, President Magsaysay resettled thousands of landless peasant families from rural Luzon to less crowded parts of Mindanao and Palawan, thus deflating the Huks. In election year 1957, with plans on tap to limit the size of land holdings and to sell portions of large estates to tenants, President Magsaysay died in a plane crash.

As for the population, it had risen from about 7.6 million in 1903 to over 28 million by 1960, and it kept growing at one of the

their presidents, who were limited to two four-year terms by the Philippine Constitution. Following Manuel Roxas, Philippine presidents were Elpidio Quirino (1949 to 1953), Ramon Magsaysay (1953 to 1957), Carlos Garcia (1957 to 1961) and Diosdado Macapagal (1961 to 1965).

Also troubling the Philippines during this postwar period were an unfair distribution of land, an exploding population, and increasing violence and lawlessness in urban and rural areas. Forty percent of the Philippines' agrarian populace were tenants, sharecroppers or paid plantation workers subsisting in often miserable conditions. In 1950, the pro-Communist Hukbalahap movement sought to end this

fastest rates in the world — three percent per year. To a great extent, advances in modern medicine together with the Catholic Church's opposition to birth control were responsible for this population explosion. The escalating crime rate in the late 1940s through the early 1960s was the inevitable result of the Philippines' government kowtowing to American interests — exacerbated by increasing unrest and overcrowding in the cities and in rural areas and, as in America, the easy availability of firearms.

OPPOSITE: When the Japanese took Manila, General Macarthur retreated to the military stronghold of Corregidor Island. ABOVE: The 12,000-man combined American and Filipino resistance forces lived in Malinta Tunnel for nearly five months.

## THE MARCOS ERA

By election year 1965, Filipinos needed a president who could solve their chronic problems. They yearned for a national strongman, brazen and daring. Enter, one Ferdinand E. Marcos, a lawyer, congressman and former World War II guerrilla against the Japanese.

Marcos was already mildly notorious: in 1952 he had been convicted, then acquitted, of murdering his father's political rival.

The murder weapon came from the armory of the university Marcos then attended, where he was a national champion in small-bore weapons; his father's defeat meant no income to finance Marcos' university education.

His questionable past notwithstanding, Ferdinand and his young wife Imelda — a former Miss Manila who was then fresh from the provinces — campaigned tirelessly throughout the archipelago and promised to make the Philippines a great nation. They would break the power of the rich and of the Catholic Church, wipe out the communist threat and deliver Filipinos from poverty. To drive their message home, the Marcos clan hired publicity agents.

"Overnight, Filipinos were besieged by propaganda of a superhero combining the qualities of Audie Murphy and John F. Kennedy, who lived in their midst, unknown until the presidential campaign of 1965," writes Carmen Pedrosa. Meanwhile Imelda's propagandists proclaimed that she was "the perfect complement to this modern day superhero — rich, young and beautiful; an Asian Jacqueline Kennedy."

Unable initially to resist the charms of this Camelot couple, Filipinos soon learned the truth. The Marcos' interests were solely aimed at enriching themselves and their friends. This they did by making corrupt deals and embezzling from government loans, and by assigning government posts to their friends who in turn practiced nepotism and embezzlement. Only during his first term in office (1965 to 1969) did Marcos do anything resembling public service — and then probably only to win re-election in 1969 (which he did, barely) — by building irrigation systems that increased rice production and by introducing improvements in public health, transportation and communications.

After 1969, Marcos concentrated on staying in power. Imelda soon adjusted to her status as First Lady, transforming herself from a shy unsophisticated rural lass to the flamboyant figure who beguiled world leaders with her flirtatious beauty: the "Steel Butterfly," the international press dubbed her. Her shopaholicism became legendary; her lifestyle was a neverending round of international, celebrity-packed spending sprees (ostensibly diplomatic missions), during which she acquired exclusive real estate and priceless antiquities as effortlessly as her infamous shoes.

"Imelda's excesses were not limited to shopping. At home, she dreamed of glamorous projects that would bring her further glory even as they bled the national treasury. Indeed, Imelda discovered the wonderful world of international bank loans in her search to fund her projects. These loans would flow to the Philippines for more than a decade, plunging the economy further into debt even as the Marcos' diverted millions of dollars to their personal assets," wrote Carmen Pedrosa.

Imelda's so-called "edifice complex" resulted in the construction of a series of grandiose concrete structures, including Manila's Cultural Center, the National Arts Center and Convention Center, as well as 14 luxury hotels — all at a time when 30 percent of the nation could barely afford the basic necessities of food and shelter; the country's per capita income was US$200 a year.

On September 23, 1972, Marcos declared martial law — and it remained in force for most of his stay in office. His stated reason was that this was the only way to stop the threat of insurrection posed by the Communist Party of the Philippines and the New People's Army (NPA). In reality, these groups controlled no more than 1,000 armed regulars, 10,000 part-time supporters and 100,000 sympathizers — in a country of more than 40 million people. Although Marcos referred to a "state of anarchy," bombings and outbreaks of violence were few (some Filipinos have even charged that Marcos engineered many of them in order to create the pretext for martial law). Through martial law, Marcos got what he had wanted all along — an amended constitution allowing him to stay on indefinitely as head of state.

In the immediate aftermath of martial law, every Philippine newspaper except one owned by a Marcos crony was padlocked and placed under military guard. Six of the country's major television stations and nine radio stations were shut down. Only one radio and one television station, both controlled by Marcos, were allowed to operate. The country was now controlled from the center, with the army and the security services as Marcos' main instruments of power. Hundreds and ultimately thousands of opposition leaders were imprisoned, among them Senator Benigno "Ninoy" Aquino, who was jailed for eight years until May 1980, when he was permitted to travel to the United States for open-heart surgery. Although Marcos ended martial law in January 1981, he ruled thereafter by presidential decree.

Like Rizal before him (whose hero's homecoming to the Philippines from Spain was promptly followed by his execution),

Aquino was catapulted to the status of a national messiah and roused the nation when, upon his return from the United States on August 21, 1983, he was assassinated on the tarmac at Manila Airport immediately after he was forcibly escorted off the plane by three government officials. The Marcos government claimed the assassin was a lone Communist agent, Rolando Galman, who soldiers gunned down on the spot. Later, many of the country's highest-ranking military officers were tried for the assassination, but all were acquitted.

In the weeks after Aquino's murder, foreign banks withdrew their funds, and the Philippines found itself massively in debt. In 1984, inflation topped 60 percent. The economy declined by five percent that year and by another five percent in 1985. This waning economy bred violent crimes committed by armed factions on both the left (represented by the Communist Party of the Philippines and its military wing, the NPA) and the right (the army, police force, certain corporations and industrialists). By the mid-1980s, the NPA counted more than 15,000 guerrilla fighters, and it was operating in the majority of the Philippines' 73 provinces, mainly in the countryside but also in some cities, such as Davao in Mindanao. Also disrupting the peace were the separatist Moro National Liberation Front, representing the dissident Muslims of Mindanao and the Sulu Archipelago.

OPPOSITE: Ferdinand Marcos during his 1985 Manila speech rally. ABOVE: Squatters bathe not far from Roxas Boulevard in downtown Manila.

## THE SNAP REVOLUTION AND PEOPLE POWER

Amid this chaos and growing international and national criticism, Marcos planned a snap election for February 7, 1986, expecting a disunited opposition, as had been the case in 1981. His opponent was Aquino's widow, Corazon "Cory" Aquino of the Philippine Democratic Party. To ensure victory, Marcos controlled the election results by having his thugs buy votes, steal ballot boxes and destroy voter registration records. But Marcos had underestimated the degree to which Benigno Aquino's 1983 murder had galvanized the nation against him and in favor of Cory Aquino. Although Marcos proclaimed himself the winner, claiming 53 percent of the vote, Aquino, addressing nearly a million supporters in Rizal Park, refused to concede. The quiet widow with the gentle smile announced a peaceful program of civil disobedience, including a strike after Marcos' planned inauguration. The tide began to turn in her favor when, on February 20, 1986, many military officers denounced the election as fraudulent. Two days later, Defense Minister Juan Ponce Enrile and the country's highest ranking military officer, Chief of Staff General Fidel Ramos (Marcos' cousin) defected from the Marcos camp and called on him to resign and cede power to Aquino.

The following day, Sunday, February 23, thousands of Manila's citizens thronged Epifanio de los Santos Avenue (known as "EDSA") and blocked the vast intersection of EDSA outside two military camps. They brought the soldiers food and wildly celebrated the overthrow of Marcos and the birth of a new Philippine republic under Cory Aquino.

Jaime Cardinal Sin, Archbishop of Manila, played a pivotal role, urging peaceful protest on the streets. Some historians have credited the People Power revolution with inspiring a wave of popular discontent around the world in the 1980s. The sight, on live television, of a million people standing in defiance against Marcos' military regime remains one of the defining images of the era.

In the morning of February 25, 1986, Aquino took the oath of office; 12 hours later, following a White House call for Marcos to step down, four American helicopters descended on Malacañang Palace to airlift the Marcoses, their family and a close friend to Clark Air Force Base and then into exile in Hawaii, where Marcos was to die three years later. Within days, Aquino opened the opulent Malacañang Palace in Manila to the public, so that Filipino people could witness the extravagant lifestyle of the autocrats who had ruled them for 21 years.

The terms "EDSA Revolution" — or "EDSA," "People Power," the "February Revolt," and the "Snap Revolution" — were quickly coined to describe the events that began the drive for "Filipinization." Toward this goal, in the first year of her administration Aquino restored the rights of free speech and a free press, released hundreds of political prisoners, reformed the constitution to restrict a president to a single six-year term, and ousted all Marcos loyalists serving as governors and mayors, replacing them with her own appointees.

After that first year, however — once a congress had been elected, essentially — the defiant widow's administration veered from reform to conservative politics, much like those of the pre-Marcos era. The question is, why? "Was she pushed that way by the military, by the Americans, by business interests? Or was that her natural resting place, where she would have ended up in any case?" wrote W. Scott Thompson in his book, *The Philippines in Crisis*.

The argument based on Cory Aquino's "natural resting place" is the more compelling, as Aquino was a member of the Philippines' richest landowning family and thus an aristocrat, whose family members included seven members of Congress, four of whom were serving under her stewardship (a brother, brother-in-law, cousin and uncle). Cory Aquino had substantial interests of her own and of her family to protect and defend. It is no accident that she chose to take the oath of office at the posh Club Filipinas, in one of Manila's richest enclaves, well surrounded by her upper middle and upper class supporters? As bluntly put by Thompson, "There was absolutely nothing in her intellectual or social preparation indicating the slightest interest in serious social reform."

And indeed, during her six-year administration no serious economic or social reforms were made. Economic problems and gross social inequity persisted throughout her presidency, which explains why no fewer than seven attempts to overthrow her government were made.

the country's electricity problem — which kept the main island of Luzon in darkness for up to 10 hours a day — by transferring control of the energy sector to private business; and he dismantled the monopolies and other regulations that had thwarted economic growth for decades. "In three years, Ramos achieved what Taiwan and Korea took two decades to do," said Srinivasa Madhur, an economist at the Asian Development Bank in Manila.

In an attempt to jump-start the country's economy, Ramos had a yard sale of sorts,

## PATH TO RECOVERY

The man responsible for putting down the seven rebellions that plagued Aquino's presidency was Fidel V. Ramos, who was elected president in 1992. Fidel V. Ramos was a former general known as "Steady Eddie," a man never seen without his trademark cigar.

Born in 1928 and a 1950 graduate of West Point, Ramos was also the country's most decorated soldier, with a reputation for getting things done. Ramos' mother was Marcos' maternal aunt. During Aquino's presidency, Ramos traveled from camp to camp, from group to group, talking her opponents down. Later, as president, he solved

selling off burdensome government properties to private and international investors. who were eagerly buying whatever they could get their hands on. He also offered tax breaks and lowered interest rates. With the result that the Philippine economy grew nearly six percent each year under his presidency. "The Ramos-led reforms, which have transformed the Philippines from an inefficient inward looking country with protectionist barriers to an externally oriented and market driven economy, continue to bear fruit," says a report published in 1995 from the British-based Standard Chartered Bank.

Craftsmen at the Crystal Corp. Glass Factory, Angeles, Clarkfield, Luzon, turning out a variety of glassware.

But the fruit was to take a fall soon long after this encouraging prosperity. Ramos and the rest of the Asian region had no way of predicting the crisis that lay ahead.

## THE ASIAN FINANCIAL CRISIS

Like a domino effect in the late 1990s, the drastic devaluation of the *baht* in Thailand in less than one week sent sparks flying throughout the entire Asian region. Before they knew it, countries like Malaysia, Indonesia, and the Philippines helplessly watched as their currencies too crashed and burned.

Many factors are to blame for the financial crisis that plagued Asia until recently, as countries begin to show signs of recovery. Some economists point to corruption and Asian governments' mishandling of funds as the major cause for the crisis. Others suggest it was fixed exchange rates, careless borrowing of large amounts of international capital, and overbuilt property markets. A lack of infrastructure and revenue, combined with agricultural yields taking a pounding from Mother Nature, contributed to defaults in loans and led to businesses going under, which perpetuated the ever-growing unemployment rate.

But thanks to a rather timely IMF-supported program and structural reforms in the late 1980's, the Philippines, unlike its neighbors, was capable of pulling somewhat ahead of the crisis — just keeping their heads above the financial tidal wave. The country took on post-crisis management responsibly, stabilizing the peso, tightening and strengthening banks and monetary policy, and was positioned for a recovery when stabilization took effect in 1998. Climbing from one percent when the crisis took hold to a 3.25 percent GDP, recovery is expected to continue.

## THE ESTRADA SHOW

A political recovery is underway as well. In 1998, President Ramos was replaced by former actor Joseph Estrada, who from the beginning admitted his infidelity and love of the bottle. But his pledge of prosperity for the country's poor was too great to dismiss, and the people loved him.

However, opposition built up after Estrada decided to bury former dictator Ferdinand Marcos at a heroes' cemetery. Not soon after, word got out that Estrada had allegedly received close to P400 million in bribes, and that he was harboring his concubines in mansions throughout the country. The country was showing sure signs of suffering from a crisis of confidence, and echoes of the past were too loud to be ignored. It was the beginning of his demise.

## PEOPLE POWER PART TWO

The year 2000 saw another victory for people power, as street protests, coup rumors, and calls for Estrada's resignation rocked the capital. An impeachment trial seemed out of the question since those in charge of overseeing the hearings remained pro-Estrada supporters. Estrada seemed to take such bitter disapproval from his people with a grain of salt, and shrugged off the alleged charges of bribery, corruption and misconduct.

Defections from the military and his cabinet prompted Estrada to encourage Congress to call a snap election to replace him. However, Vice President Macapagal-Arroyo rejected the proposal in favor of running the country herself. President Estrada was playing tough, refusing to hand over the reigns to Macapagal-Arroyo and opted instead to encourage the people to hold elections in May 2001, but the opposition stood stronger than ever, demanding his immediate resignation.

The story sounds much like a soap opera. A B-grade movie actor turned president, Estrada faced an unprecedented impeachment trial amid charges of corruption, scandal, and harboring mistresses with which it's rumored that he fathered numerous children. Years of mismanagement boiled down to one dramatic face-off: the once overly confident and cocky actor, who said that being president would be the "best performance of his life," was holed up in his palace as a united opposition stormed the gates of the Palace and forced him out of office. The opposition was composed of a country outraged by such presidential philandering, echoing too closely the years under Marcos' dictatorship.

On January 20, 2001, President Estrada and his family left out the back door, ending his tumultuous presidency, and offering the Philippines a chance of recovery under Vice-President Macapagal-Arroyo. She was sworn in later that day as the country's next president.

## VIOLENCE IN THE SOUTH

On her election, Macapagal-Arroyo faced the daunting task of continuing where previous presidents left off in trying to wage peace with Muslim separatists in the south; whose violent strikes against tourists, civilians, and government have been on the rise and continue to threaten the safety of the country.

The civil war has been a major thorn in the body politic of the Philippines. Centered in the southern island of Mindanao, separatists have waged their struggle for the past 26 years in the hopes of winning autonomy. The conflict has left more than 150,000 dead, and the recent kidnappings of divers and tourists indicates that the movement does not intend to give up easily. The bitter hostility goes back to the fifteenth century when occupation by Spanish, American, and Philippine colonists threatened to take over their traditional lands. They believe the threat still exists and continue their quest for autonomy by whatever means necessary.

An agreement brokered in 1996 between Ramos and the Moro National Liberation Front (MNLF) was to be a crucial step for lasting peace. It was to give more autonomy to Muslim-dominated regions of the southern Philippines, and in return, the rebels were to drop their demands for an entirely separate nation. Under the agreement's terms, the MNLF's 20,000-strong rebel soldiers were to be gradually integrated into the Philippine Army; an independent executive legislature would be introduced; and Islamic education would be integrated into the school system. Violence has not subsided however. A radical group, which disagreed with the peace process between the Muslims and

the State, left the MNLF and formed the more radical Abu Sayyaf Group (Bearer of the Sword). Its main purpose is to establish an Islamic state, based on Islamic law — and they are not allowing room for compromises.

## PROMISES OF WEALTH

As the Philippines proceeds through the new millenium, its cultural heritage is threatened to disappear forever. There are a few exceptions. Muslims and some re-

mote tribes are the only groups who have been unaffected by Spanish and American influences. Only about 10 percent of the country's cultural minority groups retain a traditional existence. Even the select mountain tribes of the Igorot group in the Central Cordilleras are having a hard time retaining traditional cultivation practices, as evidenced by the continuing erosion of the famed rice terraces, which in the past were maintained only through constant effort of Igorot men, women and children. Economic hardships have forced the young to adopt cash-crop farming instead of sustaining agricultural methods handed down over centuries.

Many reject the rural life altogether, and instead head for a more contemporary life in the urban areas, leaving behind the tight binds of tribal customs and practices. This is particularly true with women. Like Bangkok, Manila's sex industry stands as no secret, and stories of military men sweeping

The military contingent at the Independence Day celebrations, Manila.

into town from months at sea are still legendary too in Subic Bay and Angeles — the two former United States military bases in the country. Although no longer saturated with men in uniform looking for a good time, the Philippines is still seen as a premier place to come for prostitution, mail-order brides, and pedaphilia. Women seeking independence, or being forced by their families to make money, venture to these urban centers and become prey to abusers and sex exploiters, forcing them to work in brothels or for pimps.

Where there is a demand, there is opportunity and, unfortunately, for some women growing up in squalor it is their only option. Driving out of the city of Manila through long stretches of its outlying semi-slums and villages formerly claimed by other provinces (such as Tondo), it is difficult not to acknowledge that not all is a rosy picture of rural bliss, despite an overall improvement in the region's economy.

The past decade has seen an increase in the number of women and children being trafficked for sex throughout the entire Asian region. According to the Coalition Against Trafficking in Women Organization, the sex industry is valued at more than US$17 billion a year. Technology is partly to blame for this increase. Ordering a bride or reserving a woman is as easy as entering the three W's — www. The Internet has made the sex trade more accessible, more anonymous,

## THE ENVIRONMENT TODAY

From deforestation, irregularities in season and temperature from El Nino and El Nina, damaging fishing practices, and a recent oil spill in Manila Bay, the environment has taken quite a beating in the Philippines.

The Philippines' rainforests have diminished dramatically over the past 50 years, as the increasing population led to expansion of farming activities and large-scale logging activities became highly profitable. Indigenous people continue to be forced to relocate to less and less fertile land. Land disputes are becoming increasingly common — recently erupting afresh among the Manobo groups on Mindanao, as the island's resources are drained by foreign and Philippine commercial interests.

The jewel of the Philippine crown is unarguably its underwater ecology. This has been threatened, not solely from dynamite or cyanide fishing, but also from global warming, which has caused water temperatures to rise and the coral to become bleached, leaving it vacant of color and life. The vacant reefs have left fisherman scurrying for catch and have caused many to resort to injecting cyanide into the coral, stunning fish so they could be caught more easily. Cyanide is poison for the delicate reefs, and combined with the use of explosives to stun fish and send them floating to the surface, fishing has played havoc on the reefs throughout the archipelago. Palawan stood as the most damaged until strict measures were enforced protecting the waters off El Nido and elsewhere on the island from such practices. With support from the government, the diving and international communities, and local environmental groups, word has got out about the importance of maintaining and preserving the underwater treasures. As a result, local communities are listening — and coral rejuvenation projects have begun along much of the stretches of reef off Palawan and other Visayan islands.

and much harder to contain. Between 1989 and 1998, almost 150,000 Filipino women migrated to marry foreign husbands. Yet despite such discouraging increases, efforts are being forged to put an end to such practices: by organizations like the Coalition Against Trafficking in Women, as well as the Commission on Filipinos Overseas, who monitor the rate at which Filipinas leave the country either engaged to or married to foreignors. Of these 55,000 went to the United States and 20,000 to Australia. "Sex tours" sponsored by some Australian and German clubs have been closely monitored and many have ceased their operations. Hopefully that's a sign of changes to come in the Philippines.

Dazzling white sand at White Island, an uninhabited sandbar favored by tourists, off Camiguin Island.

# Manila

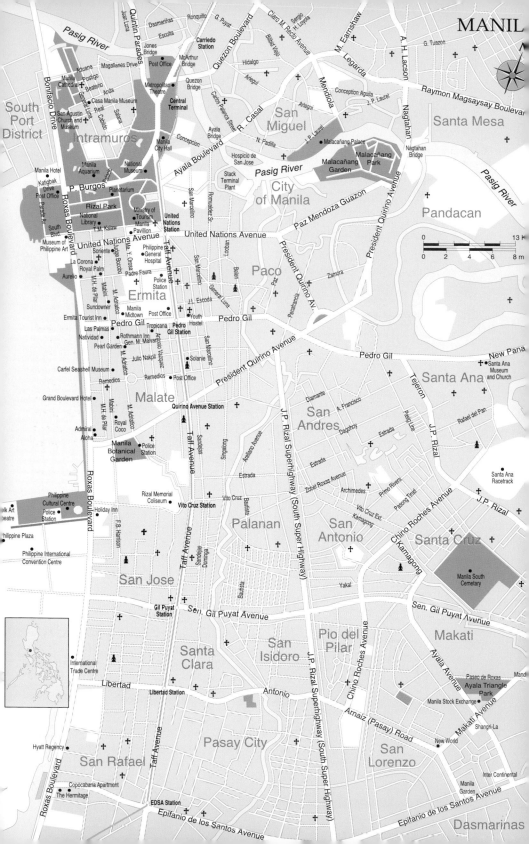

## THE CITY BY THE BAY

THE CITY OF MANILA WEARS ITS INFAMY LIKE A badge. Home to some 10 million people, this densely crowded concrete jungle has been much maligned. For many years, political and economic chaos lent the capital a certain poignant allure. This changed dramatically with the famous Snap Election and the People Power revolution in February 1986, which brought to an end the 20 years of the Marcos reign. When satellite images from Manila of almost a million determined and united citizens marching in defiance of armed tanks were beamed across the world, their spirit commanded respect and spread a wave of infectious revolutionary zeal.

James Fenton, in *All the Wrong Places*, described a scene he witnessed in the Malacañang Palace immediately after the Marcos family fled in a helicopter. On the street outside, a happy Filipino, with a whiskey glass in hand, confided in him: "You don't realize," he said, "how deep this goes. Nobody will call us cowards again. We've done it. We've had a peaceful revolution. We've beaten Poland."

Today, Manila is working hard to fulfill its role as a financial key-pin in the region, and is the headquarters of the Asian Development Bank. The economy is recovering nicely from the Asian financial crisis of the late 1990s, foreign investment has begun to flow in again, new buildings are burgeoning in the affluent business neighborhood of Makati, and the city is now liberally studded with five-star hotels to help consolidate its position as a regional leader.

Manila is in every way an extraordinary city, for all its arresting poverty and promises of wealth. It is a beacon for millions of rural Filipinos, dreaming of a better life from far away in the provinces. The city suffered more destruction from the ravages of World War II than even Dresden, so much so that most of the architectural legacy left by the Spanish has been obliterated. Despite its wholesale reconstruction, Manila retains a desultory aura of painful memories that it is only recently coming to terms with. It is hard not to empathize with a place that has endured so much.

Pico Iyer wrote in *Video Night In Kathmandu*: "Thus I left the Philippines. But the Philippines did not so easily leave me. For months, I could not get the country out of my head: it haunted me like a pretty, plaintive melody." Like Iyer, most visitors will remember Manila in a series of discrete, perhaps diffuse, images and moments: the luminosity of the sunset across Manila Bay, with its almost Technicolor hues, melting into the South China Sea; stumbling into a thirteenth-century graveyard in the shadow of skyscrapers; society matrons with bouffant hairdos eating bibingka cakes in coffeeshops; Spanish churches with gold-encrusted icons; life in the squatter communities around the khaki-colored, poisonous Pasig River; and even CNN featured dancing traffic officers at congested intersections.

The city began as small, but prosperous hamlet alongside the banks of the Pasig River, near the mouth of Manila Bay. The settlement was surrounded by flowering mangrove plants, or *nilad*, and was thus called "Maynilad" or the place where the nilad grows. It was called Manila by the Spanish who arrived in 1571 and, made it the seat of their Asian empire, constructing the inner city fortress of Intramuros.

To a newcomer's eye, Manila indeed deserves the description of a "shapeless, confused and unrelievedly twentieth-century mess strung out along a reeking bay," made of it by James Hamilton-Paterson in *Playing with Water*. One of the most perceptive foreign writers on the Philippines, Hamilton-Paterson observes wryly that "the Manila which ex-President Marcos left in late February 1986 was, like the man himself, a notorious mixture of wealth and decay."

Hamilton-Paterson continues: "In the late seventies and early eighties — that is to say, the declining years of the Marcos dynasty — the country appeared to be superficially in a state of stable anarchy brought about by the rigors of martial law and the untrammeled freedom of public officials to do pretty much what they liked. In this strange political half-life, Manila had some of the high, wild, *fin de saison* qualities ascribed to other famous cities under regimes in their lapsarian days, Batista's Havana, Faroukh's Cairo, even Mussolini's Salo."

Since then, Manila has tightened its belt. Made up of 10 cities — Manila itself, Quezon, Pasay, Makati, Pasig, Parañaque, Las Piñas, Muntinlupa, Mandaluyong and Caloocan — Metro Manila is full of contradictions. It derives much of its admirable civic order from the predominant Catholicism of its citizens, yet has a soaring crime rate with frequent kidnappings, armed robberies, and commissioned murders.

On the reclaimed foreshore alongside Roxas Boulevard, the monuments created by former First Lady and now Congress member Imelda Marcos are still regarded with pride by the average Manileño, despite having been built largely with funds earmarked for alleviating the nation's poverty. In the upper-class residential enclaves of Forbes Park, Dasmarinas Village and Wack Wack, spacious villas and swimming pools are surrounded by shrub-shrouded security guards and barbed wire, while the slum dwellers who squeeze themselves into cheap concrete caverns, burned-out ruins and cardboard sheeting face a future as bleak as ever.

## GENERAL INFORMATION

Manila's **Department of Tourism Head Office** ( (2) 523-8411 to 8430 FAX (2) 521-7374 WEB SITE www.tourism.gov.ph, T. M. Kalaw Street, Rizal Park, is open Monday to Saturday from 8AM to 5 PM. They provide nifty computer printouts for all of the Philippines' provinces, with run-downs on accommodations, transportation, and attractions. There is also a **Department of Tourism Branch Office** ( (2) 832-2964 at the Ninoy Aquino International Airport, Pasay City.

The **Philippine Convention and Visitor Corporation** ( (2) 525-9318 to 9332 FAX (2) 521-6165, Fourth Floor, Suites 10-17, Legaspi Towers 300, Roxas Boulevard, publishes the excellent and informative *Islands Philippines* series of maps and pamphlets.

For the **Tourist Assistance 24-Hour Hotline** call ( (2) 524-1660.

## WHAT TO SEE AND DO

Manila's architectural layers spill out across its seams in a contradictory muddle. Formidable traces remain of the sixteenth-century wall constructed by the colonizing Spanish. **Intramuros** (literally, "within the walls") was an impregnable, five-sided bastion that contained a hive of ecclesiastical buildings, palaces, a university, schools, a printing press, government buildings, hospitals and barracks as well as grand Iberian mansions, all surrounded by *baluartes* (battlements), *puertas* (gates), and a moat. Only Spaniards and Spanish mestizos were allowed to live inside — drawbridges went up each night.

Despite the ravages of earthquakes and wartime bombing, many grand husks and ramparts of the former stone citadel remain. Restoration and reconstruction work is ongoing by the Intramuros Administration, with many of the original gates — including the **Puerta Isabel II** and the **Puerta Real** gates — walls and cobblestone streets being repaired. Starting from Puerta Real, where the drained moat has been transformed into the city's golf course, you can wander for just over four kilometers (two and a half miles) around the walls of Intramuros, which are six meters (20 feet) high and 13 m (43 feet) thick.

Inside the city's walls, overlooking the mouth of the Pasig River, it's possible to explore **Fort Santiago**, whose history is mired in brutality. From its bastion, Miguel Lopez de Legaspi, the mastermind of the Spanish colonization of the Philippines, surveyed the construction of Intramuros. The fort was the headquarters of the Spanish military, which was ousted by British troops in 1762 and later housed Filipino Tayabas soldiers in 1843. Yet it withstood attacks by the Dutch and the Portuguese, as well as Sulu pirates. With its interrogation chambers, rat-infested hold-alls and infamous dungeons that were below the high tide level, this was a place of terror and death throughout the centuries. It was here that the revolutionary hero José Rizal was incarcerated for two months on charges of rebellion and sedition prior to his execution by the Spanish in 1896. His cell is now the **Rizal Museum**. It is open daily from 9 AM to noon and 1 PM to 5 PM. Rizal wrote his final poem, "Mi Ultimo Adios" (My Last Farewell), from his cell and had it smuggled out in the base of an oil lamp.

Intramuros — TOP: Memorare Manila 1945. BOTTOM: San Agustin Church, the country's oldest stone church, dating from 1571.

United States troops ran the fort after 1898, and it was an operational base for General Douglas MacArthur from 1936 to 1941. When the Japanese took Manila, the next violent chapter in the fort's history began. Some 600 bodies were later discovered beneath the bastion of San Lorenzo. Rumors had persisted that the Japanese General Yamashita may have hidden his legendary — or as some say, mythical — gold here. In 1988, with President Aquino's permission, American treasure hunters painstakingly searched and partially excavated Fort Santiago looking for clues, but nothing was uncovered. The fort is open between 8 AM and 10 PM — although wandering alone around its battlements at night is not recommended.

Also within the remains of the fort, the open-air **Rajah Sulayman Theater** is a venue from December to June for Filipino plays staged in Tagalog. Beneath the theater complex there is a quirky **museum of vintage cars** — those used by General MacArthur and past Filipino presidents.

Walking away from Fort Santiago, across General Luna Street, you will pass through **Plaza Roma**, a popular bullfighting arena during the eighteenth century and now the site for a modernist statue, by Filipino artist Solomon Saprid, in homage to the three Filipino priests Gomez, Burgos and Zamora, who were accused of leading an anti-Spanish revolt and were publicly garroted in 1872, sparking revolution. The Plaza Roma is bounded by **Palacio del Gobernador**, the residence of the Spanish governor-general from 1660 to 1863, which is now, despite the ravages of earthquake damage, a sturdy complex of government buildings.

Regarded as one of the most imposing church buildings in the Philippines, the **Manila Cathedral** in Intramuros is the sixth built on this site, and was itself rebuilt between 1954 and 1958 with the assistance of Vatican funds. The original cathedral was constructed in 1571, and some original walls were incorporated from this and other past incarnations of the church. The main door holds bronze bas-relief panels depicting the cathedral's history. Inside, immediately noticeable is Filipino artist Galo Ocampo's dramatic series of stained-glass windows, which tell the story of the Madonna's life

and portray her in various regional Filipina costumes. The remains of past Spanish and Filipino archbishops are entombed in a crypt beneath the main altar. The Dutch organ, with its 4,500 pipes, is one of the largest in Asia. The cathedral's congregation is majestically presided over by Manila's controversial archbishop, Cardinal Jaime Sin, known for his decisive role in the People Power revolution. In 1987, Cardinal Sin set up an ecclesiastical museum to present the history of the Catholic Church in the Philippines — the **Archdiocesan Museum of Manila** is nearby at 121 Arzobispo Street.

Several blocks away, on Calle Real, **San Agustin Church** is the country's oldest stone church and dates from 1571. It is built in High Renaissance, Mexican-influenced style, with Doric and Corinthian columns, while Augustinian motifs of an arrow-pierced heart and a bishop's mitre decorate its grand portals, which are carved out of native molave wood. Also, look for the Chinese guardian lions. Inside, a baroque pulpit and wrought-iron door are impressive. Fourteen side chapels line the nave, with a tomb and effigy of Legaspi to the left of the main altar. The remains of the great Spanish conquistadors are interred here — Legaspi, Martin de Goti, Juan de Salcedo. These and an assortment of early governors and archbishops lie in a communal vault. The ceiling, which looks like a bas-relief, is actually a *trompe l'œil*, created by a pair of Italian artists in 1875. The church was the only structure within Intramuros to survive the 1945 bombing.

Adjoining San Agustin, the **Monastery Museum** has an extraordinarily rich collection of Philippine artifacts and religious art, despite being plundered during wartime years. It was here, in the vestry of the monastery complex, that Spain formally ceded to the United States in 1898, marking the final act of the Spanish-American War. Many prominent families in Manila's early colonial history were buried within the **Pantheon**. The peaceful, **cloistered garden** to one side was planted during the eighteenth century by the Augustinian botanist, Father Manual Blanco. One of the more dramatic incidents in the history of the monastery occurred during the battle for Manila in

February 1945 — some 7,000 civilians fled here in hope of sanctuary while the fierce artillery battle between Japanese and American forces raged. Intramuros was the site of the most brutal Japanese opposition, and few of these civilians escaped the orgy of violence that occurred here.

Just off the **Plaza San Luis**, across the road from San Agustin Church, is the **Casa Manila**, a reconstructed nineteenth-century colonial mansion, its interior crammed with period furniture and adorned with charming archways and a stone fountain. The Casa Manila complex includes a restaurant (Barbara's Intramuros) as well as a small café and some antique and curio shops good for browsing. Casa Manila is open daily, except Monday, from 9 AM to noon and 1 PM to 6 PM. Closing time during the weekend is 7 PM. Further along Calle Real is the four-story crafts complex **Silahi's Arts and Artifacts**.

Reached through the Puerta Real, the 58-ha (143-acre) **Rizal Park** (also called Luneta Park after the crescent-shaped redoubt near Manila Bay) is a calm respite from traffic streaming along Taft Avenue down to Roxas Boulevard. It has a desultory, tropical charm, dotted with acacia trees and fringed by horse-drawn calesas. During the day, this is where the city stretches its limbs: a gathering place for meandering families, t'ai chi ch'uan practitioners, joggers and off-duty workers. By night it is the haunt of would-be lovers or would-be muggers. Regardless of the hour, there are always hawkers selling fresh coconuts, balloons, improbable toys or jasmine flower necklaces. During the People Power uprising, many thousands of protesters gathered here. The most prominent landmark within the park is the **Rizal Monument**. Opposite is an **obelisk** marking the site where native priests Gomez, Burgos and Zamora were executed. On the spot where Rizal was shot by firing squad in 1898, a sound and light show re-enacts the event with life-size statues and a recorded narrative. There are Chinese and Japanese gardens, a playground and a skating rink. Also nearby is a duck pond with the Philippine Archipelago rendered in concrete. On one side of the park, on Padre Burgos Street, the **National Museum (** (2) 527-1215, which is open Monday through Saturday from 8:30 AM to noon and 1 PM to 5 PM, is worth seeing for its archaeological exhibits, ethnological artifacts and natural history collection.

## THE MANILA HOTEL

Bordering Rizal Park, the Manila Hotel is a mainstay of Manila life. When it first opened in 1912, the hotel was the social center of the booming industry that accompanied the Americanization of the Philippines. With its grand, California Mission-style exterior and interior intricately paneled with warm

Philippine narra mahogany, the hotel soon became a sort of exclusive club for the elite diaspora of colonizing and traveling Americans — entrepreneurs, politicians, military personnel and engineers among them. Much unofficial business was, and continues to be, conducted at the hotel's bayside bar. Initially, social and racial barriers in the new society meant that Filipinos were neither welcomed nor made to feel comfortable here, unlike the mestizos who made up the wealthy landowning class, a divide that lingered on until the time when Manuel Quezon became President of the new Philippine Commonwealth in 1935 and instituted social policy reforms.

Ever since the Manila Hotel was reopened with great fanfare by the Marcoses in 1977 (Imelda orchestrated much of the interior design), it has resumed its role as the most exclusive place for private dinners, weddings and conferences — despite the mushrooming of many other, more obviously extravagant hotels across the city. Any Filipina society

Fort Santiago.

matron worth her salt will express profound nostalgia for the memories of the **Champagne Room** or the **Fiesta Ballroom** during the 1950s and 1960s, where lovely Filipinas clad in *ternos,* or hand-embroidered gowns, would compete for attention and dance the rigodon with partners dressed shark-skin suits or barongs and "tango shoes." The corps of international journalists who converged on Manila during the time of the Snap Election and the People Power revolt in February 1986 have equally nostalgic memories of the heady, chaotic days spent here: at the

Ernest Hemingway, Tyrone Power, Bob Hope and the Beatles have all been guests. All this and more is documented in the hotel's Archive Room, open daily.

The story behind the hotel's MacArthur Suite is a chapter in the history of Manila. When General MacArthur was invited by Philippine President Quezon to become military advisor and create a Philippine Army in the 1935, one of the American general's conditions for acceptance was that he be provided with living quarters to equal the elegance and comfort of Malacañang

time, the hotel was the unofficial press center, with some of the television networks taking over large sections of it. Later that year, in July, the hotel became the target of a "minicoup" when it was taken over for several days by armed Marcos loyalists along with some 5,000 civilians.

The hotel has seen many famous people come and go. American presidents Dwight Eisenhower (then a young major in the staff of General Douglas MacArthur), Lyndon Johnson, Richard Nixon and more recently, Bill Clinton, have stayed here, among a long list of international presidents, prime ministers and dignitaries including Emperor Akihito of Japan. The Duke of Windsor, the Rockefellers, Henry Luce, Marlon Brando,

Palace. This request resulted in the construction of a penthouse suite for the General and his family atop the fifth floor of the old Manila Hotel. MacArthur, his wife Jean and son Arthur, lived here between 1935 and 1941. In December 1941, as the Japanese invaded, this became the command post. Unable to hold off the advancing forces, MacArthur retreated to Corregidor. In a twist of fate soon after that, when Manila was declared an Open City by the Japanese, the Manila Hotel became the headquarters of the Japanese army lead by the "Tiger of Malaya," General Yamashita. The next time the MacArthurs saw their old home, in 1945, the hotel was a bombed-out shell.

## THE MANILA BAYFRONT

Alongside Roxas Boulevard and Manila Bay are an array of some of Imelda Marcos' vast "beautification projects," financed in part by large international loans.

It is said that up to 10 percent of the total cost of some of these projects went into kickbacks. During the late 1970s, in her role as Governor of Metro Manila, Imelda developed an obsession with building grand status symbols, a mania that Filipinos dubbed Imelda's "edifice complex." The **Cultural Center of the Philippines** (CCP) ( (2) 891-5610 or (2) 832-1125 gathers together Philippine ethnological treasures along with works by modern artists. Its theaters, as well as the **Folk Arts Theater** nearby, are intended to provide a showcase for both Filipino and international performers. You can pick up a schedule of events. There are seven theaters and six resident companies performing dance, drama and music. The venues at the CCP Complex include the **Main Theater**, with an abstract Ocampo-designed curtain and the **Little Theater**, which presents chamber music and plays in Tagalog, either in their original versions by Filipino authors or as adaptations from foreign plays.

Close by, the **Philippine Convention Center** ( (2) 551-7920 or 7415, usually a conference hall but also used for rock concerts, was inaugurated for the 1974 International Monetary Fund-World Bank Conference. The **Contemporary Art Museum of the Philippines** has a permanent collection of Philippine modern and contemporary sculpture, paintings and other visual arts dating back to 1910. Also on this patch of reclaimed land are the **Design Center of the Philippines** and the **Philippine Center for Trade and Exhibitions**. Here, the full spectrum of Filipino artistry is on display: weaving, woodcarving, shellcraft, jewelry making, and metalwork. Next door, the **Coconut Palace** is an unusual, attractive mansion entirely inspired by and fashioned out of the coconut tree. Guided tours in English are conducted every half hour from 9 AM to 11 AM and from 1 PM to 4 PM daily except Monday.

Within the same stretch of reclaimed land is the infamous **Manila Film Center**. Conceived by Imelda in 1981, this was to be a grand Parthenon-style showcase for the first Manila International Film Festival. Contractors were given seven months to complete the shopping-mall-size building, and the First Lady was personally in charge of the project's supervision, which had a round-the-clock timetable. At 2:35 AM on November 17, 1981, the top story of the partially completed building fell through. Hasty construction had not allowed the concrete sufficient time to set. Hundreds of day-shift workers were sleeping beneath the viewing theater's atrium, and night-shift workers were toiling on the scaffolding above. Many workers were killed instantly; some were trapped and suffocated by the drying concrete; some were rescued by their fellow workers from air pockets and stairwells up to 24 hours after the accident.

Orders from Malacañang insisted that the rescue operation be halted and that construction continue without delay. Security personnel cordoned off the site, and the next day local newspapers reported that only a minor accident had occurred; with two fatalities. Bulldozers arrived to push the mangled remains of bodies, concrete and rubble from the site, fresh concrete was poured in, and the appalling stench grew fainter.

No one is sure how many died — but workers on site, who could list their missing colleagues, thought it was over 200. The Manila International Film Festival went ahead, inaugurated with great fanfare by Imelda, but was never repeated. Within two years the Film Center was screening uncensored pornographic films in attempt recoup some of its costs. Abandoned now and rumored to be haunted, it awaits some unspecified future use.

## ACROSS THE PASIG RIVER

North of the Pasig River are some of Manila's most densely populated, vibrant and historic neighborhoods, encompassing some compelling detours within their limits.

For the elite, the Champagne Room Restaurant, of the Manila Hotel.

## Chinatown

An atmospheric, clannish Oriental warren of shops, stalls, temples and restaurants, Chinatown is not to be missed. You can spend hours wandering through its small alleys, browsing through shops selling Chinese pottery, handcrafted gold and jade jewelry and traditional medicines. Its well-stocked Chinese supermarkets, tiny teahouses, mahjong parlors, large chopstick-clattering dim sum halls, pet shops, kung fu institutes and Buddhist shrines smoky with incense create an atmosphere found nowhere else

is imposing. Built in 1596, it was severely damaged during earthquakes and wartime bombing. Only the octagonal bell tower on the present structure is original. Directly across from the church is a distinctive Chinese-style bridge, which leads across a canal, and a curious fire station constructed in the style of a pagoda.

By a twist of the city's fate, **Escolta**, the former fashionable street of Manila's Spanish era, on the fringes of Chinatown, is now a listless collection of rather dusty shops and proletarian restaurants. Nevertheless, it is

in the city. There are several good Chinese restaurants tucked away here. In general, Chinese cuisine in the Philippines is predominantly Cantonese in bigger restaurants, Fujian (where most Chinese in the Philippines come from) in smaller ones, with a scattering of Hunan, Peking, Sichuan and Shanghai restaurants to be found as well.

Chinatown encompasses parts of the districts of Santa Cruz and Binondo and is bounded by three huge **Welcome Gates**. You can get your bearings by beginning your walk at **Ongpin Street**, which runs east to west. It is the main business street, and branching off it are many beckoning alleys that snake throughout the quarter. **Binondo Church**, near the Plaza Calderon de la Barca,

a segment of the city's living history in which something of an Iberian atmosphere still lingers on.

## Quiapo

Named after the water lily, *klyapo*, this cramped, bustling district — a short walk from Rizal Avenue — is worth visiting to see the life that hums around the shrine of the Black Nazarene in **Quiapo Church**. Outside, pavement fakirs, hawkers, herbalists, fortune tellers and craftspeople gather daily in a swelter of makeshift stalls. It's fun to browse and hear stories about the potions, *anting-anting,* or amulets, and medicinal drinks — and you may be lucky enough to discover an unusual curio or bargain antique.

Inside the Mexican-baroque-style church, reconstructed in 1935, the famous **Shrine of the Black Nazarene** has a history immersed in Spanish lore. The life-size statue of Christ was carved in Mexico by Indians and transported to the Philippines in the seventeenth century by the Spaniards — who fervently believed in the statue's miraculous powers. Each day, although especially on Fridays, the shrine attracts hundreds of the faithful. One of the more dramatic occasions to attend here is the procession of the Black Nazarene on January 9. This is procession is the climax of the shrine's adoration held on the Monday and Friday of Passion Week (the week before Easter, between Passion Sunday and Palm Sunday).

**Plaza Miranda**, opposite Quiapo Church, is a popular gathering point for both entertainment and political rallies. Many large anti-Marcos rallies started at Plaza Miranda, one of which was fired upon, before ex-President Marcos declared martial law in 1972.

In the same area, you can visit the unusual, neo-Gothic-style, steel fabricated **San Sebastian Church**, built on the site of three previous churches. The first was founded in 1621; all of them were destroyed by earthquakes. The current structure was built by Recollect Fathers in 1891 who, determined that this one survive, imported prefabricated steel from Belgium. The formidable structure, inspired by the fourteenth-century Gothic cathedral of Burgos in Spain, has two soaring openwork towers and vaulted steel. Despite the heavy construction, the building has a touch of airy insubstantiality by virtue of its charming stained-glass windows.

Opposite San Sebastian Church stands the **University of the East**. Also worth visiting in this area is the underpass market (Ilalim ng Tulay) below **Quezon Bridge**. Here you will find with dozens of stalls selling a wide variety of wares such as capiz lamps, rattan bags and other handicrafts.

East of Quezon Boulevard is Manila's **Muslim quarter**, which has a 60-year-old gold-domed mosque, along with a few Muslim restaurants and coffee houses. The Arab-style bazaar nearby is a good place to buy Indonesian batik, Pakistani cloth and Egyptian perfumes.

## SANTA CRUZ AND LA LOMA

Sprawling, residential **Santa Cruz** and **La Loma** are vibrant neighborhoods full of street-life and markets — with several compelling sights within their limits. **Santa Cruz Church**, originally built in 1608 by Jesuit Spaniards for Chinese converts, stands on Plaza Locsin. Within Santa Cruz, **Central Market** is full of lively stalls, with sections for textiles, cheap clothing, baskets and all kinds of foodstuffs. In La Loma, you'll see

rows of mounted roast pigs turning on rotisserie sticks awaiting buyers on Calavite Street. Nearby, Manila's bird hustlers crowd around on the hour to watch cock fighting in the **La Loma ring**, where the unfortunate creatures fight each other to the death with razors inserted in their claws.

Like Cairo's City of the Dead, the astonishing **Chinese Cemetery**, north of Santa Cruz along Aurora Avenue and Jose Abad Santos Street, is an eerie replica of a well-kept suburb, with tombs for the dead on a grand scale. Here, house-size — and sometimes palace-

OPPOSITE: A plethora of religious items are always on offer at Quiapo Church, Manila, one of the most important centers for Catholic pilgrimage. ABOVE: The chaotic color of Chinatown, Manila.

size — tombs and crypts are maintained to preserve the spirits of their inhabitants. They stand on well-swept, signposted roads; some have gardens and letterboxes. As you stroll, you'll see that tombs are often cozy, surrounded by icons of former lives — even telephones and fax machines. Most shrines contain black-and-white photographs of the deceased in their youthful prime, set about with scraps of red paper, burning joss sticks, and supplies of their favorite food and drink for feast days and anniversaries. Often maintained by caretakers, some of whom live in

the building, many of these tombs are supplied with electricity, running water and some even run to air conditioning. The old riddle, "Would you rather be a dead Chinese or a live Filipino?" to which Manileños don't really expect an answer, alludes to the juxtaposition of the appointed and serviced tombs to the largely unserviced shanty towns of the living that surround the cemetery. Society's pecking order is also evident in the range of tombs — rows of grandiose marble "mansions" contrast with eccentric, individualistic shrines. In some cases, Catholics have requested burial here. The impecunious are relegated to a sweeping bank in the cemetery's exterior walls containing thousands of tiny burial niches.

It is easy to lose yourself in the many alleys that branch through the cemetery. You may find it useful — and safer — to hire a guide to lead you through, but agree on a price beforehand. Those in a hurry can drive around the perimeters and through the main boulevards.

After this visit, you may have had enough of cemeteries. Yet **North Cemetery**, nearby in La Loma, is also interesting and historic. Many wealthy Spanish and Filipino families are buried here and there are some impressive mausoleums — one includes two pyramids and a sphinx. As with the Chinese Cemetery, it is not advisable to come here either on your own or at dusk — it too has become home to a large squatter community.

Also in the area, the **University of Santo Tomas** resonates with history. Although the original Dominican university was founded in 1611 and lies within Intramuros, this private, well-regarded campus dates from 1927. Key figures in the history of the Philippine revolutionary movement were educated here: José Rizal, Marcelo H. del Pilar, A. Mabini and Emilio Aguinaldo; the three martyred priests Burgos, Gomez and Zamora and presidents Quezon, Osmena and Macapagal. During the Japanese occupation from 1942, the campus was used as an internment camp for Allied citizens, its survivors released three years later when American troops swept through the city. Within the university, the **Museum of Natural Science** displays an extensive and rare collection that offers insights into the archaeological, anthropological and other scientific discoveries of the region — including a collection of rare and ancient pottery.

## MALACAÑANG PALACE

The white and mahogany fretted Spanish-style mansion built in the late nineteenth century has housed several previous presidents and, before them, American governors-general. But most visitors are drawn here because for 20 years this was the home of the Marcos clan. "You want to go to Malacañang?" said my taxi driver, chortling. "You want to see Imelda's shoe collection?" Like many locals and visitors to the palace, the taxi driver was not aware that, like other controversial swathes of Manila, Malacañang had been cleaned up under President Ramos. Today, a wing is dedicated to unfolding the history of the Philippine democratic tradition, with rooms displaying the personal memorabilia of each past president.

When the residence was first opened to the public in the immediate aftermath of the departure of the Marcos family, it was proclaimed an unofficial "museum of greed." It attracted thousands of curious Filipinos and foreign visitors alike. Throughout her presidential term, Corazon Aquino left the palace essentially as

was the most luxurious in the palace. Designated the "Queen's Room," a carved coronet billowing with tulle topped her bed. The scope of Imelda's wardrobe and adornments — including some 3,000 pairs of shoes and 2,000 ball gowns — was reputedly enough to stock a large department store. Imelda is remembered vividly across the world's temples to fashion, from the Via Condotti in Rome and Avenue Foch in Paris to New York's Fifth Avenue and Los Angeles' Rodeo Drive, running up the nation's external debt for her wardrobe.

it was, fulfilling a campaign promise, maintaining it as a symbol of the staggering corruption associated with her predecessor.

During the Marcos era, millions of dollars were spent remodeling the palace into a passable imitation of a Disney-esque Versailles. Walls and floors were covered with Italian marble and Persian carpets. Huge French mirrors abounded. Rooms were strewn with reproduction Louis XIV period furniture, English antique furniture, Aubusson tapestries and Chinese treasures. A discotheque complete with a waterfall was created and paintings of the First Couple and their offspring — some by the same artist favored by the Reagans — were prominently displayed. Imelda's red-carpeted bedroom

Because of the failing health of Ferdinand Marcos, the once gracious and airy palace was hermetically sealed — to block the wafting stench of the Pasig River and the barrios that flanked it. The palace also bore all the marks of illness — with a fully operational hospital clinic set up off the ex-President's bedroom. The equipment has since been donated to a Manila hospital. It was from Malacañang that the Marcoses fled by helicopter on February 25, 1986. Two hours later, thousands of exhilarated Filipinos stormed through the gates and gaped incredulously at the lofty rooms filled with paintings by old masters — not to

OPPOSITE: Preparing for a furtive cockfight, Pasay City, Manila. ABOVE: Herbarium in Quiapo.

mention Imelda's pure gold washbasin, her many giant perfume bottles, and, naturally, the shoes.

Anyone who saw Malacañang Palace in the early days of its post-Marcos state will barely recognize it now, since so little of Imelda's fantasy palace remains. Many of Marcos' spoils — including the famous shoe collection — are stored in a semi-display state in the basement chambers awaiting adjudication. It is difficult to get permission to view this section of the palace, but it is worth persisting, for it provides a fascinating

protest when it was the scene of many clashes between riot police and demonstrators during the People Power uprising.

## ERMITA

Known for years to experienced Asia travelers as "the strip," the tourist belt of Ermita was synonymous with raunchy nightlife: a zoo of sex-trade fauna, riddled with go-go bars, massage parlors, beer stalls, peep shows and, for the unlucky, venereal disease clinics. It was also the seat of the so-

insight into the psyches of the Marcoses, especially Imelda. Ask the ticket officer or tour guide for advice about to access. The entrance to the Malacañang Palace Museum is on José P. Laurel Street, San Miguel. On official occasions the palace and the museum are closed to the public.

During the eighteenth century, San Miguel was where the Filipino gentry built their summer residences and the area — surrounded by security checkpoints — contains some buildings reminiscent of nineteenth-century colonial Spain. Close to Malacañang, seek out **San Beda Chapel**, lined with paintings, murals and carved wood. Nearby **Mendiola Bridge**, which spans a small canal, became a symbol of

called "Malate Mafia" which controlled the city's underworld and trafficked in sleazy prostitution and pedophile rackets, drugs and most other known forms of vice.

Since the post-Marcos era, reformists have stepped in and Ermita has changed. Now much of its seedier and red-light-tinged nightlife has migrated to Pasay and Quezon City. The main force behind the clean-up of Ermita is Mayor Alberto Lim, also an influential businessman.

Ermita is colorful, far more redolent of the old Manila than Makati, and it's a haven for cheap hotels, curio shops and restaurants — most tucked around Remedios Circle and Adriatico Street — attracting tourists, expatriates and young, hip locals.

## MAKATI

Makati is where moneyed Manileños work by day and play by night. As the capital's expanding commercial center, it is almost a city in its own right. Megalopolis glass office towers, corporation headquarters, hotels and malls are rapidly consuming the teeming barrios at its outer limits. Designer shops are everywhere and the malls have an endless array of corridors bursting with opulence. For visitors, this is the place to

do business or wander in the neon-lit concrete alleys at night in search of a good meal and entertainment. Like a newly transplanted heart valve, the synthetic culture of Makati beats out a pulse that is quite different to that of, say, Intramuros or Ermita, with their heady whiffs of bygone eras. Makati glitters and beckons, a skin-deep version of Manila, with slick bars and restaurants which take cues from Bangkok and Hong Kong.

Aside from hotels, restaurants and shopping malls, there are a few places to visit in Makati of historical interest, as well as a museum and some parks and gardens. The **Church of Our Lady of Guadalupe** overlooks the Pasig River near the San Carlos Seminary and is quite lovely with its antique stone façade, ornate interiors and shady cobbled courtyard. The **Ayala Museum of Philippine History and Iconographic Archives** ( (2) 812-1191, on Makati Avenue, is open Tuesday through Saturday from 9 AM to 6 PM. It contains a remarkable display of some 60 dioramas portraying key events in the nation's history — from pivotal moments in the Spanish-American War to graphic World War II scenarios and right through the tumultuous events leading up to the People Power revolution in 1986. Don't overlook the exhibition of ancient Asian boats that have sailed in Philippine seas, or the museum shop, which has a good stock of ethnic crafts and art pieces. The **American Cemetery and Memorial** at Fort Bonifacio, in Makati, is the largest American burial ground outside the United States. Here, in rank and file, are buried 17,000 soldiers who died in the Philippines and surrounding Pacific during World War II. In the circular memorial are numerous photographs and montages of famous battles in the Pacific. The cemetery lies two kilometers (one and a quarter miles) from where Ayala Avenue meets Epifanio de los Santos Avenue (EDSA).

## QUEZON CITY

The former capital of the Philippines, Quezon City is named after its founder, Manuel Quezon, the first President of the Philippine Commonwealth. Four times the size of Manila, Quezon is a city unto itself, divided up into suburban housing estates or "projects," wealthy residential complexes and dotted with swimming pools, golf courses, hospitals and churches. Its center is **Cubao**, a maze of shopping malls and department stores, restaurants, cinemas, fast food joints as well as busy farmer's and seafood markets. This is where off-duty Manileños throng to spend their leisure hours, watching sporting events at the giant **Araneta Coliseum**. The **Museo ng Buhay Filipino** (Museum of Filipino Life), in the Central Bank building on East Avenue,

The well-tended American Cemetery, Makati, last resting place for over 17,000 World War II casualties.

is worth a visit if you are in the area, but it is not sufficiently compelling to warrant a detour.

## UNIVERSITY OF THE PHILIPPINES

"UP," as most Filipinos call the University of the Philippines, is considered to be the most prestigious school in the country. Located in the large campus in Diliman, Quezon City, the state university has many distinguished former alumni, including more than a few former presidents.

The **University of the Philippines Museum** ( (2) 976060 or 976061, is open Monday through Friday from 8:30 AM to 11:30 AM and 1:30 PM to 4:30 PM. The museum has a fascinating display of photographs and ethnic artifacts from tribal communities from all parts of the Philippines.

## NAYONG PILIPINO

Close to the Ninoy Aquino International Airport, Nayong Pilipino, or Philippine Village, recreates the nation's cultural mosaic with representative architectural styles; it's an interesting and educational visit. Nayong Pilipino more than lives up to its stated aim of being a "living museum." Set within a 46-ha (114-acre) park are replicas of village houses from throughout the Philippines, concentrating on the six main regions — Cordillera, Ilocos, Mindanao, Visayas, Bicol and Tagalog. Each house contains examples of the region's arts and crafts. There are also well-known landmarks from each region, recreated in miniature, such as the Banaue Rice Terraces, Cebu's Magellan Cross, Bicol's Mayon Volcano and the colorfully decorated houses of Samal in Mindanao. Especially appealing, the complex offers a range of indigenous handicrafts from all over the country — such as ikat cloth, jewelry, bags, brassware and carved wood — that you are unlikely to find in such profusion anywhere else in the Philippines.

The Nayong Pilipino also has an aviary, an aquarium and an orchidarium (with more than 50 species of native orchids). Perhaps most interesting and unusual, though, is its **Philippine Museum of Ethnology** ( (2) 832-0593, open Tuesday through Sunday from

9 AM to 6 PM, where actors clad in the ethnic costumes of different Philippine regions and tribes wander around and interact with visitors. Visitors can participate in the lectures given here and learn how to put on the Muslim garment called *malong*, beat the kulintang gongs, or coax music from an Ifugao nose flute. The museum showcases a fine collection of ethnological specimens of ancient arts such as of carving, weaving, weaponry and crafted ornaments. Films about Philippine culture and ethnology are screened at the museum from Tuesday to Friday at 10 AM and 3 PM, and on Saturday and Sunday at 10 AM and 5 PM.

It is well worth planning your visit to coincide with a performance of the **Nayong Pilipino Dance Troupe**. A repertoire of regional dances is offered at the Mindanao Pavilion at 2:30 PM and 4 PM every Saturday and Sunday.

To get to Nayong Pilipino, take a taxi or bus from the main thoroughfare of Epifanio de los Santos Avenue (EDSA) to the main village's entrance on Ninoy Aquino Avenue. Within the premises, colorful jeepneys take you to any point in the grounds free of charge.

## SMOKY MOUNTAIN

During the Marcos regime, the ultimate symbol of the dictator's callous indifference to Manila's suffering was Smoky Mountain, a fuming 21-ha (52-acre) pile of garbage alongside Manila Bay. It is here that some 15,000 people eked out an existence — scavenging and squatting in makeshift hovels on the filthy heap. Yet Smoky Mountain continued to smolder for almost nine years after Marcos had gone. In 1994, President Fidel Ramos decided to "clean-up" Smoky Mountain — and announced that the huge garbage slum would be bulldozed and transformed into a US$650 million port, factory and incinerator complex, with apartment blocks as well. Its residents would be rehoused and given training for more dignified professions, after which they would be offered permanent housing in the rehabilitated complex.

The plan has not been entirely successful, although Smoky Mountain is almost gone. When police came to relocate the squatters, they put up a battle in which one person was killed. The new housing site and complex, complete with library, nursery and vocational centers, is all but empty. Apparently, it can be more profitable to make a living sifting and sorting through garbage than engaging in somewhat cleaner occupations, and many squatters were reluctant to give up the lifestyle. Some residents have now moved to the Payatas dump across town, which is rapidly taking on Smokey's likeness. Several years later, *Time* magazine ran an article saying that many of Smoky Mountain's former residents badly miss their old home.

## WHERE TO STAY

Manila has some of Asia's finest — and in the case of the Manila Hotel, most historic — hotels, where guests are pampered in five-star luxury. There are also plenty of moderately priced and inexpensive places to stay for those on more limited budgets.

### EXPENSIVE

#### Makati

The **Shangri-La Hotel Manila** ( (2) 813-8888 FAX (2) 813-5499 WEB SITE www.shangri-la.com, at the corner of Ayala and Makati avenues, Makati, is the capital's slickest hotel. It's an enormous marble edifice with an Italianate lobby, a health club, excellent restaurants and top-notch facilities (including one of Manila's better nightspots, the Zu disco). It also connects with an impressive shopping mall with department stores, boutiques, cinemas, restaurants and bars. Arguably as glamorous is the **Peninsula Manila** ( (2) 810-3456 FAX (2) 815-4825 WEB SITE www.peninsula.com.ph, on the corner Ayala and Makati avenues, Makati. An affiliate of the famous Peninsula Hong Kong and in every respect its equal, the Peninsula fully lives up to its five-star category. It has several top class restaurants and attentive service.

Traditionally elegant in the Mandarin style, with five-star amenities, the **Mandarin Oriental Manila** ( (2) 750-8888 FAX (2) 817-2472 WEB SITE www.mandarin-oriental.com/manila, Makati Avenue and Paseo de

Roxas, Makati, has a spectacular pool and seven excellent restaurants. The conservative and spacious **Inter-Continental Manila** ( (2) 815-9711 FAX (2) 812-4389 WEB SITE www.interconti.com/philippines/manila/hotel_manicp.html, 1 Ayala Avenue, is equipped for the business traveler with work stations, fax-scanners, swivel chairs, and office supplies in the rooms. They even have cable modems for quick access to the Internet. The **New World Renaissance** ( (2) 811-6888 FAX (2) 811-6777 WEB SITE www.renaissancehotels.com, Esperanza Street at Makati Avenue, made

its debut in 1995. This modern high-rise hotel boasts ultramodern decor and automatic controls for almost everything.

#### Ermita/Malate

The **Manila Hotel** ( (2) 527-0011 FAX (2) 527-0022 WEB SITE www.manila-hotel.com.ph, 1 Rizal Park, adjacent to Quirino Grandstand, is in a class of its own — one of the aristocrats of Asia's historic hotels. Rooms, furnished with four-poster beds and Old World fabrics, look out across the medieval ruins of Intramuros or across the spectacular Manila Bay to the rocky fortress of Corregidor. There are three major suites,

On the outskirts of Manila, Nayong Pilipino, the Philippine Village, was created for tourists.

including the Penthouse, the Presidential and the MacArthur. The Presidential Suite includes an indoor swimming pool, and a live-in butler, as well as a helipad. The MacArthur Suite, occupying a wing of the fifth floor, includes a master bedroom with a guest room, a dressing room, and a formal dining, lounge and boardroom area, with a widow's walk overlooking the bay.

The **Century Park Hotel** ( (2) 528-8888 FAX (2) 528-1811, Pablo Ocampo Senior Street (formerly Vito Cruz), recently underwent a face-lift and now stands as one of the premier hotels in the tourist belt of Malate.

Spacious and technologically advanced, the **Pan Pacific** ( (2) 536-0788 FAX (2) 526-6503 WEB SITE www.panpac.com, M. Adriatico and General Malar Streets, offers personal computers on granite desks, fax/printers and stereo systems in every room.

### Along Roxas Boulevard

The **Manila Diamond Hotel** ( (2) 526-2211 FAX (2) 526-2255 WEB SITE www.diamond hotel.com, Roxas Boulevard, at the corner of J. Quintos Street, straddles the best of Manila between the tourist belt of Ermita/Malate and the business center of Makati. It's lavish decor and early 1900s art deco/postmodern design throughout the lobby and rooms is a hit with business travelers, particularly Japanese guests. The **Westin Philippine Plaza** ( (2) 551-5555 FAX (2) 551-5610, Cultural Center Complex, Roxas Boulevard, rounds out the top-notch hotel choices in Manila proper. The Westin is a veritable beachfront resort, and has its own golf course and a huge and luxurious swimming pool. Don't miss their nightly barbecues.

### MID-RANGE

### Makati

Formerly the Nikko Manila Garden Hotel, the **Dusit Hotel Nikko** ( (2) 867-3333 FAX (2) 867-3888 WEB SITE www.dusit.com/Dusit/dnm/, Ayala Center at EDSA, Makati is popular with visiting Japanese businessmen, and is notable for its elegant Spanish-Mediterranean style. It s conveniently located in the Makati Commercial Center, with restaurants, cinemas, boutiques, and department stores only a stone's throw away.

### Ermita/Malate

There are two excellent choices suitable in this area for business travelers. **Bayview Park** ( (2) 526-1555 FAX (2) 521-2674, at the corner of Roxas Boulevard and United Nations Avenue (opposite the United States Embassy), overlooks Manila Bay and offers large rooms and polished service.

The **Holiday Inn** ( (2) 526-2552 FAX (2) 526-2552, United Nations Avenue, is good value for the price, with Internet facilities and an attractive swimming pool area.

### Along Roxas Boulevard

At the high end of the mid-range, and representative of the chain, is the **Hyatt Regency Manila** ( (2) 833-1234 FAX (2) 833-5913, 2702 Roxas Boulevard, Pasay City.

There are two other recommended international standard hotels in this area, both with good facilities. The **Heritage Hotel** ( (2) 891-8888 FAX (2) 891-8833, at the corner of Roxas Boulevard and Epifanio de los Santos Avenue, is a glossy new hotel next door to the Casino. It offers the usual amenities, including a helipad and an excellent swimming pool. The **Mercure Philippine Village Airport Hotel** ( (2) 833-8080 FAX (2) 831-7788, Nayong Pilipino Park Complex, Pasay City, is a good choice if you have to catch an early flight.

### INEXPENSIVE

### Makati

Those traveling on a shoestring budget will be pleased to find a very clean and social **YMCA** ( (2) 899-6101 FAX (2) 899-6097, on Dao Street, San Antonio Village (near Makati's Central Post Office).

### Ermita/Malate

The **Adriatico Arms** ( (2) 521-0736 FAX (2) 525-6214, J. Nakpil Street at the corner of Adriatico Street, is situated in the heart of the tourist belt. Service is friendly and always welcoming. The **Centrepoint Hotel** ( (2) 521-2751 FAX (2) 521-5331, A. Mabini Street (near Robinson's Mall), is perfect if you plan on exploring Manila's nightlife. The staff is more than happy to offer planning assistance for the rest of your trip too. The **Ambassador Hotel** ( (2) 506011 FAX (2) 521-5557,

2021 A. Mabini Street, Malate, is a charming hotel in the Malate tourist belt, with a busy 24-hour coffee shop that is a long-time favorite with Manila's politicians.

## WHERE TO EAT

Unlike its neighbors, Bangkok and Hong Kong, Manila is not regarded as one of Asia's great gastronomic cities. Yet it has a profusion of good or, in some cases, excellent restaurants. One of the most popular restaurant and bar strips is found along and

**Albert Rotisserie ℂ** (2) 815-9711, Intercontinental Hotel, Ayala Avenue, is another Mediterranean gastronomic experience. The atmosphere is elegant and the restaurant serves such palate-pleasers as fresh lobster and smoked salmon. **La Tasca ℂ** (2) 893-8586 or (2) 893-8556, Greenbelt Commercial Center, Legaspi Street, has earned a well-deserved reputation as offering some of the best Spanish cuisine in Asia.

No restaurant selection would be complete without including the top of the Italian restaurants — **Carpaccio Ristorante**

around **Jupiter Street** in Makati, which is a good place to head if you feel like browsing for a table.

Although not always essential, it's advisable to reserve a table in Manila's more popular formal restaurants and, in some cases, to check if there is a dress code.

### EXPENSIVE

#### Makati
**Le Soufflé Restaurant and Wine Bar ℂ** (2) 812-3287 or (2) 894-1269, on Greenbelt Drive at Makati Avenue, has an innovative and varied menu, and is regarded by many Manileños as the city's most elegant restaurant. Reservations are necessary. **Prince**

**Italiano ℂ** (2) 843-7286, Yakal Street, San Antonio Village. Despite its remote location, it serves the closest thing to perfect pasta in Manila. Both **Sugi ℂ** (2) 816-3885 or 3886, Greenbelt Mall, Ayala Centre, and **Zen ℂ** (2) 892-6851 Glorietta 3, Level 1 Ayala Center, dish up excellent sushi.

The five-star hotels in Makati offer some excellent dining. The Shangri-La Hotel Manila scores high for cuisine, service and style: its **Cheval Blanc ℂ** (2) 813-8888 is excellent for fine European food — predominately French — and is open for breakfast, lunch and dinner (reservations are required). Upstairs at the Shangri-La,

Manila boasts some of Asia's finest hotels. One of the best is the Peninsula Manila in Makati.

Conways serves a buffet lunch and becomes a music lounge in the late afternoon. **Spices** at the Peninsula Hotel is also especially good, with an array of sophisticated pan-Asian dishes.

### Ermita/Malate

If you are looking for a more refined version of the Filipino culinary experience and want to dress up, then **Maynila** ( (2) 527-0011 at the Manila Hotel is the place to go. It has a turn-of-the-twentieth-century ambiance and extraordinary furnishings (in-

friendly atmosphere attracts the expatriate and local communities alike. **Flavours and Spices** ( (2) 815-3029 or (2) 819-1375, Garden Square, Greenbelt Commercial Center, not only dishes out the best of Thai food in Manila, but is also the place to go for spices and condiments. For the best Chinese food that Manila has to offer, nothing beats **The Good Earth Tea Room** ( (915) 702-7786, located in the Magallanes Commercial Center. The **North Park Noodle House** ( (2) 895-3471, Banawe Avenue, Quezon City, brings in crowds like never before.

cluding capiz-decorated chandeliers). The Manila Hotel's **Sea Breeze** is perfect for a bayside meal overlooking the sea; chefs help you select and then grill your choice of meat or seafood. It is open Thursday through Saturday from 5 PM to 10 PM, although it closes during the rainy season (late July to early November).

### MID-RANGE

### Makati

**Baan Thai** ( (2) 895-1666, at the corner of Makati Avenue and Jupiter Streets, is the place to go for home-cooked spicy Thai food. The food may burn your tongue but it won't burn your pocket and the restaurant's

**Cassarola** ( (2) 816-1935, at 102 Jupiter Street, is the best and perhaps only Portuguese restaurant in Manila. Specializing in European specialties, **Europa Deli** ( (2) 878310, at 150 Jupiter Street, has delicatessen dishes featuring imported produce such as Angus beef, salmon, duckling and trout. In the Ayala Building is the chic **Giraffe Bar and Grill** ( (2) 815-3232. The food is good, though overpriced, and the raised bar is a fun spot for a pre-dinner drink. **L'Olivier** ( (2) 812-8596, No. 6750 Ayala Building, is a fashionable boutique restaurant with Mediterranean-based cuisine; there is live music for late diners every Tuesday. The traditional flavors of Luzon's Bulacan and Pampanga provinces can be found at

Restorante Barasoain ℂ (2) 812-4719 or (2) 843-9596, Mile-Long Building, Amorsolo Street at Herrera Street. At the Mandarin Oriental, **Tin Hau** ℂ (2) 816-3601 is an exceptional Chinese restaurant.

## Ermita/Malate

To sample the varied dishes that constitute Filipino cuisine, a good place to start is **Kamayan** ℂ (2) 528-1723, 523 Padre Faura at the corner of M. Adriatico Street. Guests dine native-style, with their hands, on an excellent range of traditional Filipino dishes. The

atmosphere is lively, with a band performing every night as well as appearances by a group of talented blind musicians who bear a slight resemblance to the Blues Brothers. **Zamboanga** ℂ (2) 525-7638 or 521-9836, 1619 Macario Adriatico Street, is a classic Filipino restaurant, serving essentially seafood dishes that hail from Mindanao's two Zamboanga provinces. **Bistro Remedios** ℂ (2) 523-9153 or (2) 524-3795, Adriatico Street, is another popular traditional Filipino restaurant. It is open long hours, with breakfast being the most popular time.

**Kashmir** ℂ (2) 524-6851, Padre Faura, with a second location in the Festejo Building in Makati, prepares authentic Indian food that never fails to please. There are plenty

of vegetable dishes too, and their breads shouldn't be missed.

Two moderately priced restaurants with an Iberian atmosphere offer romantic, candlelight dining in the walled city. **Barbara's Intramuros** ℂ (2) 527-3893 is located upstairs within the Casa Manila complex, opposite San Agustin Church. Nearby **Ilustrados Restaurant** ℂ (2) 527-3675, at 744 Calle Real, is elegant and formal, housed in a recreated nineteenth-century mansion overlooking a courtyard. Arrange to have a taxi pick you up after dinner as Intramuros isn't considered safe for foreigners to walk around in late at night.

Ermita has some unusual theme restaurants. At **Seafood Market** ℂ (2) 524-7756, Ambassador Hotel, Mabini Street, diners "shop" in a little supermarket for their dinner, selecting from an array of live seafood, platters of vegetables and iced beer or wine. They are then ushered into an adjoining dining area where they are served their selections. The famous **Singing Cooks and Waiters Restaurant** is a unique institution that never fails to charm. As its name suggests, at some point in the evening the "star-studded" cast of cooks and waiters break into song. There are five locations: Quezon City ℂ (2) 926 5757, West Triangle, Quezon Avenue; Pasay City ℂ (2) 832-0658 Roxas Boulevard; Pasig ℂ (2) 645-0628 FAX (2) 645-3735, Restaurant Avenue, Marcos Highway; Makati ℂ (2) 899-7528, J.P. Rizal, at the corner of Makati Avenue; and Mandaluyong City ℂ (2) 635-5944, SM Megamall, EDSA. On Remedios Circle, **Guernicas** ℂ (2) 521-4417 has a Latin atmosphere and serves good Spanish food, with flowers for the women and mariachi performers eliciting singing requests with great persuasion. By midnight, the waiters and cooks (and you) are singing along too.

## Outside the City Center

Probably two of the most unique dining experiences to be had in Manila are located outside of Makati and Ermita. The **Aviary Restaurant, Iguana Bar, Pet Museum Café and Pet Park** ℂ (2) 726-4618, Jose Abad Santos Street, Little Baguio (near Cardinal Santos

Music is an integral part of dining in many of the country's better restaurants.

Hospital), is practically a zoo. The grunts of lizards and howls of silver-crested Australian cockatoos at this zany watering hole, popular with artists and politicians, makes a night here interesting. The food is quite eclectic with a lean toward French and the beef fondue is a must-try. **L'Eau Vive in Asia** ℂ (2) 563-8558, 59, Paz M. Guazon Avenue, Paco, is a missionary settlement run by Carmelite nuns, who serve up authentic French cuisine including frogs' legs and rabbit. To warm your heart and spirit, catch the 9:30 PM prayer, when local children kneel down in front of the garden courtyard and the statue of Mary and sing along to Ave Maria.

## INEXPENSIVE

You won't be sacrificing quality at the many inexpensive restaurants in Manila. Quite the contrary — some of Manila's best local dishes are found at back-street restaurants that won't empty out your wallet while you fill up.

If a restaurant with a view is your priority, then **Harbor View** ℂ (2) 524-1571 along Gate A of Manila Bay near Rizal Park, is the place to head. You can watch the boats pass by and catch fresh bay breezes while eating their selections of Filipino seafood dishes. The very popular corner hacienda, **Café Havana** ℂ (2) 521-8097, on M. Adriatico at Remedios Street, dishes up excellent Cuban cuisine; its lunch specials and interesting bar drinks attract many travelers and expatriates. For pizza and pasta, **Italianni's** ℂ (2) 536-7961, Second Level, Robinson's Place, is a very popular and casual Italian restaurant, also noted for its focaccia and *pan de sal* bread, baked fresh daily. Under the same ownership, the equally popular **Paper Moon** ℂ (2) 895-1071, on Jupiter Street, has a friendly ambiance and serves classic antipasti and pasta dishes. **Penguin Café** ℂ (2) 521-2088, on Remedios Circle, is popular with artists and young journalists and show-cases the work of Filipino as well as foreign photographers. For Tuscan-based cuisine, **La Vecchia Trattoria** ℂ (2) 521-9431, at M.H. del Pilar Street, is a good choice. At lunch, they serve great pizzas and have an appetizing buffet.

Another interesting experience in Manila is to wander through the clusters of stalls selling all sorts of dishes. You'll find food stalls in carinderias or working-class cafés on the street or in the food halls located in the ground floor or basement of major shopping centers, such as the Shangri-La Plaza, Robinson's and Shoeman. Diners select *turo-turo*-style (*turo* which means "point" refers to the practice of pointing to make your selection) whatever looks appetizing. Dishes to sample include *sinigang* (a hot, sourish broth with meat, fish or prawns), *arroz caldo* (chicken and rice soup topped with onions), *mami* dishes (noodles prepared with chicken or beef), *rellenong bangus* (milkfish, deboned and stuffed with chopped meat and vegetables then lightly grilled), fresh or fried *lumpia* (spring rolls) and *ihaw-ihaw* (chicken, pork or seafood grilled and served on a skewer). Other tasty local delicacies include *banana-cue* and *camote-cue* (fried sugared plantain bananas skewered on a barbecue stick) and the ever popular *balut*, a partially cooked, fertilized duck's egg (definitely not for the squeamish).

## NIGHTLIFE

New York City is not the only place in the world that stays open all night. Manila's nightlife pulsates to all hours and the variety is sure to please the nightlife appetite of any visitor. With distinct scenes in each part of the city — Malate with its bohemian, laid-back air, Makati with its distinctive jet-setting scene, choosing a destination to suit your need and mood will be easy.

### HOTEL LOUNGES

Like the Spanish, Manileños live for that hour when the sun goes down and the city wakes up. At sunset, cocktail shakers start competing with each other across Manila Bay. The first place to idle over a sunset cocktail is the **poolside bar** at the **Manila Hotel**. Also within the Manila Hotel is the **Tap Room** (2) 527-0011, which performs old classic jazz favorites, or the adjoining **Lobby Bar** where Philippine politicians and journalists get together informally most Monday evenings. The more formal **Champagne Room** with its Imelda-esque decor is a place to drink some bubbly while being serenaded by the Champagne Strings band. A less formal, but no less elegant, Manileño rendezvous for drinks is the **Conservatory** ( (2) 810-3456, at the Peninsula Manila. The spacious room with its high ceiling overlooks a garden. Happy hour is from 6 PM to 8 PM and free appetizers are served.

The **Manila Yacht Club** ( (2) 521-4458 along Roxas Boulevard is also a great place to welcome the dusk, although you may need to prove that you have some nautical affiliations to be admitted. The **Calesa Bar** ( (2) 833-1234, Hyatt Regency Hotel, has a reputation for launching new and noteworthy singers, while the **Captain's Bar** ( (2) 750-8888, at the Mandarin Oriental Hotel is frequented by Manila's upper crust for its relaxing live music.

## NIGHTCLUBS AND DISCOS

From the traditional to the extravagant and outlandish, Manila's disco and club scene is alive and well. The music is very western and the crowds range from transvestites to yuppie and wannabe hippies. **Studebaker's** ( (2) 892-0959, Ayala Center, spans three levels of the Quad and is easy to find, located directly opposite the Shangri-La Hotel. The club is a mix of modernist and art deco styles, with the quieter **Fashion and Wine Bar** at its entrance. Upstairs there's a music lounge and brasserie-style restaurant, with a discotheque on the third level. In the basement of the Shangri-La Hotel, **Zu** ( (2) 813-8888 is considered the hottest nightspot in town. It combines karaoke, a sushi and oyster bar, live pop bands and an electrifying mix of styles. **Euphoria** ( (2) 815-9711, in the Hotel Inter-Continental, is another place to go to see and be seen. The young and in crowd mingle here.

If you want to practice your merengue or salsa, the **Siete Pecados** ( (2) 551-5555, at the Westin Philippine Plaza favors showy bands and Latin music. **Top of the Century** ( (2) 522-1011, at the Century Park Hotel, has well-known jazz and pop singers who are very popular. In Quezon City, **Club 690** ( (2) 712-3662 is a popular gay club with performances that range from dance troupes to Madonna impersonators. And for one of the most liveliest of scenes, put on your ballroom best for **Cats** ( (2) 811-6888, in the New World Renaissance Hotel.

## BARS

**Giraffe** ( (2) 815-3232, on Ayala Avenue in Makati, facing the Glorietta Circle, and **Venezia** ( (2) 845-1732, on the Ground Floor of the Ayala Center, are both posh places to dress in your finest outfits and come to see the crème de la crème of Manila's residents. **Guernica** ( (2) 521-4415, Bocobo Street in Malate, features Spanish music and folk tunes, and **Harry's Bar and Grill** ( (2) 842-0774, Ayala Town Center, Alabang, showcases Harry's jazz talents and his wife's finest bar food.

If Irish-style pubs are your forte and a glass of Guiness is what you crave, the **Prince of Whales** ( (2) 815-4274, in the New Plaza Building, Greenbelt, Makati, and the **San Mig Pub** ( (2) 893-8556, Garden Mall, Greenbelt Park, Makati Avenue, will deliver. Both are popular with the expat crowd.

The young and grungy of Manila tend to congregate at **Chatterbox** ( (2) 928-7539, West Avenue, Quezon City, **Club Dredd** ( (2) 912-8464, EDSA at Tuason Street. Another place that has a mix of students and professionals is **'70's Bistro** ( (2) 922-0492, on Anonas Street.

There is no need to wear high heels to see over the heads of the crowd at **Hobbit House** ( (2) 521-7604 on A. Mabini Street. The bouncer at the door, the waiters on the floor, and the bartenders are all dwarfs who eagerly rush your orders to you, pose for pictures, and see to it that you have a good time. Aside from the circus-like attendants, the bar hosts some excellent live music — including a well-known Filipino folk singer, Freddie Aguilar.

Manila also has its fair share of cafés that also serve as excellent evening hangouts. In Ermita, **Café Caribana** ( (2) 524-8421, on J. Nakpil Street, is a lively place with good and Caribbean food. The wild **Endangered Species Café** ( (2) 524-0167, on Adriatico Street, with its exotic, jungle-theme bar, puts on an eclectic choice of fare, while **Penguin Café** ( (2) 631-2088, Remedios Street at Bocobo

Street, plays a role as art gallery, outdoor lounge, café, and bar. It's quite popular with the artists around Ermita and Malate.

And no bar scene is complete without a place to play pool. **Heckle and Jeckle Café and Bar** ( (2) 890-6904, on the Ground Floor, Villa Building, Jupiter Street, is named after the two cartoon magpies. People come to this bar to play pool or to listen to the live band every Thursday and Saturday. Come between 8 PM and 10 PM to avail yourself of their drink-till-you-drop special.

( (2) 891-7856, Roxas Boulevard at EDSA, Pasay City — are open 24-hours a day and are government-sanctioned. Games include baccarat, blackjack, roulette and poker.

## SHOPPING

Authentic and inexpensive, Ermita's antique shops are concentrated along **A. Mabini Street** — their dank interiors crammed with Chinese chests, porcelain, carved Mindanao birds and lacquer ware. Some of the better stores on A. Mabini Streets are **Likha Antiques**

For a taste of what some might consider the tasteless "girlie" bars, **Jools** ( (2) 897-9097, on P. Burgos Street, Makati, is a show worthy of Las Vegas, and expats and locals say they feel comfortable bringing their visiting parents or bosses here for a night of innocent entertainment. It's a nice change from the regular sit-and-drink bars. The true strip-club scene is along P. Burgos Street.

---

### CASINOS

All three casinos in Manila — **Grand Boulevard Sofitel** ( (2) 507818, Roxas Boulevard, **Holiday Inn-Manila Pavilion Hotel** ( (2) 522-2911, Maria Orosa Street at United Nations Avenue, and the **Heritage Hotel**

( (2) 525-1620, **Padua Gallery** ( (2) 562-7772, **Riba Artifacts** ( (2) 523-0084, and **Tesoro's** ( (2) 524-3936. If you're looking for antiques, don't miss a visit to **Silahi's Arts and Artifacts**, Calle Real, Intramuros, with its wide selection of ethnic crafts and some fine antiques — probably the most extensive display of its kind in Manila.

Aside from the vibrant, bargain-stocked bazaars and shops of Chinatown and Quiapo, the curio shops in Ermita, and the fashionable boutiques in Makati, you will soon discover that Manila has developed the Asian mania for shopping malls, and a stay here of a reasonable length of time is bound to mean encountering at least one of them. Shopping bargains are as good as those found in

Hong Kong. Along EDSA, between Shaw Boulevard and Ortigas Avenue, is the one-stop-shop corner for any of your mall needs — **Robinson's Galleria**, **SM Megamall**, and the exclusive **Shangri-La Plaza**. You'll find anything from chic clothing and shoe stores, electronic and furniture stores, art galleries, cinemas, and several huge department stores here (including Robinson's, and Rustan's). Megamall is a exactly that: two hangar-size buildings joined together to form an indoor consumerist megalopolis. It even has an ice-skating rink in the basement level, next to the enormous food court.

**Harrison Plaza**, in the middle of the tourist belt adjacent to the Century Park Hotel, is huge, and Lao Center on Arnaiz Avenue in Makati is a good place to go for antiques.

If you are looking for colorful, contemporary Filipino handicrafts, try the reputable chain stores such as **Susancrafts**, as well as antique dealers such as **Jo-Liza** and **Via Antica**. Within the malls, **Rustan's**, **SM Shoemart**, **Landmark** and **Robinson's** all have well-stocked Filipiniana departments.

No travel experience would be complete without a wander through one of the local markets. **Divisoria**, the largest old-fashioned market district, is a good place to seek out bargains for local or imported fabrics, household ware, cheap jeans and discounted fashion-industry castoffs. **Cubao** in Quezon City is good for bazaars and up-market boutiques. **Santa Cruz Mission** on A. Mabini Street, Ermita, specializes in *T'boli* and other ethnic crafts, along with **Pistang Pilipino**, a large complex of about 100 shops along M.H. del Pilar in Malate.

**Duty Free Philippines** ( (2) 832-3191 to 3199, or (2) 832-3187 is one of the largest complexes of its kind in the world, and worth a visit for shopaholics. Its main branch is at the **Fiesta Shopping Center**, by the Ninoy Aquino International Airport. It is a giant treasure trove of more than 85,000 different items, with everything from Christian Dior and Bally to children's toys, sporting equipment and high fashion from both Filipino and international designers. There is a smaller outlet in the airport complex. It has a good selection of high quality Philippine-made handicrafts and furniture in addition to the usual range of luxury items.

## AROUND MANILA

If the length of your stay in the Philippines limits you to Manila, it is well worth taking advantage of the city's proximity to some of the country's most outstanding destinations. From Manila, you can explore the neighboring provinces easily by car and return by evening. Getting there is made easier by well-paved highways and expressways.

All the destinations in this section can be reached within three hours of driving. You may regard them too as stages en route while you travel onwards to further explore the island of Luzon. The Department of Tourism has information about guided tours of these nearby day-trip destinations (see too THE OPEN ROAD, page 34 in YOUR CHOICE).

### GENERAL INFORMATION

Sites around Manila are easily reached by car, although you must decide if you want to tackle the roads yourself or hire a driver at a substantially low cost. Manila car rental offices include:

Ace ( (2) 810-5147 or (2) 812-4892, Avis ( (2) 535-2206 or (2) 844-8498, Budget ( (2) 818-7363 or (2) 816-6682, Dollar ( (2) 896-9251, Executive ( (2) 832-5368, Hertz ( (2) 832-0520, and National ( (2) 897-9023.

### CORREGIDOR

You don't need to be an enthusiast of military lore to be fascinated by the battle-scarred island citadel of Corregidor, or "The Rock," as it is called by thousands of war veterans. It was the scene of some of the most grueling and bloody battles ever fought by combined American and Filipino troops against the Japanese. Reached by boat, this small, comma-shaped island fortress lies within a group of four other islands — Caballo, Carabao, El Fraille and La Monja — in the narrow entrance to Manila Bay.

Corregidor was the last stronghold of the American and Filipino forces under General MacArthur during World War II and, along with Bataan Peninsula, witnessed intensive

State-of-the-art shopping in Makati Commercial Center, Manila.

Japanese bombing and atrocities. The island, roughly the size of Manhattan, was where for more than three months the malaria-plagued troops defended their ever-shrinking territory against the numerically superior Japanese invasion. Following their surprise attack on Pearl Harbor on December 7, 1941, the Japanese bombarded United States bombers and fighter planes stationed at Clark Air Force Base, and from there invaded Luzon. Declaring Manila an "Open City" in order to protect its civilians and historic monuments from obliteration, MacArthur retreated to set up his headquarters at Corregidor, with the majority of his forces dispatched to the nearby Bataan Peninsula. He was accompanied by his family, Philippine President Manuel Quezon and United States High Commissioner Francis Sayle, along with a contingent of troops.

The decision to put up a defense from Corregidor was regarded by military strategists as one of MacArthur's bravest hedges, yet his position was ultimately hopeless. The island depended on daily barges from Bataan for water, food, medicines and ammunition. When the United States general-in-command at Bataan surrendered on April 9, 1942, President Roosevelt ordered MacArthur to Australia, inspiring his famous promise to return. The Japanese expected Corregidor to fall at the same time as Bataan. Yet incredibly, the 12,000-strong remnant of the army held out for a month before succumbing to heavy bombardment. Survivors were taken as prisoners of war on May 6, 1942. The event officially marked the end of wartime hostilities in the Philippines and the period of the Japanese occupation     until MacArthur recaptured The Rock on March 2, 1945. This date is known as *Araw ng Kagitingan,* or Day of Valor, and is a national holiday.

A former haunt of an opportunistic Chinese corsair and bands of Moro pirates, Corregidor was partially fortified by the Spanish, who built a dockyard, a naval hospital, a lighthouse and positioned guns on its battlements. After the island was taken over by United States Admiral George Dewey in 1898, it was transformed under the Americans into an impregnable warren of bunkers, barracks, office quarters and storerooms, bristling with gun towers and coastal artillery.

Today, the island has been converted into a war memorial, and you can walk throughout the ruined barracks, cannon and artillery emplacements, gaping batteries, tunnel mazes and the nineteenth-century Spanish lighthouse. Security personnel dressed in the 1930s uniform of the Philippine Constabulary add to the historical atmosphere.

### What to See and Do

You can explore the various areas — known as **Topside**, **Middleside**, **Bottomside** and **The Tail** — either on foot or by tour bus. Topside is the island's highest point and the main center of the fort. A museum of war memorabilia is housed in one of the reconstructed barracks. If you are walking, visiting all these locations and sights means covering a distance of about three kilometers (around two miles).

There is a sound-and-light show at **Malinta Tunnel**, a spooky warren of tunnels which began as an arsenal and an underground hospital and, during the siege of Manila, was used as the headquarters for the exiled Philippine government under Manuel Quezon before he escaped to the United States. **Suicide Cliff** has a Buddhist shrine to mark the place where many Japanese soldiers chose to jump to an honorable death rather than surrender.

### Where to Stay

You can stay on the island at the **Corregidor Hotel (** (32) 372-4865, a spacious hotel with air conditioning and television. **Corregidor Inn (** (32) 831-8140 is another option; an authentic reconstruction of an old inn that was destroyed during the bombing raids. Its restaurant overlooks the two historic beaches.

### How to Get There

From Manila, the trip to Corregidor takes 45 minutes by boat from the PTA Cruise Terminal at the Cultural Center of the Philippines (beside the Folk Arts Theater) on Roxas Boulevard. Day trips are available through **Sun Cruises (** (2) 831-8140 or (2) 831-5736, departing in the early morning and returning in the late afternoon. From Corregidor, **outrigger canoes** manned by local boatmen take visitors to the fortress islands of Fort Drum, Caballo and La Monja.

## RIZAL PROVINCE

Bounded by Metro Manila, many of Rizal's western suburbs have blurred into the capital's urban sprawl, among them the fishing port of **Navotos, Pateros** (which produces *balut*, the Filipino delicacy of fertilized duck's eggs) and **Las Piñas**, with its remarkable bamboo organ. Named after the national hero of the Philippines, José Rizal, the province is mostly flat but becomes hilly and rugged as it joins the foothills of the Sierra Madre.

Whether you are driving out from Manila, or returning from Laguna Province or Quezon, there are several places to stop and see in Rizal, especially the towns of Angono and Antipolo, set amongst the foothills. **Angono** is an artist's commune and is the home of Carlos "Botong" Francisco, one of the more well-known Filipino folk artists. It is a peaceful and bohemian community, with many ateliers and **workshops** to visit. **Antipolo** is otherwise uneventful aside from the religious celebrations that dominate the town every May, when devotees flock to the Shrine of the Virgin of Antipolo, feted for the image of the Madonna that was credited with miraculously saving galleons from stormy seas. Between 1641 and 1748 the Madonna was taken aboard eight return voyages. Believed to be the guardian of safe journeys, she has a large following.

Nearby, **Cainta**, **Pasig** and **Taytay** are notable as the towns captured by the British troops and Indian sepoys in 1762. The towns were handed back to the Spanish in 1763.

Another historical quirk, the **Morong Church**, four kilometers (two and a half miles) beyond **Cardona**, is one of the finest churches in the region, with many oriental touches to its architecture left by the Chinese artisans who completed it in 1615.

### Las Piñas

Just outside Manila is one of the oldest churches in the country. **Las Piñas Church** was built during the Spanish colonial period by Father Diego Cera, a Recollect Friar. Its bamboo organ, the only one of its kind, was built between 1816 and 1822, and its continued existence — it has survived earthquakes, typhoons and neglect — is a testament

*Manila*

to the durability of the natural fiber. A week-long **Bamboo Organ Festival** is held each February, attracting organists from around the world. Sometimes, usually in December, concerts are held in the Las Piñas Church grounds, under starlight from colorful lanterns, or *parols*. In Las Piñas, don't miss visiting the **Sarao Jeepney Factory** — home of the nation's famous jeepney. The factory here offers guided tours through various stages of the jeepney's manufacture.

If you wish to make a short detour to see one of Cavite's more interesting historic

towns, then drive nine kilometers (five and a half miles) further to the early Spanish town of **Kawit**, just 23 km (14 miles) from Manila, to see the **Aguinaldo Shrine**, which commemorates the life of General Emilio Aguinaldo. His house and its original furnishings have been turned into a museum, with an eclectic collection of Filipino and American national icons — American eagles mixed with Filipino flags. Aguinaldo's grave is here, too. On June 12, 1898, it was from his balcony that the First Philippine Republic was proclaimed, and the new Filipino flag was raised. The Filipino hero led the resistance first against the Spanish and later against the Americans until he was overpowered at Biak-na-Bato in San Miguel. Both Aguinaldo's presidency and the First Philippine Republic were short-lived. In 1901, after his capture, Aguinaldo issued his final edict, ceding rule to the Americans and recommending that Filipinos make the best of the situation.

A taxi weaving its way through Manila.

# Central and Northern Luzon

IF MANILA CAN BE COMPARED TO A BAR GIRL SINGING along to a Simon and Garfunkel song, then the rest of the island of Luzon is a teetotaling, provincial matron observant both of Saint Jude and tribal spirits. Considered the nation's heartland, Luzon encompasses a vast swath of territory and offers many faces of the multifaceted Filipino personality.

Geographically, Luzon is the main island of the largest island group in the Philippines, extending from the Batan Islands in the north, less than 200 km (120 miles) from Taiwan, through the islands of Luzon, Mindoro, the Calamian Group, Palawan, and Balabac Island, 55 km (33 miles) north of Borneo. This cluster of disparate island provinces shares — like the rest of the nation — a perplexing welter of tribal cultures, languages and dialects. Its landscapes differ, too, ranging from the famous pea-green rice terraces of Banaue in northern Luzon to the primeval black cliffs and dazzling pristine waters of remote Palawan — which is itself an archipelago of almost 2,000 islands.

The largest island in the Philippines, Luzon is more than 100,000 sq km (38,610 sq miles) in size and is home to half the country's population of 72 million. Its central plain is dubbed the nation's "rice bowl" — where luminous tones of green rice paddies and spectacular layered terraces undulate toward the horizon. This is one of the country's richest agricultural regions, with plantations of tobacco, sugarcane, mangoes, coffee, and coconuts.

Luzon is often neglected as a destination. Perhaps that's because it can seem almost too dense, too much of an expedition, as opposed to a simple jaunt to a beach-resort like Boracay or Cebu. Yet it has much to offer aficionados of tribal culture, remote beaches and Spanish baroque architecture.

Home to the Ilocanos people in the north and Tagalogs in the central plains, Luzon's population also includes many distinct ethnic groups whose lifestyles have changed little for centuries. Among these groups, tucked amidst the vertiginous Cordillera Central are the Ifugao tribespeople, architects of the best-known of the spectacular sights in the province, Banaue's canyon-like stonewalled rice terraces.

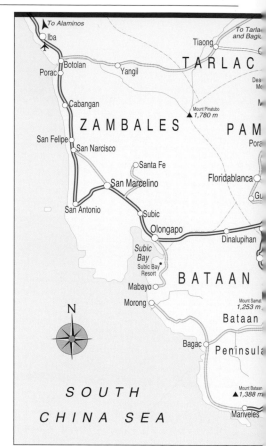

Excursions throughout Luzon offer a glimpse of the country's rugged splendor and of its people's soil-bound lifestyle. North Luzon's sites include the burial caves of Sagada and the town of Vigan, with its well-restored sixteenth-century mansions and churches. And as anyone who has witnessed the crucifixion rituals in Pampanga can attest, Central Luzon is renowned for the feverish intensity of its religious rituals. After all, Mount Pinatubo's wrathful energies are close by.

## CENTRAL LUZON

North of Manila begins Luzon's vast central plain — a giant rice-rich region that knits together the provinces of Bulacan, Pampanga, Tarlac, Nueva Ecija and the eastern flank of Pangasinan. Closest to Manila, the two provinces of Bulacan and Pampanga have much to offer, especially if you are traveling with children, who will appreciate the emphasis on colorful fiestas and prettily

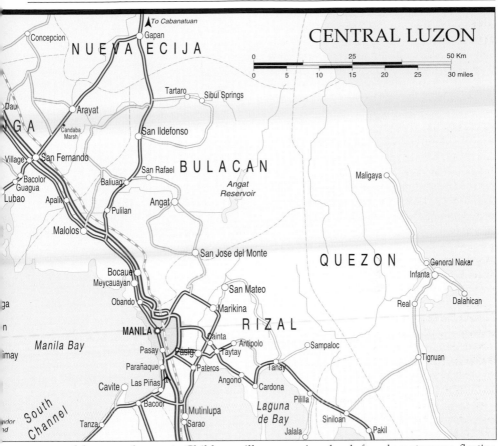

wrapped, homemade sweets. Children will especially enjoy visiting the only town in the world that celebrates Christmas every single day of the year. Both Bulacan and Pampanga mark Holy Week with passionate intensity, although these rituals, with flayings and crucifixions — with real nails — are probably not suitable for children.

## BULACAN PROVINCE

Bulacan is especially worth seeing if your visit coincides with the month of May or July, which is when festival fever overtakes the province. May's highlights are the three-day **Obando Fertility Rites** festival in the fishing town of Obando and the **Pulilan Carabao Festival** (see FESTIVE FLINGS, page 51 in YOUR CHOICE). On the first Sunday in July, the river town of Bocaue overflows with pageantry and flotillas of kaleidoscopic hued outriggers for the **Pagoda Sa Wawa Festival**, celebrating the Holy Cross of Wawa. The cross

was miraculously found a century ago, floating on the river's surface, and it is the star of the procession, borne along on a own boat.

All these towns are easily reached by driving from Manila: Bulacan's capital, **Malolos**, is only 28 km (17 miles) away. It isn't the province's main attraction, but it is noteworthy for being the seat of government for Emilio Aguinaldo's first Philippine Republic. Sweets are sold everywhere throughout Bulacan — sticky, sugary and swathed in intricate paper wrappings in bright colors. Ask for *puto* (rice cakes), *ensaimada* (sugared buns), and look for the bite-size cakes made of freshly grated coconut.

## SAN FERNANDO

While Bulacan is noted for its sweets, Pampanga Province has a rival flair for painstaking and ingenious folkloric artistry. This is amply demonstrated in the province's delightful **Giant Lantern Parade**, held in the provincial capital of San Fernando on Christmas Eve. Enormous five- to ten-meter-wide (16 to 33 feet) *parols,* or paper lanterns, are marvels of folk design and electronic wizardry, all lit up in moving colors and mounted on trucks for the night procession. The parade starts at 11 PM and ends with an award for the best lantern, in the town's main plaza after midnight. Villagers insist that the winning lantern is destroyed after Christmas Day, so that its design remains secret and irreplicable.

A string of small towns close to San Fernando — especially **Apalit, Bacolor** and **Guagua** — reflect the Spanish influence in Pampanga, with finely wrought churches and wooden houses. Completed in 1670 **Betis Church**, in Guagua, is a masterpiece of the province, with an ornately carved retable (raised ledge behind the altar), elaborately frescoed ceiling and ecclesiastical architecture. Bacolor's church, built in 1754, is also one of Luzon's best preserved.

**Paskuhan Village**, on the outskirts of San Fernando, is obsessed with Christmas all year round. As artificial as a Christmas bauble, Paskuhan was constructed in 1980. The town is dedicated to endlessly re-enacting nativity scenes and to the production of Christmas decorations made from native materials. Just an hour from Manila by car (75 km or 47 miles), this village teems with shops, stalls and cafés that sell Christmas paraphernalia and delicacies, Filipino style.

### Where to Stay and Eat
Although San Fernando otherwise is not a place to spend much time, if you have come to see either Good Friday's gory lashings and crucifixions or the more upbeat lantern festival, plan on staying overnight at the **Pampanga Lodge** ( (45) 602033 or 615908, which has the overwhelming advantage of location: its balconies overlook the main plaza and church courtyard. The lodge offers simple, rustic accommodation and basic meals. It may be difficult to reserve ahead, so begin your planning early.

### ANGELES

Up until quite recently, the main center in Pampanga province was the city of Angeles,

which mushroomed into a raunchy "R&R" (rest and relaxation) satellite for nearby **Clark Air Force Base** during the Korean and Vietnam wars. It was rivaled only by Olongapo, which serviced Subic Bay Naval Base in neighboring Zambales.

Clark began in 1902 as Fort Stotsenburg, a United States Cavalry detachment. The base then became the headquarters of the 13th United States Air Force, the largest American military facility outside of the United States, covering over 550 sq km (212 sq miles) and employing more than 9,000 Americans and 18,000 Filipinos.

In its heyday, Angeles, like Olongapo, was a watering hole and playground for the troops. With its thousands of bar girls, strip clubs, night clubs, restaurants and hotels, the promise of cheap sex and music lured a steady stream of male patrons. (Clark, incidentally, had the highest re-enlistment rate of any American military base.) Since the Aquino government (as landlord) terminated the United States' lease on the Clark Base in 1991 (as well as that of Subic), Angeles' malls, garish fast food outlets and rows of go-go bars have taken on a surreal, abandoned look. Accelerating the lease termination was the deadly eruption of Mount Pinatubo — the most devastating last century — which inflicted much misery and loss of life, as well as draping a pall of economic depression over the region.

In the aftermath of the disaster, Angeles looked like a moonscape, smothered in ash and debris. Because of the eruption, Clark Air Force Base was abandoned four months ahead of schedule and thoroughly looted. Local officials and foreign investors bade farewell to an era of freewheeling prosperity. Yet despite having seemingly landing in the obituary column, Angeles appears to be reinventing itself now. The city is showing signs of economic recovery, it is rebuilding and improving its infrastructure, offering Mount Pinatubo tours and resurrecting former bars, nightclubs and bordellos to reconjure its former attractions. Many Australians, who make up the bulk of the tourist traffic here, are finding it irresistible. Much of the activity that used to be associated with Ermita in Manila before it was cleaned up by Mayor Lim has moved here.

The increasingly popular **International Hot Air Balloon Festival** is held each January or February at Clark Air Field.

### Where to Stay and Eat

Angeles has a profusion of hotels, bars and restaurants, either reconstructed from the damaged originals or brand new. The most luxurious place to stay is the **Holiday Inn Clark Field (** MANILA (2) 845-1888 FAX (2) 843-1363, a five-star hotel with excellent amenities and recreation facilities. The **Oasis Hotel (** (45) 322-3301 or 322-3303 FAX (45) 332-1309 WEB SITE oasis-hotel.theshoppe.com, in the Clarkville Compound, is another top choice.

Angeles has several inexpensive hotels favored by those in search of traveler's tales and the authentic Angeles experience. Two good ones, both with swimming pools, are the **Sunset Garden Inn (** (45) 888-2312 FAX (45) 888-2310 Malabanas Road, Clarkview, and the **Swagman Narra Hotel (** (45) 602-5133, Orosa Street.

Finding a decent meal is not difficult in Angeles. There is a profusion of bars, restaurants and cafés. The time-honored label of best restaurant in town is always conceded to the **Maranao Grill Restaurant (** MOBILE (45) 202-5847, in the Oasis Hotel at Clarkville Compound.

### How to Get There

Philippine Airlines flies to Clark International Airport from Hong Kong, Bangkok, Jakarta, Singapore, Kuala Lumpur, Taipei, Tokyo, Brunei and Seoul. Domestic flights also arrive at Clark from Manila. By road, Angeles lies 80 km (50 miles) away from the capital, a journey of about one and a half hours.

---

### MOUNT PINATUBO

Tucked away in the Zambales Mountains — at the juncture of Zambales, Pampanga and Tarlac provinces — Mount Pinatubo had been peacefully dormant for some 600 years. Its eruption on June 15, 1991 was a national catastrophe, that took vulcanologists by surprise. Volcanic activity continued in spurts until September the same year. The first rumblings began on June 9, but no one predicted the epic devastation that would follow: an explosion that vomited detritus 40 km (25 miles) high, accompanied by waves of violent earthquakes, typhoons and deadly avalanches of *lahar* (mud) and ash.

In what was the Philippines' worst volcanic explosion last century, some 900 people died — including the Ayta tribespeople living on the volcano's slopes — and 250,000 were left homeless, as more than a hundred villages were engulfed, many completely buried under mud and lava flows, especially in Pampanga. Since the eruption, millions of tons of ash sit on the volcano's slopes, sliding inevitably downwards, continuing

the saga of destruction of villages within its radius. Many of the villages have constructed dikes to hold off mud flows. Temporary shacks still house many of those left homeless. Vulcanologists claim the 1,700-m-high (5,577 feet) Mount Pinatubo is by no means dormant, and that it may not be until the year 2010 that the volcano once again resumes its deep sleep.

Making the best of the situation, hotels and tour operators in Angeles offer **jeep tours** to Mount Pinatubo, west of the city. It is a riveting experience to survey the extraordinary geological carnage that took place during the eruption, as you walk along the crater's ravines, looking down over huge swells of hardened lava and ash, eerie formations, and half-submerged villages.

If you remain curious and fearless and want to swoop into the volcano's still-active crater, aerial tours are also available (inquire at the tourist office). It's possible to do a round-trip hike through the fields to

Preparing to race water buffaloes at the annual Carabao Fiesta in Pulilan.

the crater lake in one day, but it will be exhausting and you'll be racing against the sun. A better option is to camp for the night at the lake.

## General Information

Inquiries about Paskuhan Village and surrounding areas can be directed to the **Department of Tourism** ( (912) 961-2612 FAX (912) 961-2612, Paskuhan Village, San Fernando, or to the **Paskuhan Tourist Office** ( (45) 602031 (/FAX (45) 613361.

To hire a car for the day to explore Mount Pinatubo's surroundings, contact **Avis** ( MOBILE (45) 301-1885, Don Juico Avenue, in Clarkview.

## Where to Stay

Overnight tours can be arranged through any travel agency; they'll provide tents and food to camp at the crater lake. A cheaper option is to go to Angeles City yourself and ask around for local tour operators.

The **Woodland Park Resort Hotel** ( (45) 322-3529 on MacArthur Highway, Pampanga, is friendly and reasonably priced, and can help you organize your trek to the crater.

## THE BATAAN PENINSULA

Although parts of the Bataan Peninsula have been rapidly industrialized, the Bataan Peninsula, along with the Zambales coastline, will have a special allure for war buffs and those in search of deserted beaches with fine sunsets over the South China Sea. Fiercely contested during World War II, the strategically located Bataan Peninsula lies at the entrance to Manila Bay, ringed by impressive and formidable volcanic mountains, among them Mount Pinatubo. Until November 1992, the peninsula was also home to the other major United States military base — the **Subic Bay Navy Base**.

In the words of General MacArthur, "No soil on earth is more deeply consecrated to the cause of human liberty than the island of Corrigedor and the adjacent Bataan Peninsula." In Bataan, after holding out for three months, the outnumbered Filipino and American troops surrendered to the Japanese on April 9, 1942. Of the 64,000 Filipinos and 12,000 Americans, at least a tenth died in the months to come, some of starvation and disease and some by brutal torture at the hands of their Japanese captors. Many perished on the horrific forced 112-km (69-mile) trek that became known as the "Death March." Throughout the province, historical markers commemorate sites of battles and bombings, the route of the Death March and wartime encampments.

## What to See and Do

Many of the interesting places to visit in the province recall the Battle of Bataan. Near the border with Pampanga, the town of **Hermosa** has the First Line of Defense marker, while **Pilar** was the scene of intensive fighting. Hermosa is also notable for the **Roosevelt Game Reserve** nearby. On **Mount Samat**, the Dambana ng Kagitingan (Altar of Valor) is a dramatic giant cross, made of concrete and steel, 95 m (312 feet) high and clearly illuminated at night. It honors the war dead. On clear nights, it can be seen from as far away as Manila. The viewing gallery offers vertiginous vistas for kilometers across land and sea. Wreath laying ceremonies are held each year commemorating the Fall of Bataan and Corregidor. The provincial capital, **Balanga**, is where General Edward King of the United States Armed Forces officially surrendered to the Japanese.

## Where to Stay and Eat

**Montemar Beach Club** ( MANILA (2635-5099 or (2) 635-7499 FAX (2) 635-6699, Barangay Pasinay, Bataan, is the most pleasant place to stay in Bataan. This secluded resort has a wide and private beach tucked into the shore within a headland. Water sports, bird watching and fishing are popular activities here, and there are swimming pools, tennis courts, a playground and a nine-hole golf course. The resort has two good restaurants. Rates are moderate.

## How to Get There

As well as driving or taking regular buses for the three hour-long trip from Manila to Bataan's capital Balanga, it is possible to get to Bataan by boat from Manila. **Sun Cruises** ( (2) 635-5099 or (2) 635-7499 FAX (2635-6699, PTA Cruise Terminal, Cultural Center of the Philippines, Roxas Boulevard, Manila, makes regular stops at the beach resort between Balanga and Mariveles.

## THE ZAMBALES COAST AND OLONGAPO

One hundred and twenty-eight kilometers (79 miles) from Manila, Zambales offers an authentic slice of coastal life. Its thin coastline has spawned a string of small fishing villages, supported by fishing, making *bagoong* (fermented fish sauce) and harvesting salt, and by their cottage industries. Craggy mountains range behind the coastline, making a natural barrier for the province. Most of the indigenous tribes — the Zambals and the Ayta — melted away into Luzon's interior with the arrival of the more dominant Tagalog and Ilocano settlers.

In Zambales, Olongapo — a three-hour drive from Manila — has always been closely tied to **Subic Bay**, 19 km (12 miles) away, and the former home of the United States Seventh Fleet. This was the biggest overseas base and supply depot for the United States Navy until November 1992, when it finally closed. Many freely admit this has meant economic disaster for nearby Olongapo, like Angeles, where almost everyone — from bar girl to office worker — depended on the Americans for their income.

### General Information

The Tourism Department offers some interesting tours, such as "ecotrips" into the jungle and visits to the Calapan Negrito settlements, as well as cruises on reconstructed Spanish galleons and guided tours of the former Subic Bay base. The Subic Bay Zone **Visitors Center (** (47) 252-4154, is at the Second Floor, Building 662, Barryman Street.

### What to See and Do

Since the closure of the naval base, Subic Bay has been turned into a free port, attracting a great deal of Taiwanese investment and mushrooming new resorts, factories and duty free malls. The **Subic Bay Freeport Zone**, mobilized energetically by Chairman and Olongapo Mayor Richard J. Gordon, has been provided with hefty grants and a loan package from the World Bank and the Asian Development Bank. As a result, the former military airport in Cubi

Point — Subic International Airport — is now the country's most modern airport, while the Barrio Tipo Highway has greatly improved road links to Manila. The city was for a long time known for its active nightlife — centered on **Magsaysay Drive**, a strip full of raunchy go-go bars, once nicknamed "Sin City" — but also a performance Mecca for legions of talented Filipino musicians. Now that the Americans have departed, their place is being taken by vacationing Japanese, Taiwanese and Australians. With its infrastructure in place, the base is now a Special Economic Zone awaiting investment and promoting its future as a convention center. Not far from the former base is a large stretch of tropical jungle, where tribes known as Negritos live in the style of their ancestors and where United States troops used to do their survival training. It's possible to arrange overnight jungle tours. Don't expect decent beaches around Subic Bay — you will need to head north to San Miguel (near San Antonio) and farther afield up the Zambales coast. Aside from Olongapo and Subic Bay, as you travel up the coast, small fishing villages and beaches become gradually less populated, and exposure to local life here is a compelling draw. The provincial capital of **Iba**, 83 km (51 miles) from Olongapo, only really comes alive during the **Kalighawan Festival**, celebrated every March with agricultural and beauty contests — the beauties and the beasts. You can give Iba a miss as a place to stay.

### Where to Stay and Eat

The most luxurious and comfortable accommodation option is the **Subic International Hotel (** (47) 252-2222 MANILA (2) 243-2222 FAX (2) 243-0852 WEB SITE www.subichotel.com, Santa Rita Road, Subic Bay Freeport Zone, which caters primarily to business travelers and is expensive. At moderate prices, **Crown Peak Garden (** MANILA (2) 816-4411 FAX (2) 819-5925 WEB SITE www.crownpeakgardens.com, Upper Cubi, Subic Freeport, has incredible views of Triboa Bay and Olongapo City. The complex is made up of 12 hotel buildings, all named after precious stones.

Barrio Barretto has clusters of bars and restaurants relatively close to the sea, and several private hotels and resorts. The inexpensive **Marmont Hotel (** (45) 5571 here has a restaurant, nightclub, swimming pool and gymnasium. In Olongapo, many cheap hotels line Magsaysay Drive and Rizal Avenue. The best of the bunch are probably the **Plaza Hotel** and the **Diamond Lodge** (no phones), both inexpensive and located on Rizal Avenue.

### How to Get There

Subic Bay International Airport receives regular flights from most Asian capitals, with

flights from Manila hourly. Otherwise, air-conditioned **Victory Liner** buses **(** (2) 833-0293 ply the route from Manila, 128 km (79 miles) away, throughout the day; it's a three-hour journey. There are also regular bus connections to and from Angeles, San Fernando and Baguio. Jeepneys shuttle continuously between the former base area of Subic Bay and Olongapo.

## PANGASINAN PROVINCE

The oddly shaped Pangasinan province has a slow tempo and is known for its salt production, oysters and fish farms. Its main attraction, particularly for divers, is the **Hundred Islands National Park**, actually composed of about 400 coralline islands strewn along the coastline in the Lingayen Gulf; many of them are still unexplored.

The most popular of the islands — for clear waters, snorkeling and diving — are **Quezon Island**, **Cathedral Island**, **Devil's Island**, so named for its mysteriously deep waters, and **Shell Island**, with its fine white shell-strewn sands. The jumping-off point is the wharf town of **Lucap** and the village of **Alaminos**, where fishermen ferry tourists and divers on their *bancas* out to the island of their choice. It is possible to camp on some of the larger islands, a more atmospheric experience than staying in either of these towns. Divers should contact the **Philippine Commission on Sports Scuba Diving (PCSSD) (** (2) 599031, Department of Tourism Building, T.M. Kalaw Street, Rizal Park, in Manila.

## LA UNION PROVINCE

This thin slice of Luzon's west coast has become a popular beach destination and a jumping-off point for scuba divers keen to explore the Lingayen Gulf. Non-divers will enjoy it too — its towns have a tropical sleepiness, lush with bougainvillea and flame trees. But don't expect the sublime beaches and pristine ambiance that are found elsewhere in the Philippines.

The popular beaches are centered around **Bauang**, which is a convenient stop en route to Baguio. The main highway follows along the coastal strip. You could base yourself for a day or two in Bauang, enjoying the beach strip before heading up to the mountains. San Fernando, the provincial capital, and Agoo aren't recommended as places to stay.

### Where to Stay and Eat

In Bauang, the **Villa Estrella Beach Resort (** (72) 413794 FAX (72) 413793, at Paringao, is well-maintained, with a modern Spanish-colonial feel and a decent restaurant. Another recommendation is the **Bali Hai Resort (** (72) 242-5679 or (72) 242-5680 FAX (72) 888-5480 WEB SITE www.balihai.com.ph, also at Paringao, which has air-conditioned rooms and pleasant duplex cottages, as well as a restaurant and swimming pool. Both are moderately priced.

## How to Get There

Philippine Airlines flies regularly from Manila to San Fernando, but sometimes cancels flights during the typhoon season (August to late October). From Manila, by car or bus, the drive to Bauang takes five or more hours. From San Fernando, jeepneys make the trip to Bauang in 30 minutes.

## BAGUIO

Resting on a summit of the Cordillera Central, Baguio lies 250 km (155 miles) north of Manila, a six- to seven-hour drive through increasingly dramatic scenery.

Beloved by Filipinos as a holiday retreat, Baguio was developed as a vacation resort at the turn of the twentieth century by homesick colonial Americans. It retains traces of American influence in its architecture and also in the strange American twang discernible in the dialect of the indigenous Igorot, whose grandparents were under the tutelage of American missionary teachers.

At an altitude of 1,500 m (4,920 feet), Baguio is a sylvan realm of year-round cool breezes, pine forests, panoramic views, lovely Spanish houses and flower-strewn parks — the perfect summer retreat. It is, indeed, regarded by Manileños as their summer capital. Baguio also has a following for its faith-healing practitioners, who claim to "open" the skin of their patients and to "operate" with their bare hands.

This region — which also includes the nearby destinations of **Sagada**, **Bontoc** and **Banaue**, as well as many small villages of great interest — can easily keep you amused for at least five days, and it is a good place to relax and slow your pace.

### GENERAL INFORMATION

The **Tourist Information Center (** (74) 442-7014, on Governor Pack Road, Baguio, can provide free maps and tell you about workshop tours and visits to surrounding Igorot tribal villages.

It is easy to get around the hilly city by foot, if you have strong calf muscles, or by jeepney or taxi. To rent a car, try **Avis (** (74) 442-4018, Padilla Building, Harrison Road, or **Hertz (** (74) 442-3045, on Session Road.

*Central and Northern Luzon*

**Cyberspace**, at the Mount Crest Hotel, is a cool and comfortable place to check e-mail. They charge P100 per hour and P50 per hour on weekends. It's open from 8 AM to 1 AM daily.

Baguio is a good starting point for exploring **Sagada** and **Banaue** — which have the cachet of being the former realm of headhunters. They are a day's excursion away, farther north. Jeepneys and buses connect the main towns and travel across the provincial borders to Cagayan Valley, Ilocos Sur, Ilocos Norte and Abra.

Getting around Baguio is also fairly simple. It is the only city in the Cordillera region that has taxis, and rides within central Baguio cost about P80. Jeepneys usually begin and end their routes near the public market.

### WHAT TO SEE AND DO

Baguio — which sprawls across almost 50 km (31 miles) — is still recovering from a fatal 1990 earthquake, which inflicted much damage, devastating hotels, parks and a golf

OPPOSITE: A newspaper vendor touts the latest headlines in Baguio. ABOVE: Camp John Hay, a government-run tourist resort, with restaurants, playing fields and sports facilities.

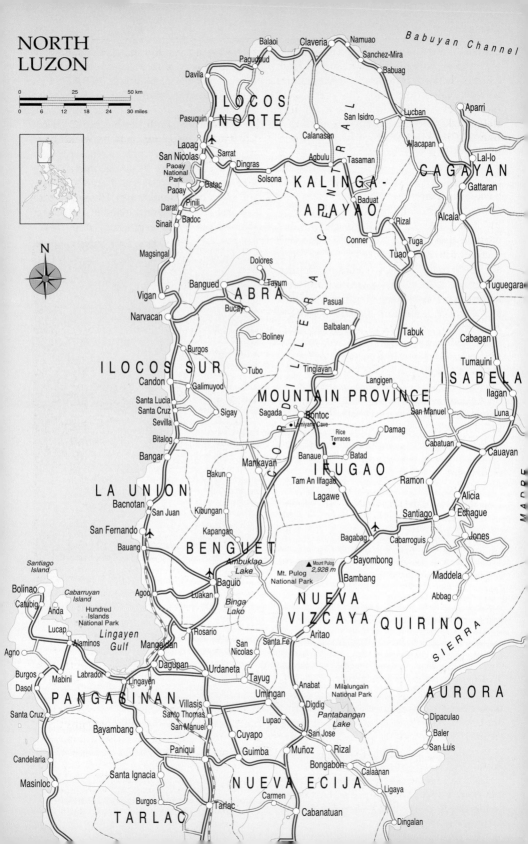

course. Nevertheless, it is rebuilding itself, and its key attractions have not changed. Most of the interesting cafés and shops are located downtown. In the city, you can explore relics of faded Americana and militaristic parks and poke around the vibrant **Baguio City Market** which, as well as selling mountain produce and brassware, has stocks of ethnic fabrics, woven items, silver, jewelry, Igorot woodcarvings and Ifugao baskets and craftware. It is also crammed with carinderias serving inexpensive Filipino food. At Christmas time, this market becomes the focus for celebrations.

Both **Burnham Park** and the **Cathedral** are worth seeing. The park is named for the American architect who created Baguio's layout, and has a pretty orchidarium and terrace restaurant. The Cathedral is notable as an icon of endurance during World War II — 5,000 citizens sheltered here while the city was under siege, and the church grounds are full of war dead. Previously known as Imelda Park, the **Baguio Botanical Gardens**, on Leonard Wood Road, offer beautiful panoramic views. Close by, **Wright Park** is known for its horseback riding trails — horses and guides are available for hire.

The **Baguio Mountain Province Museum**, which is next door to the Tourist Information Center on Government Park Road, explains much of the history and cultural traditions of the region's minority ethnic tribes. It also has exhibits from other tribal groups within the archipelago.

The **Good Shepherd Convent**, run by Belgian nuns who provide a home for unwed mothers, sells various souvenirs along with fruit preserves. In the nearby garden-farming suburb of **La Trinidad**, a visit to **Narda's** ( (74) 442-2992 on Upper Session Road, run by weaver Narda Capuyan, is a chance to see her designs based on a blend of ethnic themes and patterns, with unusual clothes and other items for sale. Igorot cloth is woven on traditional backstrap looms at the **Easter Weaving School** ( (74) 442-4972 on Easter School Road. The **St. Louis Silver Shop** ( (74) 442-2139 on Assumption Road, sells well-crafted silver items.

Baguio City encompasses both the **Philippine Military Academy** (the West Point of the Philippines) and **Camp John Hay**,

formerly the rest and recreation station of United States military troops. Since being turned over to the Philippines in 1991, it has become a government-run tourist resort complex, with restaurants, playing fields and sports facilities. Both the **Baguio Country Club** and **Camp John Hay** have excellent 18-hole golf courses.

Camp John Hay has an important history: it was here that World War II started and ended in the Philippines. This was where the first Japanese bomb was dropped and where General Yamashita moved his head-

quarters, along with the puppet government under José Laurel. Yamashita spent the last weeks of the war in Baguio in an underground warren, before being overpowered by United States and Filipino forces and finally returning to Camp John Hay to sign the Japanese surrender at the United States ambassador's headquarters on September 3, 1945.

For the best view of Baguio and its surrounding mountains, climb up **Dominican Hill** to the **Diplomat Hotel**, which used to be a Dominican seminary. Many stories are told about the building — it was previously

Baguio, the country's premier hill station. Here, boats for rent in Burnham Park. The comprehensive orchidarium in the park is also worth a visit.

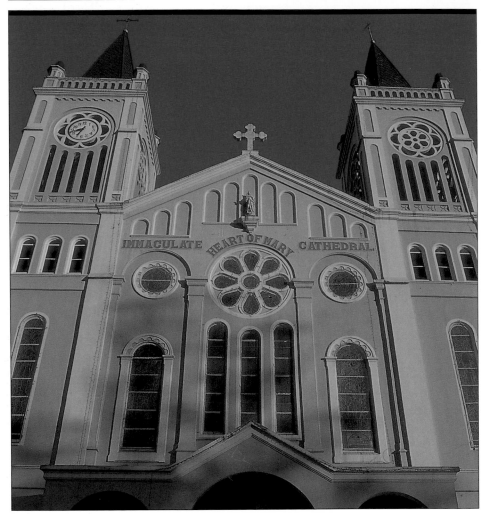

owned by one of the country's most famous faith healers, the late Tony Agpaoa, who practiced his faith "surgery" here. En route, you'll pass rows of antique shops, perhaps worth a browse, while the nearby **Lourdes Grotto**, 225 steps up the hill, becomes a frenzied pilgrimage site during Holy Week.

**Balatoc Mines** ( (74) 447-2610, on Abanao Street, give visitors a chance to explore the life of a gold miner. The non-operational mines are a 40-minute drive southeast of Baguio. Check out the miners' gear and then board a guided train into the mine.

**Tam-Awan Village** ( (73) 446-2949, fifteen minutes from Baguio, displays reconstructions of traditional grass-roof houses. It offers a great opportunity to glimpse the way of life of the Cordillera's Ifugao peoples.

### Faith Healers

Fake or faith? That seems to be the question plaguing the residents of Baguio for years now, since stories of "Albulayos" (or herbalists) practicing unconventional healing methods with only their hands as instruments made waves across the world in the 1980s.

Albulayos have lived in remote villages in this region for centuries, and have been looked upon by the community as medicine men, concocting herbal medicinal remedies for simple ailments like colds, fevers, and aches. This new generation of "psychic healers," who are mostly congregated in Baguio City, are a bit more ambitious; claiming to expel tumors and other life-threatening diseases with their hands — no tools or anesthesia necessary! Many residents, including Baguio's mayor, remain skeptical, claiming it's a bunch of hocus pocus. However, the city's more prominent faith healers justify their practices by preaching that ancient priestesses or "babaylan" would summon the Gods to aid them in healing their believers.

Whether or not current faith-healing practices are an extension of ancient rituals, you can choose to see for yourself what exactly goes down during a "surgery." Simply ask a taxi driver in town if he knows of a healer. You can undergo a healing yourself for a hefty fee — or just watch (also for a hefty fee!). The faith healing, or performance — however you like to look at it — is not for the faint-hearted. Skeptics say that cow's blood and pig intestines are used as realistic "props."

## WHERE TO STAY

Baguio has scores of inexpensive hotels and guest houses, and just as many restaurants, cafés and nightspots, catering to seasonal swarms of Filipino tourists.

### Mid-range

The city's newest big hotel, **Concorde** ( (74) 443-2058 FAX (74) 443-2060, Europa Center, Legarda Road, is a unique work of sleek modern architecture. Amenities include a beauty salon, convenience store, car rental, on-call doctor, laundry, boutique, travel agency and much more.

The **Prince Plaza Hotel** ( (74) 442-5082 FAX (74) 442-5093, on Legarda Road, offers large rooms with excellent views of the highlands, and its Shabu Shabu restaurant dishes up good local cuisine.

### Inexpensive

Once a family residence, **Casa Amapola** ( (74) 443-7911, on First Road, is now a pension; with cozy lounges and chalet apartments with verandas and kitchens. **Munsayac Inn** ( (74) 442-2451, on Leonard Wood Road, is a haven of quietness and solitude. The rooms are decorated in local handicrafts.

Probably the most popular hotel with budget-conscious travelers is the **Swagman Attic Inn** ( (74) 442-5139, 90 Abanao Street,

which is managed by Australians. **Burnham Hotel** ( (74) 442-2331 or (74) 442-5117, 21 Calderon Street, has a peaceful feel. Agreeably furnished and with a good Chinese restaurant, it offers very good value.

## WHERE TO EAT

Traditional Cordillera cuisine and mountain brews are served at **Café By The Ruins** ( (74) 442-4010, opposite Baguio's town hall — the café is worth visiting to sample its excellent seasonal specialties, *tapuy* (rice

wine) and *basi* or *salabat* (ginger tea). **Ionic Café** ( (74) 442-3867, along Session Road, is a hip place where Baguio's gen-exers and hippies hang for a cup of Joe. It has a full bar and serves salads, pastas and sandwiches. **Biscotti et Cioccolate** ( (74) 442-7420 on Nevada Square near Club John Jay, offers pretty good coffees, pastries, and home-cooked dinners. The two owners are artists, and have decorated the interior with their own paintings. A great place to write or catch up on some reading. And for Chinese food, the **Star Café** ( (74) 442-3148 on Session Road, has tasty, inexpensive fare.

OPPOSITE: The glowing and well-maintained façade of Baguio Cathedral. ABOVE: Vegetables for sale in Bontoc market, en route to Banaue.

## HOW TO GET THERE

Philippine Airlines (PAL) ( (74) 442-2695 or (74) 442-6627 flies from Manila Domestic Airport to Baguio's Loakan Airport daily; the flight takes 50 minutes. The airport is about 12 km (seven miles) from downtown Baguio.

If you rent a car, or come by bus, the 246-km (153-mile) journey — which becomes increasingly scenic — takes up to seven hours. It's not a good idea to try to travel by road during the rainy season, when landslides become a problem along the high mountain passes. Several bus companies, including Victory Liner and Pantranco, run day and night services.

## SAGADA

The enchanting village of Sagada is a backpacker's dream. Tucked amongst mountains some 1,530 m (5,025 feet) above sea level, Sagada is in the midst of a lush region of waterfalls, underground pools, mysterious caves, tribal burial sites, hiking trails, and "hanging coffins." At the edge of the village are fruit orchards and rice terraces (though nothing compared to Banaue's terraces) and the occasional *dap-ay* — a circular stone meeting place where village elders once gathered to discuss communal matters. Savor Sagada's clean air, its lack of telephones and laid-back nature, and the striking surrounding scenery. You don't want to miss visiting this most charming traveler's hangout.

## WHAT TO SEE AND DO

The lure of cave exploring attracts not a few spelunkers to Sagada, though some people may not relish the thought of wading through icy underground rivers. Most of the burial caves do not demand such exertions and are located within half an hour's walk of the small town.

For centuries, according to Igorot tribal custom, the dead have been set in wooden coffins and placed so as to be exposed to the light — often in cliff-side cave mouths or attached to pegs halfway down a cliff — in the belief that this would allow their

spirits to roam free. Probably the most dramatic cave open to tourists is the beautiful **Matangkib Cave**, which contains numerous sealed coffins from 20 to 600 years old; the older coffins are much smaller, since the bodies were laid to rest in a fetal position. Sadly, many of the coffin lids have been pried off and the skulls removed — apparently the work of decades of tourists wanting to claim souvenirs. Located in a gorge, Matangkib is set above an underground river, and the sounds of rushing water can be heard echoing below it. Occasionally the cave is closed, so be sure and check with Sagada's **Environmental Guides Association** in the town hall.

**Sumaging**, also known as the "Big" or "Marcos" cave, is the largest, and is considered the most exciting for adventure spelunking — a dizzying maze of winding paths, water pools, narrow passages and huge limestone formations. Don't be intimidated, however, anyone can explore of this cave. Just hire a guide at the town hall and be prepared to scramble and get grimy!

**Lumiang Cave** is the most visited, for rather macabre reasons: placed at the cave's wide entrance are numerous piles of coffins, some of which lie open, revealing decayed bones and clothing fragments. Another place to view the coffins is the **Hanging Coffins View Point** — where coffins can be seen hanging like bats against a sheltered section of limestone rock.

Set amidst rice terraces and only 25-minutes from town, **Bokong Waterfall** is popular among both locals and visitors. The falls are small but spill into a deep pool — an ideal spot for a picnic or quick dip. **Bomod-ok** is a bigger waterfall, but farther away. To get there from Sagada, walk along the road that passes the Banga-an Elementary School. Another hour's walk will take you down the path through the village of **Fidelisan** and some rice terraces to the waterfall.

## WHERE TO STAY AND EAT

Sagada is the most appealing place to stay in Central Luzon — rather than Baguio or Banaue — because of its spectacular views of the mountains, rice terraces, hiking trails and for the calm pace of village life. However, don't come to Sagada expecting first-class accommodations and dining. Neither phones nor hot water have made their debut here. To many visitors that is what's so endearing about the village. What it lacks in amenities it makes up for in charm.

There are a number of guesthouses here that cater especially to foreign tourists — as opposed to vacationing Filipinos — and café food can be good. Try the **Olahbinan Resthouse** or the friendly **Green House**. The **Masferre Restaurant and Lodging** has a loyal backpacker following and very good

**The Log Cabin**, down the hill from Shamrock, will give you delicious European-style food, including lasagna and omelets.

## HOW TO GET THERE

Most visitors to Sagada arrive via Banaue or Baguio City, from where there are regular buses to the terraces and Sagada.

A **Dangwa Tranco** bus ( (2) 731-2859 leaves Cubao terminal once a day for the nine-hour trip to Banaue, the first leg of the Manila–Banaue–Sagada route (13–14 hours).

local cuisine. **St. Joseph's Rest House** is the largest in the area, and has excellent views of the town and the Episcopalian church. **Sagada Prime Hotel**, a five-minute walk past the Municipal Hall, is Sagada's first official hotel. The rooms are spacious and there is a large restaurant serving meals and drinks at reasonable prices.

Travelers congregate at the **Rock Cave**, near the Underground River, which has a cozy, pub-like feel, with a fireplace. **Shamrock Café** provides breakfast, lunch, dinner and snacks, and in the evening guitar players, some locals, some tourists, add to the warm atmosphere. Lots of tourists come here, so it's a good place to share information with other travelers.

A daily jeepney leaves Banaue every morning for the two- to three-hour ride to Bontoc. In Bontoc, jeepneys leave from outside Nellie's Eatery on Bontoc's main street several times a day for the two-hour ride up to Sagada.

A number of bus companies travel the popular direct route (six hours) from Manila to Baguio. **Victory Liner** ( (2) 833-0293 or (2) 833-5020 leaves Manila hourly and is air-conditioned and comfortable. From Baguio, several early morning buses depart from the Dangwa Terminal starting at 6:30AM. The trip to Sagada takes you along the hair-raising Halsema Highway, also known as the Mountain Trail.

Igorot tribal chief in front of his home in Sagada Town.

## BANAUE

Banaue is known for its spectacular and meticulously carved rice terraces, a testament to the determination of the Ifugao, the most ancient mountain tribe in the area. The Ifugao (literally, "eaters of rice") have lovingly maintained these terraces, with their water-retaining dikes, for hundreds, perhaps thousands, of years. The staple grain they reap is said to have been a gift from their deity, Kabunyan, and in return the Ifugao built the terraces, both a source of their survival and a magnificent stairway to their god's heaven.

### WHAT TO SEE AND DO

Clearly, the main attractions are the rice terraces themselves. If measured from end to end, the terraces would stretch a total length of 22,400 km (13,888 miles). They rise up to over 1,500 m (4,900 feet). The ideal time to visit is from March to May, when the terraces are green with rice shoots and the scenery is superbly lush. Trekking is the best way to experience the terraces, although the **Banaue View Point** has panoramic views for those just passing through. Tourism has flooded this formerly hermitic tribal region, and it is feared that the Ifugaos may soon find catering to tourists more interesting than tending to the fields. The tribespeople, who you will encounter here and in their villages, seem to have accepted that their colorful attire and patterned headdress make them natural targets for picture-snapping tourists — and they expect some pesos in return.

Nearby **Batad** is surrounded by beautiful tiered and contoured rice terraces and there's a large cascading waterfall 20 minutes from the village. Not far from Batad is **Cambulo**, a relatively untouched Ilfugao village. The first 12 km (seven miles) from Banaue can be covered by vehicle, but you have to walk the remaining four kilometers (two and a half miles). The tough hike is rewarded with breathtaking views across the terraces and the village with its thatched huts. It can be accomplished as a day trip, or you can stay overnight in Batad.

**Tam-An Village**, just behind the Banaue Hotel, is a recreation of a typical Ifugao village, and traditional beads and woodcarvings are fashioned and sold here. The original Tam-An is only a few meters away, where at many of the dwellings visitors can see the ancestral skeletons beneath their raised floors. A well-marked trail from Banaue follows a two- to three-hour circular path through the rice terraces to the Ifugao villages of **Bocos** and **Matang Lag**. The Ifugao are remarkably talented artisans, and it is fascinating to watch a variety of crafts being made in village workshops. At Tam-An and Matang Lag, you can watch handicrafts, copper, silver jewelry, fabrics — including hand-woven blankets — being created using traditional techniques. Finally, **Guihon Natural Pool** is wonderful in summer for a swim and a picnic.

### WHERE TO STAY AND EAT

The best place to stay in the area, the **Banaue Hotel (** MANILA (2) 812-1984 FAX (73) 386-4087, is a tastefully furnished 90-room establishment, with private balconies overlooking the rice terraces. It has a restaurant, swimming pool and sun terrace, and rooms range from moderately priced to expensive. You can also use the facilities — notably the swimming pool — if you stay at the inexpensive **Banaue Youth Hostel**, which is under the same management. Book the hostel at the same contact numbers and addresses as the Banaue Hotel. The **Banaue View Inn (** (73) 486-4078 is a small and quaint inn above the town, nestled in the mountains. There is a family museum containing anthropological documents and memorabilia on tribal life in the area.

### HOW TO GET THERE

Banaue is 348 km (216 miles) from Manila. From October to May, **Aerolift (** (2) 817-2369 flies from Manila to Bagabag, the nearest airfield to Banaue, almost two hour's drive away.

Another way is to take a Philippine Airlines flight to Baguio City and then make a six-hour journey by bus or car onwards to Banaue. The drive takes you on a beautifully scenic trip through the Cordillera Central. The last — winding — stretch between Bontoc and Banaue, a 50-km (31-mile), two-hour journey across the Mount Polis range, is one of the

The fabulous 2,000-year-old Banaue rice terraces.

country's most spectacular experiences, with vertigo-inducing and awe-inspiring views across the emerald canyons. This drive is as impressive as the destination itself.

## ILOCOS REGION

Consisting mostly of La Union, Ilocos Sur, Abra and Ilocos Norte provinces, the region of Ilocos sprawls across northwestern Luzon. There is a strong Spanish influence in the architecture, called "earthquake baroque," which evolved to withstand all-too-frequent violent typhoons and tremors. This stoical style can be seen in the grander homes and churches. This is a region of stately, if faded, cobblestone towns founded in the sixteenth century, balustraded Castillian-style houses with porticoes and courtyards, grand Augustinian churches, and tobacco, garlic and rice plantations — dry and arid in the summer and waterlogged during the rainy season.

### VIGAN

If you are going to choose one destination in Ilocos, make it Vigan, the capital of Ilocos Sur and the third-oldest city in the Philippines. Here, the Spanish influence is at its most visually appealing. This well-preserved colonial town has cobbled streets, spacious plazas and beautiful Spanish houses, many built by Chinese mestizos, with narra wood floors, high ceilings, intricate grillwork, *azotea* (tiled patios) and *capiz* (shell) windows.

Vigan began as the religious and political capital of Northern Luzon towards the end of the sixteenth century, founded by 22-year-old conquistador, Juan de Salcedo, a grandson of Miguel Lopez de Legaspi, the former governor-general and founder of Manila.

### What to See and Do

Vigan is easily explored on foot, though horse-drawn calesas still serve the city's residents. Start with **Vigan Cathedral**, also known as Saint Paul's Cathedral. Built in 1574 and rebuilt in 1800 — in then current earthquake-baroque style — the façade features Chinese Fu dogs, reflecting Vigan's Chinese heritage, and its main altar is lined with beaten silver panels. The cathedral's bell tower stands apart in Plaza Burgos, on

the south side of the cathedral proper. Adjacent to the cathedral is the **Archbishop's Palace**, an eighteenth-century building with capiz windows and fretted carvings. It was used by Filipino revolutionaries in 1896 and taken over by American troops three years later. Nearby, the **Ayala Museum** has a remarkable display of antiques and artifacts from the local Tingguian tribe and the Ilocanos. **Burgos Museum**, no phone, Burgos Street, is housed in a colonial-era residence that was the birthplace and home of revolutionary martyr-priest Father José

Burgos. The museum showcases dioramas, artifacts, and paintings, as well as period furniture, and is open Tuesday to Sunday from 9 AM to noon and 1 PM to 5 PM. **Salcedo Plaza**, opposite Vigan Cathedral, is a park with an obelisk commemorating Vigan's young conquistador founder.

On Quirino Avenue, **Syquia Mansion** is the most exceptional example of Vigan's colonial architecture, built in 1830 for a Chinese merchant. It later became the residence of Elpidio Quirino, who was the president of the Philippines from 1948 to 1953. You will see many beautiful houses though, not open to public view, as you stroll around town — Vigan is frequently used as a film set. **Mena Crisologo Street** is especially pretty. Rotund *burnays*, traditional pottery urns, are still made in small workshops along Rizal Street. About 10 minutes from town, you can watch weavers at work in their homes making *binakol*, weavings that incorporate a traditional psychedelic-looking, geometric design.

### Where to Stay and Eat

The best place to stay in Vigan is the **Cordillera Inn** ( (77) 722-2526, 29 Mena Crisologo Street, a restored colonial home with a good restaurant. Otherwise try the **Villa Angela** ( (77) 722-2914, Quirino Boulevard at Liberation

## LAOAG AND ILOCOS NORTE

The attractions of typhoon and earthquake-prone Ilocos Norte can be summarized in one word: Paoay. This small town, which lies 20 km (12 miles) south of the provincial capital, Laoag, is a beautiful place to see, reflecting the taste and ambitions of the Augustinians who founded it in 1593.

### General Information

Because of its airport, Laoag, the capital of

Street, a turn-of-the-twentieth-century house filled with antiques. The rooms are probably the most distinctive of all the hotels in the area, with high ceilings, large four-poster beds, and mosquito netting, and the house has a wonderful garden. Both are in the inexpensive-to-moderate price range.

### How to Get There

Vigan is a seven-hour drive from Manila. Various buses make the journey, including **Philippine Rabbit** ( (2) 363-0677 and **Times Transit** ( (2) 731-4180. An alternative is to fly to Laoag airport on Philippine Airlines. The alternative is to fly to Laoag Airport, from where jeepneys leave to Vigan. The jeepney ride takes an hour and a half.

Ilocos Norte, is a hub for those visiting the far reaches of Luzon. The **Department of Tourism** ( (77) 290467, Ilocano Heroes Memorial Hall, can provide information on the tourist sites to see in the area, including Paoay National Park.

### What to See and Do

Paoay's centerpiece is **Paoay Church**, the finest example of earthquake-baroque style in the province, with its massive lateral buttresses, exterior staircases and façade designed to withstand the wrath of the elements. It also has unusual oriental crenellations and niches reminiscent of Indonesian temples.

Paoay's Spanish church — made of coral with a sugarcane juice and lime mortar.

The secret of the church's strength is its unusual construction: its thick coral rubble walls are sealed with a mixture of sugarcane juice and lime mortar. The bell tower is imposing — it was used by the Katipuneros and later by local guerrillas in World War II as a hideout and lookout tower. The **Paoay National Park** with its large lake provides another incentive to visit the area.

Laoag has some interesting Spanish-colonial buildings and churches too, including the **City Hall**, the **Tobacco Monopoly Monument** and the Renaissance-inspired

design of the **Cathedral of Saint William**, built between 1650 and 1700. It's a good place to browse through antique shops, and an especially good spot for pottery, santos, figurines and Ilocano woven cloth.

Between Paoay and Laoag, **Batac** was the boyhood home of former president Ferdinand Marcos. The colonial Marcos family home has been turned into a museum–shrine, **Balay Ti Ili**, and displays Marcos memorabilia. Once he had scaled the presidential heights, Marcos returned to Batac to build his **Malacañang del Norte**, a giant palace that is now also a museum.

It was, however, at **Sarrat**, near Laoag, that Marcos was born — a typical provincial town with its main claim to fame being the large

Augustinian **Sarrat Church**. The town was transformed in a frenzy of construction when it was used as the venue for the wedding of Marcos' daughter, Irene, in 1983. Imelda demanded that the entire town — and an additional 3,000 workers — toil day and night for two months to turn what had been a scruffy, sleepy village into a splendid, "aristocratic" town lined with Spanish mansions. Laoag's international airport was built for the wedding, as well as the five-star Fort Ilocandia Resort Hotel, with its lavish casino. A few days after the wedding, a violent earthquake caused great damage to many of the buildings and the church.

### Where to Stay and Eat

Somewhat kitsch, **Fort Ilocandia Resort Hotel (** (77) 221166 to 70 FAX (77) 422356 or MANILA (2) 816-4411 FAX (2) 819-5925 on Suba Beach, the region's main beach destination, hotel is a self-contained complex with a golf course, swimming pool, restaurants, disco, beach buggies and casino. The Marcos clan adored it. It is expensive and 10 minutes out of town. Inexpensive and unexciting accommodation can be found within Laoag itself at either the **Modern Hotel (** (77) 2348, Nolasco Street or the **Texicano Hotel (** (77) 21125 on Rizal Street.

If you prefer more rustic accommodations, go to **Pagudpud**, 60 km (37 miles) north of Laoag, which has one of the most pleasant beaches in northern Luzon; Saud White Beach. Simple nipa cottages on the beach — such as the **Villa del Mar Ivory Beach Resort** (no phone) — offer peaceful and basic amenities at inexpensive prices.

### How to Get There

Laoag's international airport caters primarily to tourists from Taiwan, drawn by the delights of the Ilocos beaches and the casino at the region's premier resort, the Fort Ilocandia. From Manila, the daily Philippine Airlines flight takes an hour.

Driving, by car or bus, from Manila takes 10 hours. **Philippine Rabbit (** (2) 363-0677 and **Times Transit (** (2) 731-4180 are the most reliable bus companies.

ABOVE: A band precedes a funeral procession in Vigan. RIGHT: Jeepneys skirt the sinking tower in Laoag, Ilocos Norte.

# Southern Luzon and Mindoro

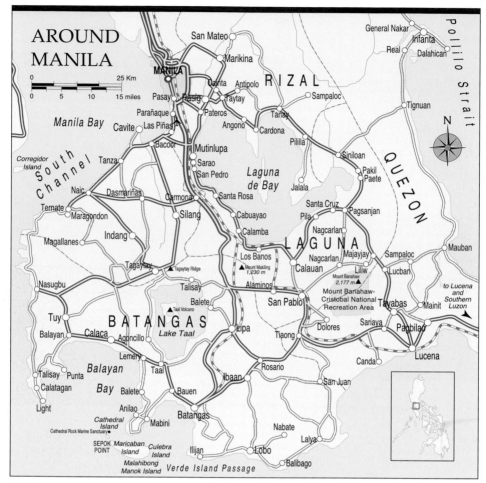

AROUND MANILA

0       25 Km
0    5   10   15 miles

Manila Bay

Corregidor
Island

South Channel

Manila Bay

San Mateo
Marikina
MANILA
Cainta  Antipolo
Pasay  Pasig  Taytay
Parañaque  Pateros
Las Piñas  Angono
Bacoor  Mutinlupa
Sarao
San Pedro
Carmona  Santa Rosa
Silang  Cabuayao
Calamba
Los Banos
Mount Makiling
1,230 m
Talisay  Alaminos
Balete  San Pablo
Lipa
Tiaong
Rosario

RIZAL
Sampaloc
Tignuan
Tanay
Cardona
Pilila
Siniloan
Laguna
de Bay
Jalala
Pakil
Paete
Santa Cruz
Pila  Pagsanjan
Nagcarlan
LAGUNA  Majayjay  Sampaloc  Mauban
Nagcarlan
Calauan  Liliw  Lucban
Mount Banahaw
2,177 m
Mount Banahaw-
Cristobal National
Recreation Area  Tayabas  Mainit
Dolores  Sariaya  Pagbilao
Canda  Lucena

Tanza
Naic  Dasmariñas
Ternate  Maragondon
Magallanes  Indang
Tagaytay  Tagaytay Ridge

Nasugbu
Tuy
Balayan  Calaca  Agoncillo
Lemery
Talisay  Punta  Taal
Calatagan
Light  Anilao
Cathedral
Island
Cathedral Rock Marine Sanctuary
SEPOK  Maricaban
POINT  Island
Malahibong
Manok Island

BATANGAS
Lake Taal

Balayan
Bay  Balete
Bauen
Batangas
Mabini
Nabate
Lalya
Culebra
Island  Ilijan
Verde Island Passage

Ibaan
San Juan
Lobo
Balibago

QUEZON

N

Pollilo Strait

General Nakar
Infanta
Real  Dalahican

to Lucena
and
Southern
Luzon

WITHIN A RELATIVELY SHORT DISTANCE SOUTH OF MANILA, Luzon quickly shows a side of the island that contrasts sharply with the hectic bustle of the capital. This is a land of tiny villages nestled alongside great lakes or snaking along volcanic slopes, where boys row visitors in small wooden canoes up the river rapids to Pagsanjan Falls and hikers set out to walk around the volcanic crater of Lake Taal. Just over an hour from the edges of Manila, the views from Tagaytay Ridge — the breathtaking sight of Taal Volcano rising from within the crater lake of a larger volcano — instill a profound sense of the landscape's volatile beauty.

Past Lucena City, Southern Luzon is easily distinguishable as the peninsula jutting southeast like an arm into the Pacific. This southern peninsula has an altogether different attitude from its northern brother.

This part of the island is best known for the festering volcanoes — Mount Iriga, Bulusan Volcano, and, of course, the giant Mount Mayon near Legazpi — that have left their distinctive scars on the landscape. Mayon last spewed lava, ash, and steam into the atmosphere and down its slopes as recently as March 2000. The region is also a convenient jumping-off point for travel to Mindoro and the Visayan islands.

Composed of two provinces — Mindoro Occidental and Mindoro Oriental — the island of Mindoro faces, to the north, the Verde Island passage and Luzon's diving resort of Batangas and, to the south, the islands of the Visayas. Puerto Galera, a beach resort on Mindoro, is one of the most popular destinations in the Philippines. Away from its coastal villages, the dense jungle interior is home to Mangyan tribes. There

144

are also several reserve areas in Mindoro Occidental for the endangered *tamaraw*, a fierce buffalo species found nowhere else in the world.

Somewhat more off the beaten track is beautiful, less-touristy Marinduque Island — a destination for adventurous island-hoppers, and one which offers ample opportunity to live out Robinson Crusoe fantasies.

## THE CAVITE COAST

On the Cavite coast are two of the most exclusive beach resorts convenient to Manila. This is a pleasant area for a few days of relaxation, and a good base from which to explore the surrounding sights of **Tagaytay** and **Cavite City** or even venture as far as **Pagsanjan** in Laguna.

Close by, too, is the small fishing village of **Naic**, where the triggerfish, called *papacol* or *baget*, around nearby Carabao and Fraile islands draw keen game fishermen and anglers, especially between June and September. Past Ternate, nearby **Maragondon** is notable for its old church with an ornate carved interior, where Andres Bonifacio and his brother, leaders in the late-nineteenth-century armed revolutionary brotherhood against the Spanish — the Katipunan — were detained before being executed by General Aguinaldo on nearby Mount Buntis.

Often overlooked by visitors passing through it en route to the Batangas Peninsula, the historic city of Cavite demands a brief stop, if only to see its old of Spanish forts, cobblestone alleys, and dilapidated, formerly grand mansions. The ruined bastions on the headland once repulsed Moro pirates. Founded the same year as Manila (1571), Cavite was an important maritime and Jesuit center in the early colonial period. Here, giant galleons, constructed from the wood of molave trees, were destined to sail all the way to Mexico filled with exquisite goods from China. Cavite has a long tradition of maritime trade links dating back to the thirteenth century, when Chinese junks often moored here to barter for exotic goods. When the Philippines declared its independence from Spain, the first American naval expeditionary force arrived at Cavite, as the new leader in the archipelago

poised to take control. Because of its strategic port, Cavite was also a prime target for the Japanese when they invaded in 1941.

## WHERE TO STAY AND EAT

**Puerto Azul Resort** ( (95) 574731 or ( (95) 574036 ( MANILA (2) 525-9246 FAX (95) 597074, beyond the coastal town of Ternate, is a five-star resort set within a private forested estate fringed by bays. With its health spa, swimming pool, championship golf course, tennis, squash and badminton courts and

water sports equipment, this resort is clearly a destination for sports enthusiasts. Rooms are quite comfortable, rates are expensive. The restaurant is good if overpriced. The Puerto Azul also has more luxurious (and more expensive) suites.

Adjacent to Puerto Azul, amid the green hills surrounding a picturesque bay, is the **Caylabne Bay Resort** ( (95) 732-1051 FAX (95) 818-4089. More upscale than the Puerto Azul, the Caylabne Bay has condominium-style hotel rooms and suites with up to three bedrooms, as well as a private marina and a helipad. It buzzes with activity on weekends, filling up with unwinding Manila executives, politicians and socialites. The resort includes a busy bar and restaurant.

## VOYAGE TO THE VOLCANO'S RIM

The outer rim of an extinct volcano, shrub-covered **Tagaytay Ridge** is a popular weekend retreat for Manileños and is dotted with

Cavite is a major port for fishing; here, the piers serving *bancas*.

country houses and hotels. You can stroll along the ridge walkways with its many picnic spots, go horseback riding, or tour nearby flower and fruit farms. While in Tagaytay, you may want to sample dishes concocted from the unusual local mushrooms. They're sold at wayside stalls and apparently do *not* have hallucinogenic qualities.

From Tagaytay Ridge itself are many vantage points affording breathtaking views across **Lake Taal** and **Taal Volcano**. Despite its picturesque appearance and small size — the summit is only 406 m (1,332 feet) high — Taal Volcano has been one of the most active and devastating volcanoes in the archipelago. From the vantage point of Tagaytay Ridge, it is generally considered safe to witness the drama of its occasional fuming or even spewing of molten sparks. If the idea of exploring Taal Volcano up close interests you, take the winding and bumpy road down from the ridge to the lake's edge, where boatmen will ferry you across. Make sure you are happy with the agreed price at the outset. Lake Taal is also famous for its tiny fish — *pandaka pygmea* — the smallest of all known vertebrae, measuring only 1.3 cm (half an inch) at their most mature.

A drive from Manila to Tagaytay Ridge, Lake Taal and Taal Volcano will carry you through the provinces of Rizal and Cavite. From Lake Taal, you can easily continue on to the diving Mecca of Batangas, which is also popular with watersports enthusiasts and those travelers in need of some peaceful beachside relaxation.

## WHERE TO STAY AND EAT

If a day's visit is not enough, the location's popularity and the summer festivals that take place here have led to quite a few hotels and hostels sprouting up in this area.

The most exclusive and expensive hotel is the **Taal Vista Hotel** ( (46) 413-1223 to 27 FAX (6346) 413-1226 MANILA ( (2) 817-2710 FAX (2) 818-8208, Aguinaldo Highway, Cavite, Tagaytay City. This large hotel is set in beautiful tropical gardens, with big sliding glass windows to take in the view, and it has good amenities. In the same range, the **Ridge Resort and Convention Center** ( 632-9551 has pleasant cottages, a swimming pool and a tennis court and a restaurant serving predominately French cuisine. Inexpensive to moderately priced accommodation is available at the cosy **Villa Adelaida** ( MANUAL EXCHANGE 267 or ( MANILA (2) 810-2016 to 2019, in Foggy Heights. Villa Adelaida has a modest swimming pool and a friendly restaurant.

A tourist attraction in itself, the luxurious **Palace in the Sky** was built by late President Ferdinand Marcos and his wife Imelda for a visit by President Ronald Reagan. Although millions of dollars in public funds were used to build the structure during the early 1980s, the project was dropped when the Reagans abandoned their state visit amid growing protests over Marcos's authoritarian rule. The so-called palace, built at the highest point of a dramatic ridge overlooking Lake Taal and Taal Volcano, was extensively renovated in 1997 under a program led by the then first lady, Amelita Ramos. It has been rechristened **People's Park in the Sky** ( (46) 413-1295. Expensive.

Close to Lake Taal and Taal Volcano is the ultimate Philippine golf resort. The **Banyan Tree Nasugbu Evercrest Golf and Country Club** ( (43) 473-4411 or ( MANILA (2) 712-9293 is a luxurious golf retreat tucked in mountain highlands. Here golfers can play on "The Masterpiece," an 18-hole championship course designed by Arnold Palmer. From the luxurious resort you can take a climbing tour of the volcano or go out to the ridge on horseback. There is a swimming pool, sauna, massage, Jacuzzi and a kid's club. Call the resort for information about special golf vacation packages.

Note that prices for accommodation in the Lake Taal area tend to go up at all hotels by about 20 percent on the weekends.

## HOW TO GET THERE

Tagaytay Ridge is about an hour and a half's drive south of Manila. To drive there, take the South Expressway to the Carmona or the Santa Rosa exit; it joins up with the Aguinaldo Highway, which leads to the town of Silang and right into Tagaytay. There is a regular bus service between Tagaytay Ridge and Manila.

## LAGUNA PROVINCE

Just over an hour's drive south of Manila, Laguna province is regarded by many Manileños as the preferred place to live — within commuting distance of Manila — to escape the polluted air of the traffic-clogged metropolis. This means that the larger towns in the formerly unspoiled province, renowned for its beautiful freshwater lakes, rivers, waterfalls, mineral springs, coconut plantations, and rainforests, are rapidly

There are two ways to approach Laguna: either after exploring the Cavite and Batangas regions, or directly from Manila via Rizal province, winding through a string of communities ranged around the enormous, heart-shaped Laguna de Bay. Covering 922 sq km (356 sq miles), this is the largest freshwater lake in the country, encircled by the foothills of the Sierra Madre in the east, the plain of Metro Manila in the northwest, and a phalanx of volcanic mountains in the south, including the reportedly supernatural Mount Banahaw, in nearby Quezon province.

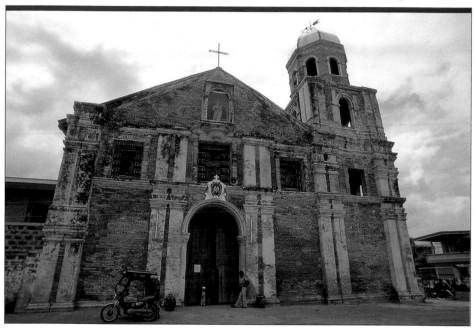

urbanizing, heralding the environmental blights of economic "development." Yet there is still much natural beauty to appreciate, especially around the Mount Makiling and Pagsanjan regions. Laguna's small towns have a decidedly Spanish feel and a gentle, tropical pace.

Laguna's lakeside communities came under Spanish control in 1571, led by Juan de Salcedo. Religious control was exerted by powerful Franciscan friars, who dotted the province with missions. The friars were feared and plotted against by the native inhabitants. Along with Cavite, Laguna was one of Luzon's flashpoints for the revolutionary movement in the nineteenth century.

### LAGUNA DE BAY

Originally part of Manila Bay, Laguna de Bay was formed as the earth's crust tilted upwards. Although many small rivers flow into the lake, it has only one major tributary, the Pasig River, crawling along, becoming increasingly polluted as it flows 16 km (10 miles) to meet Manila Bay. This water highway allows easy passage for cargo boats and *bancas* laden with produce. Fertile waters and lakeside orchards have always been the raison d'être of Laguna de Bay, which supported thriving communities long before the arrival of the Spanish.

A colonial church in Kawit, Cavite. In many parts of the Philippines, the faith is there, but the funds are not.

From San Pablo, perhaps the most impressive way to view the area's **seven crater lakes** is by walking along the roads that wind around them. Along the way, the villages of **Majayjay**, **Liliw** and **Nagcarlan** are all worth a look too.

Natives were forced by Franciscan missionaries (who were understandably reviled by the local population) to build the fortress-like Spanish baroque church in the village of **Majayjay**. The edifice has a most unusual design with three stories, and triple perimeter walls that are six meters (20 feet) thick, and the entire construction is buttressed by massive stone. Liliw is a little artisan town, where you can inspect its distinctive locally made shoes. The small village of **Nagcarlan** has unusually narrow, colonial three-story houses, a pretty baroque church and a curious 400-year-old crypt, which was later used by anti-Spanish revolutionaries, led by Andres Bonifacio, to hold secret meetings with other Katipunan members.

There is reason to stay longer: the beauty of **Mount Makiling**, which legend says is the home of the spirit Mariang Makiling. The upper slopes of the 1,000-m-high (3,283-foot) mountain are a national park full of forested pathways and, some magnificent giant trees. It's alive with strange birds, flying lizards and exotic butterflies.

### Where to Stay and Eat

If you wish to stop and test the waters, the **City of Springs Resort Hotel** ( (49) 536-0731, 35 North Villegas Street, is a good choice. It has a decent restaurant and various swimming pools. The **Lakeview Health Resort** ( (49) 536-0101, located at 1 Lopez Street, is another option. Both are inexpensive. You can stop for a few hours or stay overnight.

**Hidden Valley Springs Resort** ( MANILA (2) 818-4034 or (2) 840-4112 FAX (2) 812-1609, Limao Alaminos, Laguna, is a peaceful, forested retreat, two hour's drive from Manila, where a series of spring baths, set amidst a green forest filled with wild orchids and tropical ferns, has been turned into a resort — an oasis of cultivated tropical paradise. Paths wind through rainforest and open out to a series of cascading pools, with picnic huts and changing rooms. There are five pools of volcanically thermal, yet clear, mineral

water, with temperatures generally ranging from 29°C to 31°C (84°F to 88°F), fed directly from fissures in the rocks. While it is possible to stay overnight, rooms are overpriced for what they offer, and most visitors come for the day. For all that, it is an exceedingly beautiful place and worth the visit.

## PAGSANJAN FALLS

A raft ride up the seven-kilometer-long (four-mile), alternately serene and tumultuous Pagsanjan (pronounced Pug-sung-han) River

and its rugged gorge to reach the 91-m (299-foot) falls is one of the most invigorating and easily accomplished day trips from Manila, 102 km (63 miles) away. It is also somewhat adventurous, involving braving some not insignificant rapids and dodging boulders, with energetic *banqueros* (boatmen) at the helm. Expect to be frequently soaked to the skin; bring plastic bags to protect your valuables, and bring a change of clothes. Sunscreen lotion is also essential.

Numerous boat operators make the trip, most of them well-intentioned and well-organized locals. Yet complaints from tourists about being overcharged, robbed and harassed by *banqueros* are too numerous to ignore. Be aware that you should choose any freelance captains with caution. It's advisable to organize your boat trip to the Pagsanjan Falls while you are in Manila, working through a reputable travel agency or tour operator. You can arrange to go either as part of a group or on your own. If you haven't prearranged your trip in Manila, your hotel in Pagsanjan can offer recommendations.

The river journey takes about an hour each way, and the boats depart and alight at the clearing opposite Pagsanjan's church. Initially, a row of *bancas* are towed up the river by a motorized boat to encounter the first set of time to disembark and clamber across the river stones to the Pagsanjan Falls, where you are given 20 minutes to explore nearby caves, admire the falls, swim or take photographs. The return journey negotiating the series of 14 rapids is the most adrenaline-laden part of the trip, during which you will have to rely on the alacrity and experience of your *banqueros*. Rafting enthusiasts will prefer to tackle the rapids during the rainy season, especially from August through September, when the river is at its highest, with a challenging current.

rapids. Thatched nipa huts dot the riverbank, and you'll probably see villagers pausing to look up and wave. As you continue farther, the scenery becomes densely tropical, with forest furrowing the river edge and strange shrill calls of unseen birds. This part of the river was used as a location shot for Francis Ford Coppola's *Apocalypse Now*: it was here that the film's harrowing final sequence took place, in a replicated Khmer temple complex used as the resting place of antihero Kurtz. It is no coincidence that Oliver Stone shot his Hollywood movie *Platoon* in Laguna.

Passing through the gorge, the riverbanks become dramatic cliff faces as the tempo of the rapids increases. After being navigated through them by your trusty *banqueros*, it's

## Where to Stay and Eat

To enjoy the serenity of the river setting, it makes sense to stay overnight, so that you can make your river journey before the arrival of buses of day-trippers. Located in rustic surroundings, the most luxurious place to stay is the **Pagsanjan Rapids Hotel** ( (49) 808-4258 ( MANILA (2) 834-0403 or 834-0404 FAX (2) 832-1212, on General Taino Street, Pagsanjan, which has comfortable amenities and a good restaurant. Rates are moderate. The **Pagsanjan Village Hotel** ( (49) 645-2116, on Garcia Street, is a comfortable, inexpensive place to stay, with air conditioning. The **Willy Flores Guesthouse**

A *banqueros* navigates the seven-kilometer (11-mile) river trip to the thundering Pagsanjan Falls.

(no phone), also on Garcia Street, is popular; the management is friendly and it's extremely cheap.

## CALIRAYA LAKE

If river rafting doesn't appeal, but fishing and bird watching does, Caliraya Lake, near Pagsanjan, is a peaceful and enjoyable place and has the lure of a luxury resort. The large, tree-fringed man-made lake has many types of fish in its depths — bass, mullet, carp and catfish. Angling season is between October

and February. At the lakeshore, it is possible to hire a boat and fishing guide, either by the hour or the day. Windsurfing equipment, water skiing and horseback riding is available also.

Visit the nearby lakeshore towns of **Paete** and **Pakil**, known for staging the colorful Turumba Festival in May, and also for their carvers who fashion intricate woodwork and filigree sculptures of doves, butterflies and trees.

### Where to Stay
Filipino politicians and magnates retreat to the private **Lake Caliraya Country Club** ( (912) 306-0667 MANILA ( (2) 810-9557 or (2) 892-7777 (expensive).

## CALAMBA AND LOS BAÑOS

Perched over Laguna de Bay, the village of Calamba, 29 km (18 miles) from Manila, revels in its role as the birthplace of José Rizal, the physician and martyred nationalist leader who on his execution became a

saint-like figure for many Filipinos. A replica of Rizal's house — a two-story nineteenth-century Spanish style building — has become the **Rizal Shrine**, exhibiting the revolutionary's original furniture, books, photographs and other family memorabilia.

Numerous **hot mineral springs** dot the Los Baños area, fed by the thermal sulfur waters of dormant Mount Makiling. Thought to be curative, these waters inspired early Franciscans to build a hospital here in 1602 — the **Hospital de Aguas Santas** — which was later taken over and renamed Camp Eldridge by the Americans in 1903. During World War II, the Japanese turned Los Baños into a concentration camp. Fortunes were later reversed when General Yamashita was tried and executed as a war criminal at Camp Eldridge.

These days Los Baños is dominated by its many spa resorts, as well as by a variety of campuses — among others, the University of the Philippines has several agricultural research institutes located here, and the International Rice Research Institute set up by the Ford and Rockefeller Foundations — all attracted to the region by the exceptionally fertile volcanic soil found here. As for spas, you can't miss them as you drive along the highway from Calamba through Pansol to Los Baños.

## VILLA ESCUDERO

About two hours drive from Manila is the lush coconut-plantation hacienda-style resort of **Villa Escudero** ( MANILA (2) 521-0830 or (2) 523-0392 FAX (2) 521-8698. The resort is in **Tiaong**, off the road at 10 km (six miles) south of San Pablo, Laguna's biggest city on the highway to Lucena, at the Laguna–Quezon provincial boundary. This is a pleasant place to stay overnight and offers a taste of the life led by Spanish plantation owners. The huge plantation is still a working enterprise, operated by some 300 families. The Villa's **museum** is an extraordinary repository of the Escudero family's heirlooms, including stuffed wildlife, Spanish and Mexican religious icons, antique Chinese porcelain, nineteenth-century calesas, ethnic artifacts,

Grandstand views of the 91-m (299-foot) Pagsanjan Falls from a raft platform.

clothing and World War II memorabilia. The late Don Arsenio Escudero was an avid collector, and this private museum is said to be one of the largest collections of Spanish, Filipino and Chinese treasures.

You can opt for a two-hour carabao-cart tour of the museum, village and plantation, or you can stay at Villa Escudero's inexpensive cottages. There is a unique restaurant here where the tables are ankle deep in a freshwater stream. As you dine, you can dip your feet into water — a pleasant and rustic sensation on hot tropical days.

## MOUNT BANAHAW

Hardly ever active, but imposing nonetheless, this 2,177-m (7,142-foot) volcano sits on the boundary between Laguna and Quezon provinces and is the centerpiece of the surrounding national park. It is undeniably a spectacular hike, yet its reputation hovers firmly on the side of the supernatural: myths, superstitions and tales of strange happenings abound, attesting to the mountain's magical powers.

Long before the arrival of the Spanish, Mount Banahaw was believed to have great spiritual power by the native people of the area, who still live around its flanks and worship a type of folk Christianity in Banahaw's springs and caves. Many claim the mountain exerts its own forceful electromagnetic and energy field, and several sects have highly apocalyptic viewpoints about the site. During Holy Week, worshippers ascend the mountain to bathe in its springs and hold ceremonies in the 30-m-high (98-foot) cathedral-like cave known as the Kuweba ng Dios Ama (Cave of God the Father).

Mount Banahaw historical lore also merges into myth. In 1841, the Spanish retaliated violently against the rebellious Cofradia de San José movement in Quezon (then called Tayabas) and the survivors became *remontados*, or those who return to the mountains, living on the isolated slopes of Banahaw and nearby Mount Cristobel, in some ways behaving like the occult sect members who live on the mountain today.

Climbing Mount Banahaw takes at least four days. It is not advisable during the rainy season, when leeches are everywhere and landslides are common. There are several routes up the mountain, from **Lucban** and **Dolores** in Quezon and various points from Laguna. The main trailhead is in the village of **Kinabuhayan**. It is recommended to have a guide with you from the National Parks and Wildlife Station in the town of Santa Lucia, a 30-minute drive from San Pablo.

Even spending half a day on your own in Kinabuhayan and walking part of the way along the trail will give you a sense of the mysterious energy and beauty of Mount Banahaw.

## BATANGAS

South of Cavite, but still easily reached in less than three hours from Manila, the province of Batangas has a pretty coastline, undulating with small bays and beaches and fringed by clusters of coral gardens. While its sands are not as spectacular as Boracay's and its waters are no longer as pristine as Palawan's, Batangas is nonetheless justifiably renowned as an easily accessible destination for serious divers, especially for its famous Cathedral Rock Marine Sanctuary, off Balayan Bay.

### WHAT TO SEE AND DO

Batangas city is 124 km (77 miles) from Manila. Nearby **Balayan Bay** is regarded as one of Asia's premier diving grounds, and is also popular with windsurfers. The area's reputation has grown alongside the popularity of scuba diving in the Philippines, and many of the conservation efforts now beginning to be put into practice elsewhere in the archipelago were initially pioneered here. Most of the diving and beach resorts in the region are found at **Anilao**, a *barangay*, or suburb, of Mabini, located on sheltered **Janao Bay**, a smaller bay at the eastern end of Balayan Bay. Anilao is bursting with makeshift outdoor cafés, stalls, small traveler's hostels and offices renting out all manner of boats — from Hobiecats to yachts with full bar service — and every kind of water-sports equipment, as well as serious diving outfits. Despite the long, bumpy road out to Anilao and the unimpressive beach, it is firmly on the international divers' map. Around the point of Balayan Bay and north to Nasugbu are dotted several more small resorts and additional, more pleasant, beaches, also worth investigating for nearby dive sites.

The small town of **Taal** is also interesting. This former Spanish capital of Batangas has many colonial two-story houses and a lively market. Look for the local chocolate and peanut-brittle candy (*balisongs*), fan knives and *piña*, the fabric woven from pineapple fiber and fashioned into the Filipino national dress, the *barong tagalog*. If you've been following the trail of the province's

early revolutionary history — adjacent Cavite was a key player in the anti-Spain revolution — then all the more reason to visit the idiosyncratic **Agoncillo House**, the home of Marcela Agoncillo, the woman who sewed the first Philippine flag and who pawned her jewelry to donate the proceeds to the revolution.

The towns of **Batangas** and **Balayan** are particularly famous for their annual postharvest thanksgiving parades featuring roast pigs, or *lechons*.

### Diving

Around Anilao are many compelling dive sites, including the spectacular **Cathedral Rock Marine Sanctuary**. This entirely man-made sanctuary features a coral garden in the form of a sunken amphitheater which was cultivated from seeded corals. It is also unusual in that its plentiful varieties of fish are attracted by daily fish-feeding.

Other diving spots include **Sombrero Island**, which has a wide hat-brim-like underwater rim perfect for shallow diving, while **Maricaban Island** is also good for snorkeling and has a resort (see below). The Verde Island Passage contains the two other marine sanctuaries in the region: **Culebra Island** and **Malahibong Manok Island** — both of which have many species of coral and reef fish in their narrow rock ledges, which are studied by marine biologists from a nearby base. **Verde Island** itself, a beautiful and idyllic place, is indented with alluring coral drop-offs and, on the south side of the island, it is possible to see the sunken remains of a Spanish galleon. Due to its proximity to the diving resort of Puerto Galera (easily accessible by ferry to and from Batangas across the strait in Mindoro Oriental), you may meet divers who have journeyed across for day diving excursions, or you may decide to make the opposite journey (see PUERTO GALERA, page 158 below). When diving in most of these sites, it is advisable to have an experienced and licensed guide with you to ensure safe navigation through strong and sometimes unpredictable currents.

### WHERE TO STAY AND EAT

Most of the onshore dive camps and resorts offer inclusive packages that include inexpensive accommodation in cottages, tents or huts, simple meals and full scuba facilities. They also run courses so that beginner divers can gain PADI certification. Among the many resorts, two are especially recommended: **Aquaventure Reef Club (** (2) 899-2831 FAX (2) 813-1967, Bagalangit, Anilao, Mabini, caters primarily to divers, particularly Japanese tourists who come to learn the ropes. The facility is professional, rooms are cozy, and the entire resort feels very native, as bamboo furnishes most of the rooms and the restaurant. Prices fall in the

Tranquility in the Hidden Valley Springs Resort, a popular spa hideaway.

inexpensive to moderate range. **Eagle Point Resort** ( (043) 986-0177 or 0178 ( MANILA (2) 813-3553 FAX (2) 813-3560 WEB SITE www .eaglepoint.com.ph is a bit more expensive than Aquaventure Reef Club, ranging from US$60 to US$150 for a suite. It is located on the tip of the Calumpang Peninsula on Balayan Bay, and offers native style air-conditioned cottages and an excellent diving facility and shop. It also boasts three pools.

If you prefer to laze on the sands, you'll want to head for the most pleasant beaches on the Batangas Peninsula; they're found on the more sheltered west coast. Both Nasugbu and Matabungkay are good western-shore bases, with high-quality resorts and possibilities for diving, snorkeling and fishing.

Nasugbu, idyllic and quiet, is dotted with several private beaches and resorts. Highly recommended is the well-located and tastefully landscaped **Maya Maya Reef Club** ( (918) 272-0738 FAX (912) 322-8554 WEB SITE www.mayamaya.com, Balaytique, Nasugbu. Rates are moderate to expensive. Incidentally, Nasugbu is where 8,000 American troops came ashore in 1945 and advanced on Manila. It is easy to rent a pump boat from the town's port at Wawa and find your own private bay.

The mid-range **Matabungkay Beach Club** ( MANILA (2) 752-5252 or (2) 752-2525 FAX (2) 840-3811, at Matabungkay, Lian, is a well-organized, if holiday-camp-style resort. Facilities include a clubhouse style restaurant, tennis courts, swimming pools, water sports facilities — including catamaran sailing, fishing, windsurfing and snorkeling — a gymnasium with sauna and a massage parlor.

In the western corner of Batangas, **Calatagan** is the site of the picturesque, family-friendly resort of **Punta Baluartes** ( (2) 635-5099 or (2) 635-7499 FAX (2) 635-6699. There are a variety of air-conditioned nipa cottages and suites, some tucked away like tree houses on the hillside, others framing the beach. Good water sports facilities (aqua-bikes, jet skis and even a glass-bottom boat), a swimming pool, golf course and tennis court as well as a horseback riding program and a playground for the children. These and other amenities make

this a pleasant place to spend several days, although this is not a spot that is especially geared for enthusiasts of scuba diving. Rates are moderate.

## How to Get There

Batangas is 110 km (almost 68 miles) south of Manila. It is best to take one of the many buses that regularly leave Manila's major bus depots, including **BLTB** ( (2) 833-5501 stationed on E. Delos Santos Avenues (EDSA), Pasay City. Batangas is accessible

from neighboring provinces such as Cavite, Laguna, and Quezon by land via public buses also and jeepneys. Ferrys and other watercraft connect Batangas to Mindoro and other nearby islands.

## QUEZON AND AURORA

East of Manila, the thin, boot-shaped province of Quezon has a long, exposed coastline that runs down to the Bondoc Peninsula. It was named after Manuel Quezon, president of the Philippine Commonwealth. Farther north, across the isolated reaches of the Sierra Madre, is Aurora, the province named for Quezon's wife. This province has a small following as a surfing destination. Somewhat off the beaten track, Aurora is chiefly a conduit for travelers who pass through it to Lucena on their way to catch a ferry to the islands of Marinduque and Romblon.

Quezon is justifiably famous for its **Pahiyas Festival** — a folkloric extravaganza and one that very young children enjoy participating in — celebrated in mid-May in the towns of **Lucban** and **Sariaya**. During the festival, many house fronts are wreathed with brightly colored leaf-shaped rice wa-

sells a wide array of handicrafts made by local tribes.

## WHAT TO SEE AND DO

The secret of Sorsogon Province — until recently a little-known destination, at the southernmost tip of Luzon — has been discovered. Since a diver captured on video the migration of whalesharks into the mouth of the Donsol River, tourists have been flocking to the sleepy town for the chance to swim with them.

fers, called *kiping,* and garlands of fruits and vegetables to celebrate the year's harvest.

## LEGAZPI

A trip to Legazpi, the capital of Albay Province, can provide two of the most incredible adventures of a lifetime: trekking the formidable Mayon Volcano, considered the world's most beautiful and symmetrical volcano; and swimming with the gentle giants of the ocean, the **whalesharks** at Donsol. Other points of interest here include Legazpi's **St. Raphael Church**, where the altar is made out of Mayon's volcanic rock, and the town's **local market**, which

Whaleshark interaction tours can be arranged through the **Sorsogon Tourism Council** ( (56) 221-1357 or (56) 221-1173. Or try **WWF Philippines** at ( (2) 433-3220 to 3222 FAX (2) 426-3927. The **Bantay Butanding Project** ( (52) 481-0608 can provide further information.

While there is no guarantee that you will see one of the gentle giants, local fishermen, seeing an opportunity to profit from this natural phenomenon, make sure to keep track of the whalesharks' whereabouts.

The **tourism office** in Legazpi ( (52) 482-0712, Regional Center Site, can organize hikes and guides for the three main volcanoes in

A brilliantly decorated porch celebrating Pahiyas, the Rice Harvest Fiesta, Lucban, Quezon.

the area — the mighty Mayon, Bulusan Volcano, and Mount Iriga. Hiking **Mount Mayon**, at 2,462 m (8,125 feet), is a fairly difficult climb and you should be a seasoned hiker to attempt it. The incline to the summit is pretty consistent, with the last portion requiring climbers to be roped together to avoid slipping on the loose cinders and lava. Gas masks or an improvised cotton mask should be used at the summit to protect your lungs from the hot, poisonous gases that leak out. Do make a stop at the volcanology station right at the start of the climb. Hiking 1,559-m (5,079-foot) **Bulusan Volcano** is not too difficult, though, and 1,462-m (4,823-foot) **Mount Iriga**, which suddenly appears like a giant in the midst of a forest, is just a long walk.

Declared a national park in 1935, Bulusan Volcano is cloaked in rainforest that harbors rare plants and animals. Ten minutes from the national park is another favorite nature hop of Sorsogeños. **Palogtoc Falls** is modest in size, but it flows all the way to a natural pool that has become a favorite swimming hole among the locals especially on hot summer days.

**Rizal Beach** near Gubat is considered the Boracay of the Bicol region because of its long stretch of white beach in a perfectly symmetrical cove. The water is crystal clear, calm and safe for swimming.

## WHERE TO STAY AND EAT

**Hotel La Trinidad (** (52) 523-8054 FAX (52) 521-1309, Rizal Street, is fairly standard although some consider it the best hotel in the area. The main attraction is the convenient on-site cinema, which usually shows pretty outdated flicks. Rooms are large and carpeted, and all have private baths with hot and cold water.

You'll find many dining options simply by taking a stroll down Rizal or Penaranda streets. Two must-try local specialties are *Laing*, a spicy mixture of shrimp and pork rolled in taro leaves and stewed in coconut milk, and the Bicol express, minced beef tartar with chili peppers. Try **WayWay Restaurant** on Penaranda Street. **My Brother's Place** on Rizal Street is popular with tourists and backpackers for the San Miguel beer and live music.

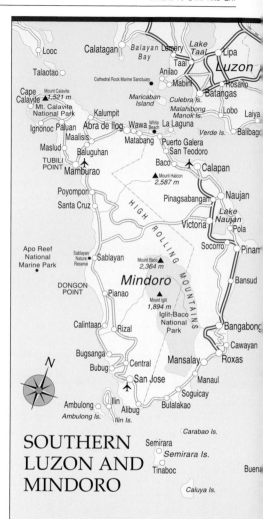

**SOUTHERN LUZON AND MINDORO**

## HOW TO GET THERE

There are two options when choosing to fly into the Southern Luzon region. First you can use Naga as the jumping-off point to other destinations in the region, particularly Legazpi (about a two-hour bus ride away) or Mount Isarog National Park. Asian Spirit, Philippine Airlines, and Air Philippines have flights to Naga, although be sure to check schedules as service here is sometimes interrupted. For a more reliable option, all three airlines have daily flights into Legazpi too. Pacific Air offers more expensive charter flights from Manila to Legazpi.

Legazpi City is a 14-hour bus ride from Manila, usually an overnight trip. From

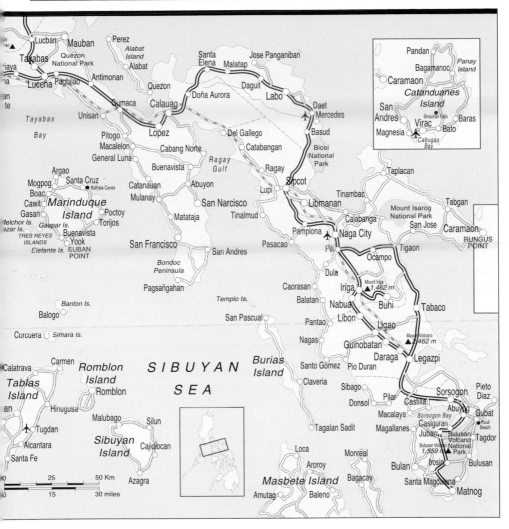

Legazpi it is another hour bus ride to Sorsogon. **JB Bicol Express** ℭ (2) 834-0927 and **Philtranco** ℭ (2) 833-1369 have services from Manila to Legazpi.

## MINDORO

Despite its proximity to Luzon and Manila, the mountainous island of Mindoro was sparcely settled until the twentieth century — largely due to particularly fierce strain of malaria that was rife across the island until the combination of anti-malarial medicines, pesticides and insect repellants. The clearing of forests for pasture reduced the problem. The few settlements that were established were generally restricted to coastal ports.

Such a low human impact has meant that Mindoro is the only place in the world where the tamaraw has been found. This small — and fierce — relation to the water buffalo was first documented by Europeans in 1888, at which time they were abundant across the island. Numbers fell dramatically over the twentieth century, though, through hunting and the destruction of forests, until conservation efforts began in the 1970s.

The best known of Mindoro's tamaraw reserves is within **Iglit-Baco National Park** near Mount Iglit, close to the settlement of Puy-Puy; another, also near Mount Iglit, is just outside **Sablayan**; and, within the reserve of **Mount Calavite**, in the island's northwest point is a third.

## PUERTO GALERA

A pretty former seaport, Puerto Galera has become increasingly "discovered" and now vies with Boracay as one of the most popular beach and dive resorts in the archipelago.

Located on the north shore of Mindoro Oriental, Puerto Galera town is knitted together by a string of coastal villages including Sabang Beach, Big La Laguna and Small La Laguna, and has a lovely natural port. "PG" as expatriates and locals affectionately call their playground — plays host to incredible opportunities for diving and snorkeling, lounging at the beach, and rowdy nightlife.

In the sixteenth century, the Spanish regarded Puerto Galera as an ideal cove for protecting their fleet of great ships from tropical storms, which is why it became known as "port of galleons." This has become a diving and beach playground, where you can also go treasure hunting and take cruises in restored Spanish galleons.

### General Information

There is no tourist office in Puerto Galera, although **Swagman Travel (** (912) 347-6993, at Sabang Beach, do a pretty good job of providing maps and answering travelers' questions. Swagman also has a branch at Small La Laguna Beach **(** (912) 306-6585. Telephone calls can be made from either branch.

### What to See and Do

Diving is the main attraction in Puerto Galera, and dive shops and undersea activities abound. Nearly all of the local dive shops have good facilities and equipment as well as their own dive boat.

Experienced divers are usually keen to explore the most popular, though somewhat distant, internationally renowned site at **Apo Reef National Marine Park** to the west of Sablayan. For beginners, however, Puerto Galera is an excellent place to learn.

Beach exploring is a natural here, and you can take your pick. The busiest beaches are **White Beach** and **Sabang Beach**, both of which have many restaurants, discos and bars and are lively at night. **Big La Laguna Beach** and **Small La Laguna Beach** are

enticing too, either for swimming or snorkeling over coral reefs. You do your beach exploring either by jeepney from Puerto Galera to Sabang, or by hiring a *banca*.

### Where to Stay and Eat

Because it is becoming so popular, Puerto Galera's hotels and restaurants are undergoing a state of flux. Simple nipa cottages with basic facilities abound, but increasingly more elaborate resorts are sprouting up. Prices vary, depending on how successful the season is. Of the many choices, one resort stands out: **Coco Beach Resort (** MOBILE (917) 377-2115 or (917) 890-1426 FAX (2) 526-6903, Puerto Galera, is the largest and most luxurious, with its bamboo cottages, swimming pool and landscaped terraces that descend to a private beach and coral reef drop-off. It offers exceptional value and its inexpensive to moderate rates include buffet breakfast and transport from Manila on the Coco Beach Express, a bus/ferry transfer that runs daily.

#### SABANG BEACH

Said to be the best and most comfortable hotel along Puerto Galera's beaches, **Atlantis Resort Hotel (** (912) 308-0672 is a contemporary Spanish-Mediterranean hotel that resembles a Greek isle. It is known for its five-star dive shop and excellent restaurant, **Ristorante de Franco**, where you can savor tender steaks, homemade pizzas and other excellent Italian-influenced dishes. Located right on the beach, **Big Apple Dive Resort (** (912) 308-1120 is a traditional-style resort popular with European divers. They have a nice pool and billiard room, and all rooms have air conditioning. **Le Bistrot Brasserie and Pizzeria** (no phone) serves delicious French-European dishes and an assortment of French, Californian, or Australian wine. For authentic Thai red, yellow, and green curry, head to **Relax Thai Restaurant**. And for Filipino cuisine, **Tamarind Restaurant and Music Pub** (no phone) serves up everything tamarind — and lots of seafood dishes including crab and lobster.

#### SMALL LA LAGUNA

With seaside breezes and views high up on a cliff, **El Galleon (** (912) 305-0652 features a triangular pool alongside a huge palm tree and a pavilion restaurant that dishes up excellent international cuisine. It's popular with divers, as its famous owner, Allan Nash, also owns Asia Divers and the **Point Shooter Bar**, a watering hole where everybody who's anybody parties.The nearby **Portofino Resort (** (973) 776704, feels more like a condo or apartment with its hacienda-like units that are complete with fully stocked kitchens and sumptuous bathrooms (some even have jacuzzis). The stone pool, only a stone's throw away from the ocean,

## How to Get There

There are no flights to Puerto Galera directly, although Philippine Airlines flies daily to San José and Mamburao and Pacific Airways flies to Calapan, the closest airport to Puerto Galera. If money is no object, you can hire a private helicopter or a seaplane for the flight from Manila for around US$1,000. Call **(** (973) 497503 for more information.

Most people make the excursion to Mindoro in two legs: from Manila to Batangas via taxi or bus (a two-hour journey), and then

is the best around. The restaurant dishes up great steaks and Mexican cuisine, and there's a friendly bar.

BIG LA LAGUNA

**La Laguna Beach Club and Dive Center** MOBILE **(** (973) 855545 FAX (973) 878409 has lovely landscaped gardens and offers comfortable and air-conditioned rooms, although they are somewhat basic, and a swimming pool. The restaurant prepares a huge range of international and local cuisine. The PADI-IDC-rated, five-star diving center offers courses in several languages. There are 20 dive sites within a 15-minute *banca* ride of Big La Laguna, and an 18-m (60-foot) liveaboard *banca* is available for charter.

by ferry from Batangas to Puerto Galera. A daily through-trip starts at 9 AM in front of the Centrepoint Hotel in Manila. The air-conditioned bus takes you to Batangas City Pier just in time to catch the **MB *Si-Kat II* Ferry**. Other reliable ferry options are **Viva Shipping Lines**, which leaves Batangas numerous times a day, or **DSL Fastcraft MV *Blue Eagle***, which is the fastest ferry, taking about one and a half hours.

Two things to consider when traveling by ferry are the weather and the condition of the vessel. At the first threat of a typhoon, ferry service will be cancelled and you can

Borrowing ideas from traditional Philippine handicrafts, many hotels combine simplicity with luxury.

find yourself stranded for days on end. Be sure to check the condition of the ferry before boarding. You can certainly tell the difference between the newer less rusty vessels and the older, rickety boats that are on their last leg. Never stay on a ferry if you feel it is overbooked.

## MARINDUQUE

The delightful outlying island of Marinduque is rarely visited by tourists outside of its festival season. This in part accounts for its unpretentious and rustic charm. Marinduque is an ideal choice for an island-hopping excursion from Mindoro, and it offers a taste of life in the busy island backwaters.

The towns of Boac, Gasan and Mogpog on this heartshaped island come alive for the **Moriones Festival** at Easter, when traditional masks, helmets and outlandish costumes imitating Roman centurions are paraded (and sold to tourists) with abandon as the colorful re-enactment of the crucifixion takes place. Although most of the island's towns perform passion plays, the largest and most outstanding is held at Boac from Easter Thursday to Easter Sunday. Aside from its festivities, Marinduque's **village markets** are great for buying carved birds, ornaments and baskets.

### WHAT TO SEE AND DO

**Boac**, Marinduque's provincial capital, is situated on the west coast. It is a sleepy settlement, dominated by a large church building, and dotted with wooden houses that seem to be staving off encroaching tropical foliage. Horse-drawn rickshaws are commonplace, and village life — which may seem dull at first — reveals a seething bed of intrigue the longer you stay and the more you pay attention to the local, clannish gossip. Much of the town's activity centers around **The Lady of Biglang Awa** (Sudden Mercy), a shrine credited with miraculous powers. For at least a day during your stay, visit the **Tres Reyes** (Three Kings) **Islands**, which lie off the coast of Gasan, 13 km (eight miles) south of Boac. Of these islands, Gaspar Island, Melchor Island and Baltazar Island are 30 minutes

away by hired outrigger *banca* and are perfect for swimming, fishing and snorkeling. Only experienced divers with local guides should attempt to explore the complex network of underwater caves that lie beneath these islands.

On the northern coast, the town of **Santa Cruz** is worth visiting for its Spanish church, built in 1714. **Bathala Caves**, 10 km (six miles) away are an interesting detour, and **White Beach** at Poctoy near Torrijos, is a little further on, although jeepneys can be scarce for transport. South of Marinduque, Japanese investors have created a private club on **Elefante Island**, complete with golf course, named the Fantasy Elephant Club ( MANILA (2) 893-8280 FAX (2) 894-5725. You can visit via boat from Lipata.

### WHERE TO STAY AND EAT

The island's main cluster of guesthouses and eating places is in Boac, but don't expect great luxury on Marinduque.

The best place to stay on the island is the **Sunset Garden Resort** ( MANILA (2) 801-6369, in Pangi, about two kilometers (one and a quarter miles) outside Gasan. It has cottages with bath and fans, and boasts the island's best restaurant.

In Boac, the **Susanna Inn** ( VIA OPERATOR 1997 has comfortable rooms with air conditioning and bath; there's also a restaurant. The **Aussie-Pom Guest House** (no telephone) in Caganhao (between Boac and Cawit) offers basic, spacious rooms and snorkeling equipment for the nearby (pebbly) beach.

### HOW TO GET THERE

You can fly to Boac from Manila with Philippine Airlines, a daily 30-minute flight. Otherwise, there is a daily boat service from Pinamalayan in Mindoro for Gasan, leaving at 8:30 AM, a journey of three and a half hours. It is also possible to make the longer boat journey from Lucena in Quezon to Balancan, in northwest Marinduque.

During Holy Week, a Passion Play is presented with great realism. Here, a young Marinduque resident reenacts Christ's last steps.

# Cebu and the Visayas

AT THE HEART OF THE PHILIPPINE ISLANDS, BETWEEN Luzon and Mindanao, the Visayas entice travelers to go island hopping, to explore the history of colonial towns with their ornate Spanish churches and ancestral homes, and to experience some of the more spectacular undersea landscapes that the country has to offer. Others prefer to stay put and simply laze about in any one of the Visayas many beach resorts. Most are designed to resemble villages of *nipa* huts — a palm thatch and bamboo version of a hotel cabana.

The Visayas comprise six of the major 11 islands in the Philippines, as well as many smaller islands, and are divided up into 14 provinces. The main islands are Cebu, Negros, Panay, Bohol, Leyte and Samar. Reliable and efficient boat services operate around the islands, and the short connections make it practical to move around from island to island, unlike the large distances necessary to cover in some other more far-flung parts of the archipelago.

## CEBU

Lying in the middle of the Visayas island group, Cebu province comprises 167 islands, many of which are startlingly beautiful and are well known to divers. The historic city of Cebu is the regional center of the Visayas, and over the past few years has undergone an economic transformation, which Cebuaños refer to as "Ceboom." Despite its rapid development and increasingly industrial skyline, Cebu has a relaxed ambiance and is well endowed with fine architecture from its rich Malay and Hispanic past, reflecting too the ancestral wealth associated with surrounding sugar cane, mango, tobacco and hemp plantations.

In the thirteenth century, "Zubo" or "Sugbo" as it was then known, was a precolonial port town visited by Asian and Arabic traders. In 1521, Portuguese navigator Ferdinand Magellan made it his base on his explorations and incursions throughout the archipelago. He was welcomed by King Humblon and Queen Juana, who were converted to Christianity. By 1565, Cebu was made the Spanish headquarters, led by Miguel Lopez de Legaspi, and for six years it was the capital of the Philippines.

When the Americans took over the Philippines in the late nineteenth century, they met with fierce resistance in the Cebu region, leading to the Toledo Bay skirmish in 1900. Cebu's strategic position in the center of Philippines also made it a prime target for the Japanese, who first bombarded it and then made it a base. Some of World War II's bloodiest battles occurred here in the Antuanga and Babag hills, before the Japanese surrendered.

Cebu is also one of the nation's high-profile seaside resorts, blossoming with tropical flowers and fringed by clustered coral reefs. The island is 300 km (186 miles) long and 40 km (25 miles) wide and has reasonable coastal roads.

## CEBU CITY

The oldest colonial city in the Philippines, don't expect the city of Cebu to be a peaceful backwater free of the development problems and social ills associated with Manila. It is doing its best to put up as many new hotels, shopping complexes and skyscrapers as it can, while the reclaimed Mactan Export Processing Zone is bristling with new factories and industrial estates. Still, the city retains much charm and piquant beauty and its historical buildings, façades and sites are preserved with care.

### General Information

It is a 30-minute drive from Mactan International Airport to downtown Cebu City, and jeepneys ply the route frequently. The convenient **Department of Tourism** office ( (32) 254-2811 FAX (62-32) 254-2711 is directly opposite Fort San Pedro. There is also a tourist information counter at **Mactan International Airport** ( (32) 340-2486.

The best way of getting around Cebu City is by taxi — they're clean, air-conditioned, metered and, for the most part, the drivers are honest. The Spanish-colonial *tartanilla*, or horse-drawn carriage, is still used in some parts of the city. Although you might want to take one, it can be distressing to observe how skinny and overworked the horses are. Negotiate your fare before taking off.

Magellan's Cross in Cebu, marking the spot where he converted King Humblon to Christianity.

The local dialect is Cebuano or Bisaya, although English and Tagalog are widely spoken. For any **emergencies** dial ☏ (32) 95676 or (32) 74642.

For **Internet** access, Cebu is one of the best and cheapest in the region. Sky Net Computer Internet Services on Sanciangko Street is a popular place, but closes quite early. The @netdepot Café, on Sikatuna Street, is open until 10 PM; it's air-conditioned and costs about P30 per hour.

## What to See and Do

Most of Cebu City's sights can easily be seen in a half-day on foot or by taxi, or a whole day if you wish to take your time. **Mactan Island**, a 20-minute drive away, is a world unto itself of beaches, resorts and diving attractions (see below).

**Fort San Pedro** ☏ (32) 96518, open daily 8 AM to noon and 1 PM to 5 PM, is a good place to begin a tour of the city. Originally built as a fortress by the Spanish as their stronghold against Muslim raiders, it has been used as a barracks for Filipino revolutionaries and the American army, and a as Japanese internment camp for prisoners of war. It is the country's oldest and smallest fort, built in 1565. From Fort San Pedro, it's only a 10-minute walk to Plaza Rizal, where **Magellan's Cross**, the original cross brought over by the famed Portuguese navigator, is housed. It was originally planted there by Magellan to mark the spot where King Humblon and Queen Juana and 400 of their entourage became the first Filipinos to be baptized, in 1521. In the eighteenth century, this cross was pillaged by devout Catholics who believed that even tiny wooden chips from it had miraculous powers. Ceiling murals inside the shrine depict the first Catholic mass held in the Philippines.

Several blocks away, the **Basilica Minore del Santo Niño** houses a gem-festooned statue of the child Jesus, given by Magellan to Queen Juana. It is said to be the oldest religious relic in the country.

Cebu has a number of small, but worthwhile museums. The **Cebu City Museum**, on Osmena Boulevard, has the most extensive and regionally representative display, with many collections donated by Cebu's old families. **Casa Gorordo** ☏ (32) 255-5630,

on Lopez Jaena Street, was the former residence of Cebu's first Filipino bishop and recreates the style of a Cebuano household in the nineteenth century. The **Sala Piano Museum**, at 415 Gorordo Avenue, has pianos of all sizes and styles. The **Osmena Residence**, on Osmena Boulevard, is the family home of former president, Sergio Osmena, and displays his memorabilia and antique collection. Included too are some historically interesting effects that belonged to General MacArthur. **Jumalon's Museum**, located at 20 Macopa Street, Pardo, is remarkable for its collection of mosaics made from butterfly wings, bound to intrigue lepidopterists. They are the work of Professor Julian Jumalon, who collected together damaged butterfly wings from all over the world to create his artworks.

Cebu's **Taoist Temple** ☏ (32) 93652 sits atop 99 steps in the affluent suburb somewhat self-consciously named Beverly Hills, with views across the city. Another place of interest is the **University of San Carlos** ☏ (32) 72419, which was established in 1565 by the Jesuits, and is the oldest school in the country. Within its museum and grounds, it sports a wide collection of archaeological, ethnic, botanical and zoological exhibits.

From here, via the city's main boulevard of Colon Street, the **Carbon Market** is worth seeking out for its warren of bazaars, which can turn up some interesting bargains. It is also fun to browse in the section of the market that sells fresh fruits, flowers and sweets. Sample some of the region's mangoes, fresh or dried, *otap*, a crunchy sugar coated biscuit and *turrones*, a rolled wafer filled with peanut or cashew candy.

Fashion accessories and rattan furniture are top exports from the Philippines, and consequently Cebu has become a major port of call for international business people who buy direct from factories in the Mactan export zone. Standards of quality and workmanship are high. In particular, look for ethnic handicrafts such as basketwork, modern rattan and antique furniture, ceramics, *capiz* (shell), coral and fossil stone jewelry. Bear in mind, however, that in some parts of the world the import of coral and shells is forbidden; it might be prudent to choose a souvenir which is more ecologically sound. Lists of manufacturers and exporters are available at the Department of Tourism office, and you can call ahead to arrange a visit.

## Where to Stay

The beach resort area of Mactan (see below) is where most visitors choose to stay, rather than Cebu City, which, although its tropical setting and sandy bays are appealing, is rapidly becoming overdeveloped.

Overlooking the city from the Nivel Hills, **Cebu Plaza Hotel (** (32) 231-1231 FAX (32) 231-2071, Nivel Hills, Lahug, Cebu City, is regarded as Cebu City's premier business address. It is located anything from 10- to 20-minutes' drive from Cebu's central downtown area. Although it has great views, there is no beach in sight. In terms of accommodation, amenities, landscaped gardens and price, it does fall somewhat short of what the Shangri-La Mactan can offer. **Waterfront Cebu City (** (32) 232-6888, Waterfront Drive, Cebu City, is the newly opened glitzy place to stay for business travelers and gamblers. The Filipino Casino is one of Asia's largest, attracting high rollers from Hong Kong, Japan, and other nearby Asian countries. Both are expensive.

Both **Cebu Marriott Hotel (** (32) 232-6100 FAX (32) 232-6101, and **Park Place Hotel (** (32) 253-1131 FAX (32) 634-7509, both on Fuente Osmena, are typical mid-range, high-rise hotels with good facilities and a convenient location.

The best choice in the budget range is in the **Montebello Villa Hotel (** (32) 231-3681 FAX (32) 231-4455, Banilad, Cebu City. Although located in suburban surroundings, it has large gardens that are a pleasant respite from the city.

## Where to Eat

**Lantaw Gardens (** (32) 231-1231, Cebu Plaza, Nivel Hills, has an open-air garden and a buffet that serves good local cuisine and some European dishes as well. For seafood, the **Golden Cowrie (** (32) 92633, Salina at La Guardia Street, has a variety of fish prepared with local Philippine spices and sauces. One of the most popular places to eat is the **Lighthouse Restaurant (** (32) 78126, on General Maxilom Avenue, which business travelers and local Filipinos like to frequent for the

authentic Filipino dishes. **Ginza Japanese Restaurant (** (32) 231-6019, Old Banilad Road, is an exceptional 20-year-old dining establishment where, for a hefty price, the "super boat" sails to your table loaded with fresh sushi and sashimi. According to the jolly old Chef and owner Alfredo, **Idea Italia (** (32) 232-4292 Level 1, Ayala Center, is the most authentic Italian cuisine in Cebu. The closest thing to a seafood wharf, **Seafood City (** (32) 213793, JY Square, Salinas Drive, allows you to customize your fish selections. Simply browse the aisles of live fish and seafood with your shopping

cart, make your selections and choose how you want it prepared. And if you are missing your cup of Joe, **Vienna Kaffeehaus (** (32) 253-1430, Ground Floor, Wayne's Inn, Banilad, Mandaue, is the perfect recreation of a Viennese coffeehouse, complete with Viennese food, newspapers, and magazines. Breakfasts here are quite popular with locals and tourists, particularly the blueberry pancakes.

## Nightlife

Nightlife in Cebu City, as in Manila, caters to all persuasions. Like the capital city, there are after-dinner diversions galore; the only

Basilica Minore del Santo Niño, Cebu City, houses the oldest relic in the country — a gem-studded statue of the child Jesus.

difference is that in Cebu the prices are lower. Bars and lounges at the main hotels are popular meeting places, especially **Bai Disco** ( (32) 231-1131 at the Cebu Plaza Hotel. Here and at **Balls Disco** ( (32) 79305, General Maxilom Avenue, the fashionable set dance to strobe lights and the latest rock sounds including live bands.

For bars, try **Prince William's Pub**, on North Escario Street, and **St. Moritz** ( (32) 231-0914 off Gorordo Avenue, for a Euro pub atmosphere. **Thunderdome** ( (32) 54534 is a midtown bar favored by locals because of

### How to Get There

**Philippine Airlines** ( (32) 254-3870 in Cebu City, has daily flights to 22 domestic destinations within the Philippines, including Manila, an hour's flight. **Grand International Airways** ( (2) 893 9768 to 9774 has twice-daily Airbus flights between Manila and Cebu and also to Davao. **Cebu Pacific Air** ( (2) 636-4838 to 4845, controlled by the super-rich Gokonwei clan, has been given the government's go-ahead to launch a Manila–Cebu service too, and has ambitious plans for five daily flights (on Boeing 737s) to Cebu,

its first-rate sound system. **Tops** on Busay Hill, about three miles north of the Cebu Plaza Hotel, is also popular with locals, offering splendid views of the city and distant islands. It's one of the more romantic spots, especially at sunset.

The **Philippine Dream** ( (32) 340-3888 is a huge cruise ship anchored at a deep-water dock close to the airport. This floating entertainment complex has restaurants, bars, and discos. For casinos, the **Waterfront Cebu City Hotel and Casino** ( (32) 231-1404 or (32) 231-5652 is the premier place to try your luck. The **Montebello Villa Hotel** ( (32) 231-3681, Banilad, has a small casino too, but it doesn't compare with the Waterfront casino.

with routes to Davao and other southern cities to follow. From Cebu City, there are many inter-island flights daily to key provincial destinations throughout the archipelago.

Internationally, Cebu is on the scheduled route networks of Asiana, Cathay Pacific, Japan Airlines and SilkAir, as well as Philippine Airlines. There are direct flights from Sydney, Japan, Hong Kong, Malaysia, Guam, Singapore and Taiwan.

Cebu's port is the gateway to the southern Philippines. Manila is 22 hours away via most of the standard ferries. All the major lines have trips between Cebu and ports all over the archipelago. For high-speed ferry service, **WG&A Superferry** ( (2) 894-3211 or (2) 893-2211 has an excellent, brisk service linking Manila with Cebu and a number of other destinations within the Visayas. Other high-speed ferry services are: **Delta Cat** ( (32) 232-1356, **Negros Navigation** ( (32) 253-3831, **Supercats** ( (32) 95661, and **Waterjet** ( (32) 232-1356. **Aboitiz Shipping** ( (32) 253-3143 and **Escano Lines** ( (32) 77253 are also fairly reliable, if slower.

## MACTAN ISLAND

Connected by bridge to Cebu City, Mactan Island boasts several luxury resorts, dozens of small, locally-owned beach resorts and some well-patronized scuba diving centers.

You do not have to be an experienced diver to appreciate the beauty of many of the island's most spectacular and accessible dive sites. Mactan is a diving Mecca, and its sites are good for beginners. **Olango Island** is accessible by boat from Mactan, and gets high ratings from experienced divers for its underwater life. It is also rich in bird life.

### Where to Stay
EXPENSIVE
Many regard the **Shangri-La Mactan Island Resort** ( (32) 813-8888 FAX (32) 813-5499 WEB SITE www.shangri-la.com, Punta Engano Road, Mactan Island, as the finest the Philippines has to offer. It has five-star accommodation and facilities, a range of plush restaurants and bars, an excellent health club, interesting shops, all the conceivable amenities for business travelers, and beautifully-landscaped gardens leading down to a white sand beach. It is the newest, biggest and most luxurious of all the Mactan resort hotels and usually the hotel chosen by those who have come to do business in the nearby export zone. It caters to families with its "Mactan Gang" all-day childcare program.

**Plantation Bay** ( (32) 340-5900 FAX (32) 340-5988 WEB SITE www.plantationbay.com, Marigondon, Mactan Island, is the newest entrant, billing itself as the "penultimate tropical lagoon resort." It has a wide expanse of private land overlooking an undisturbed powdery beach, with 38 elegant native-style bungalow suites nestled around a lagoon. Each of its 188 rooms is furnished with four-poster beds, embroidered linen and indigenously crafted Filipino furniture, with

spacious private balconies. As well as all water sports, the resort offers evening cruises on its 18-m-long (60-foot) twin-deck boat. There is a luxurious freshwater pool with built-in whirlpools, as well as tennis courts, a miniature golf and a health spa.

The charming **Cebu White Sands Beach Resort** ( (32) 340-5960 FAX (32) 340-5969, Maribago, Mactan Island, retains a turn-of-the-twentieth century ambience, with an antique collection proudly displayed throughout the lobby and the rooms. Rooms are spacious, the pool and gardens are simply gorgeous. The small beach has a bar.

MID-RANGE
Moderately priced alternatives abound, with four-star hotels in both Cebu City and along the Mactan beach strip. In Mactan, **Cebu Beach Club** ( (32) 254-5570, Buyong, Lapu-Lapu City, is one of the most pleasant options, with its curved network of air-conditioned guest rooms, lagoon-style swimming pool (with Jacuzzi) and pleasant restaurant and beach bar. **Mar y Cielo Beach Resort** ( (32) 253-2232 FAX (32) 492-0128, Barrio Angasil, Mactan, is an elegant, comfortably mid-size resort with a tranquil setting, pleasant views and native-style air-conditioned bungalows, furnished Maranaw or Cebu style. Its central pavilion has three restaurants, which serve seafood, European and Japanese cuisine.

Small and personal the **Maribago Bluewater Beach Resort** ( (32) 492-0100 FAX (32) 492-0128, in Maribago, Mactan, has 40 grass-thatched bungalows set around a white beach with a lagoon-shaped pool. **Costabella Tropical Beach Resort** ( (32) 253-0828 FAX (32) 253-0565, Buyong, Mactan, is a comfortable, relaxed resort with a pleasant beach setting. **Tambuli Beach Villa and Club** ( (32) 232-4811 to 19, Mactan Island, is a branch of the Bohol Beach Club on Bohol Island and is comprised of rooms within the beach club and larger cottages within the Beach Villa, both on the longest stretch of beach of any of the resorts on this part of the island.

INEXPENSIVE
**Club Kon Tiki** ( (32) 492-3189 FAX (32) 340-9934, Maribago, Lapulapu City, caters to

Plantation Bay Hotel, on Mactan, Cebu.

divers and budget travelers. You'll get a basic room with peace and seclusion. The hotel is located on a cliff so there really isn't any beach here.

## Where to Eat

For the ultimate in Philippino and European cuisine on Mactan Island, the Shangri-La's Mactan Island Resort offers three restaurants and a coffee shop. Its **Cowrie Cove (** (32) 231-0288 is the best place around to sit under the stars and savor sizzling seafood. Fresh catches might include blue marlin, grouper, lobster, prawns, or squid. Roving guitarists add to the ambience. Also at the Shangri-La, **The Garden Patio** (same number) has no walls, only panels that slide back to take in the view of rolling lawns and the bougainvillea in full bloom. The menu is extensive, serving anything from sushi to freshly baked breads and pastas. Their homemade ice cream is a must! Both are expensive.

If you check in to one of Cebu's resorts other than the Shangri-La, you may find yourself somewhat entrenched. Sampling the restaurants and bars of resorts other than the one you're staying in can be made difficult by obstacles along the beach such as security guards, rock clusters and fences. With the exception of the Shangri-La Mactan, most of the restaurants and entertainment begin to wear thin after a day or two. In Mactan, it can be fun to take a taxi ride to the seafood market cafés that surround the monument in Punta Engano—where Magellan was slain by local chieftain Lapu Lapu in 1521. **Anton's** (no phone), on the pier beside the airport road junction, is also good (inexpensive).

## CEBU'S EAST COAST

Because Cebu Island has so many beaches, dive sites and some picturesque towns, hiring a car to explore is a good idea. The eastern coast has many beautiful sandy bays, and **Sogod**, a one-and-a-half-hour drive north from Cebu, has dramatic cliff scenery, caves and beautiful secluded bays as well as some pleasant places to stay.

The more luxurious resorts either on Mactan itself or dotted along the coast have well-equipped dive centers and qualified instructors. There are equally plenty of facilities available for riding Hobiecats, jet skiing, or windsurfing at most resorts.

If you rent a car or decide to take a tour to the southeast coast resort area of **Argao**, make sure you stop at **Carcar**, south of Cebu City, a little town which has a beautiful **Spanish baroque church** dating back to 1876, facing a plaza lined with Spanish **colonial mansions**. The countryside, too, is attractive in this more rural part of the island. On the way, **Naga** is worth a stop to see its main church made out of coral and limestone and festooned with carved angels and gargoyles.

## Where to Stay

If you're looking for peaceful luxury or simply peace, there are several resorts a few hours' drive from Cebu City and Mactan. The most exclusive and attractive of these is in Culumboyan near Sogod. The **Alegre Beach Resort (** (32) 254-9800 or (32) 231-1198 FAX (32) 243-4345 is an upmarket (and expensive) resort run by the same group that runs the Cebu Plaza, located a 90-minute drive north from Cebu. It is perched on a dramatic cliff overlooking two white sandy beaches, with luxurious cabanas set amidst well-landscaped gardens. The Alegre has good tennis courts and a pleasant swimming pool for those wary of swimming in the sea. Also in the Sogod area, the inexpensive **Cebu Club Pacific**

( (32) 212291 FAX (32) 231-4621 is a good base for exploring the surrounding beaches.

In Dalaguete, a two-hour drive south of Cebu, the **Argao Beach Resort** ( (32) 72620 MA-NILA (2) 522-2301, set on landscaped rolling grounds overlooking Cebu Strait, is a good base for watersports fans. It has a good diving center and instruction for would-be divers and windsurfers, as well as Hobiecats and paddleboats for rent. The resort has a 15-m (49-foot) glass-bottom boat that allows you to see Camay Reef. Boat trips for diving and island hopping are regularly scheduled.

## MOALBOAL

On the southwestern side of Cebu, the small fishing village of **Moalboal** attracts serious divers with its amazing variety of sites, with coral gardens, caves, wide variety and shoals of fish and sea snakes. Moalboal is probably one of the most fascinating diving destinations in all of the archipelago, and the area is filled with hiking opportunities to beautiful waterfalls. Horseback riding in the countryside and the friendly faces of the local villagers add to its charm.

From Moalboal you can access sites on **Pescador** and **Badian** islands, with their rich and colorful coral formations.

### What to See and Do

Visitors come to Moalboal for the excellent diving and adventure sports possibilities, as the beaches were washed away about 10 years ago when a violent typhoon swept in.

Divers come specifically for the opportunity to explore Pescador Island. Some say it's the best site they've ever seen. Without a doubt it is quite impressive. An enormous mountain of coral balloons from the sea floor and the area is rich in marine life, including sharks. Another excellent dive is the underwater mountain of coral found at Sunken Island. Although not as dramatic as Pescador Island, this is for more advanced divers, as the strong currents make navigation tricky. The House Reef is close and is where divers prefer night diving, while White Beach is more challenging — with caves, overhangs, and wall dives that plummet to impressive depths.

If diving isn't part of your plan, horse trekking, river and rock climbing, volcano trekking, mountain biking, canoeing, and sailing can all be arranged through **Planet Action Adventure** ( (32) 474-0024, located on Panagsama Beach. Trips range from easy half-day activities to extended hardcore challenges, and can be custom-tailored to fit your level of adventure. You can also rent mountain bikes for about US$5 a day to discover the island independently.

### Where to Stay and Eat

The small, bungalows close to the sea here are popular with budget travelers. **Sunshine Pensione House** ( (918) 773-3021, **Quo Vadis Beach Resort** ( (918) 770-8684 or (918) 771-1853, and **Hannah's Place** ( (918) 771-3439 offer modest nipa-hut style lodging with hot water and air-conditioning along Moalboal's main strip. **Cabana Resort** ( (918) 770-7599 is the closest thing you will get to a real hotel here. It has a modest beach as well.

For such a small town, Moalboal offers a surprising variety of eats. **Love's Bar and Restaurant**, at the far south end of the beach, is a cozy place to eat local cuisine. They can also organize picnic lunches and barbecues for day trips to White Beach or Kawasan Falls. **Visaya Bar and Pizza House** serves Swiss and German food and pizza, while **The Last Filling Station**, in the middle of the beach, is known for pita sandwiches, macrobiotic selections and great people-watching.

For more luxurious accommodation, **Badian Island Beach Club** ( (32) 253-6364 or (32) 253-6452 FAX (32) 263-3385, Badian Island, is an upmarket, well-run, and beautifully-landscaped resort perfect for a peaceful island getaway. It's a 10-minute boat ride from Badian town, which is eight kilometers (five miles) south of Moalboal. Nearer to Badian town, **Cebu Green Island Club** ( (32) 95-935 FAX (32) 231-1269, Lambug, Badian, Cebu, is a moderately priced resort that also has a golf course within its grounds.

### How to Get There

A few air-conditioned buses leave for Moalboal from the South Bus Terminal in Cebu City every day. The trip takes three hours and costs just over US$1. Your other option is to arrange private transport from your resort or hotel in Cebu City or Mactan Island.

Roadside foodstall, in the heart of Cebu.

# BOHOL

Southeast of Cebu, across the Tanon Strait, the rounded island of Bohol is notable for strange geological formations and lush, tropical forests, rich in exotic flora and fauna.

Bohol is a pleasant place to stay for a day or two, to enjoy the atmosphere of its small coastal towns, Antillan mansions and colonial churches. Like Cebu, there are a variety of resorts here, most notable is the Bohol Beach Club, and many good dive spots.

Bohol is a good base for visiting the spectacular marine sanctuaries and coral reefs around the smattering of beautiful islands that dot the Cebu Strait and the Bohol Sea and Camotes seas: the best known is Panglao Island. Whales and dolphins are frequently sighted in these waters, while in the deeps are large manta rays and hammerhead sharks.

The rare tarsier monkey is a native of Bohol; reputedly the world's smallest primate, it can fit into the palm of a human hand. Flying lemurs, the size of large house cats, are another endemic species on Bohol, although their numbers too have been decreasing at a worrying rate as their natural habitat is destroyed to develop villages and tourist complexes on the island. Lemurs are also hunted down for native hotpots.

Butterflies are their most exuberant in Bohol from November to May, which is when scores of enthusiastic Japanese butterfly hunters have been known to descend on the island.

## GENERAL INFORMATION

There is no tourism office in Bohol's capital city of Tagbilaran, but **Bohol Travel and Tours** ( (38) 411-3840 or **Sunshine Travel and Tours** (no phone) on Panglao Island can arrange island tours and handle ticket bookings, visa information, and accommodation.

For **emergencies**, dial ( 166 for police and ( (32) 340-5643 for a rescue helicopter. Camp Lapu-Lapu in Cebu City ( (32) 310709 has a decompression chamber. Ramiro Hospital ( (38) 411-3515 and Tagbilaran Community Hospital ( (38) 411-3324 are small but have decent facilities; otherwise, Cebu City is the best bet for any health emergencies.

Tagbileran is home to many **cybercafés**, especially around Divine Word College on C. Galleres Street. B&J Internet Café, and nearby AC Goldchips Internet and Met Internet are all open 24-hours and are very cheap, starting as low as P20 per hour of use.

## WHAT TO SEE AND DO

Bohol is most famous for its **Chocolate Hills** — exactly 1,268 perfectly shaped mounds (one wonders who bothered to count them all) that undulate throughout the townships of **Carmen**, **Batuan** and **Sagbayan** in the center of the island. These hills, which range in height from 40 m (131 feet) to 120 m (394 feet), derive their name from the effect each summer, when the sun burnishes the tussock grasses a dark brown. They are at their most chocolaty between February and May and are green after July, when the monsoons keep them lushly carpeted. There are all sorts of local legends about the phenomenon. Scientific speculation has it that the hills are formed by buckling limestone caverns beneath the earth's surface, or that as a massive volcano self-destructed, it spat huge balls of stone, which were then covered in limestone and lifted up from the ocean bed to assume their present abode. Whatever their origin, the Chocolate Hills of Bohol are one of the region's great wonders. You can either get there by guided tour from Tagbilaran or rent a car. The island's highlights are easily seen in a day or two.

Bohol's sleepy capital, **Tagbilaran**, has both a Hispanic and a Moorish air with its Jesuit churches and colonial stone and tile-roofed mansions. Tagbilaran's **city market** is interesting for its variety of woven mats, winnowing baskets, buri hats and handicrafts made from capiz and coconut shells. The market is also a good place to find exotic shells themselves. The **Bohol Provincial Museum** has a dusty grandeur. Once the mansion of Carlos P. Garcia, a former president of the Philippines, it has been turned into a showcase for ethnic relics, papers and political memorabilia.

In **Bool Barrio**, a couple of kilometers south of the city center, a commemorative marker records the famous "blood compact" that took place here. It was here that Spanish

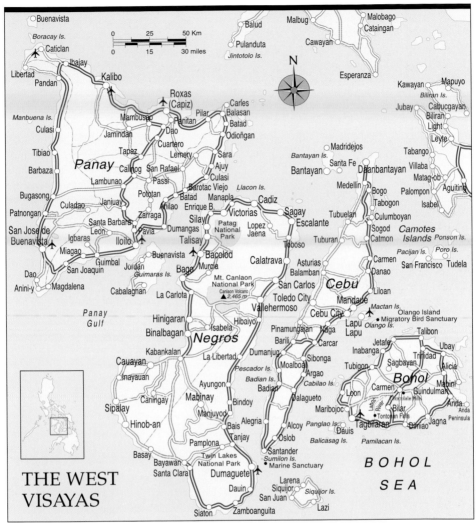

THE WEST
VISAYAS

conquistador Miguel Lopez de Legaspi and the island's chief, Sikatuna, drew their own blood, mixed it with wine, and drank it, sealing a pact of peace between their people. Each June, this place becomes the scene of a colorful re-enactment of the blood compact ceremony during the Sandugo, or "One Blood," Festival.

Along the main road out to the Chocolate Hills along the southeast coast, **Baclayon Church**, six kilometers (three and three quarter miles) away from the city center, was built in 1595, and is the oldest stone church in the Philippines. There are faint remnants of the gold-leaf work on the carvings adorning the central and side altars, which house antique *santos*. The original

ivory faces were stolen in the 1970s. An adjacent **convent** has a small museum with some Spanish icons, native religious art and ecclesiastical garments, as well as librettos of church music printed in Latin on animal skin. You'll need to rouse the priest to get permission to enter. The town of Baclayon itself is interesting, too, for its taste of rural island life.

The manmade forest at **Bilar** shows off a wide variety of exotic plants, and offers a chance to glimpse the remarkable tarsier monkey, a shy nocturnal creature which does not often survive in captivity. Sadly, most of those captured by poachers in the pet trade die, and pitiful stuffed tarsiers seem to be a popular commodity.

From Tagbilaran, it's a short detour to the nearby town of **Maribojoc**. The **Punta Cruz Watchtower**, with its adjacent cross stills, stands guard over the bay, just as when it was used by the Spanish to watch out for Muslim pirates.

An idyllic way to spend a sunny afternoon in Bohol is to float down the winding **Laboc River** to **Busay Falls**, watching the scenery drift by, hearing the sound, and breathing in the scent of the jungle. The Bohol Beach Club (see WHERE TO STAY AND EAT, below) organizes these river safaris.

Along the eastern coast of Bohol, the region around the **Anda Peninsula** is unspoiled and has some breathtaking coves to explore. This area remains almost entirely undeveloped. Archaeological finds around in this region date the earliest human remains here to around 10,000 BC, and many dugout molave wood coffins have been found, some decorated with reptile heads or flattened skulls in accordance with ancient burial practices.

The recently opened well-stocked bar at **Club Zone** on C. Gallares Street draws a hip crowd. **Melanie's Cocktail and Music Lounge** is the place to come to sing the night away.

### Excursions

**Hinagdanan Cave**, a 20-minute ride by bus or jeepney, is an eerie underworld of stalactites and stalagmites that form sculptures in an underground pool, lit by natural skylights.

Although on the face of it **Dauis Church** seems unremarkable, it has certain following within the Philippines for the supposedly restorative powers of its natural spring, which bubbles up from under the main altar.

The largest island near Bohol, located off its southwestern tip near Tagbilaran, **Panglao Island** has been recently singled out for special priority in newly conservation-minded government tourism plans. It's a quaint, quiet, safe beach destination that affords an opportunity to see true Filipino life in the nearby villages. Alona Beach is the place to stay on the island, with its long stretches of white sand and world-class diving opportunities around the many surrounding islands. Alona beach has yet to be overrun with tourists and shooter bars, and it's probably the loveliest beach around after Boracay.

The surrounding islands of **Balicasag** and **Pamilacan** — as well as **Cabilao** and **Pangangan** farther south — are justifiably sought-after destinations by divers, although simply enjoying their natural beauty is wonderful also. Balicasag Island, only 45 minutes by pumpboat from Alona Beach, is probably the best for scuba diving. The island is a national park, and its surrounding waters are declared a fish sanctuary. It's a great day trip: rent a boat for about US$25 for the day, catch some fish, and have a picnic on the island. Any of the resorts can arrange boat rental.

## WHERE TO STAY AND EAT

### Mid-range

**Alona Kew White Beach Resort** ( (912) 516-2904 on Panglao Island is the nicest of the native-style cottages that populate the beach here. It is situated in the heart of everything, and is the only resort that actually has beach furniture for guests' use. Also on Alona Beach, but away from the main drag, **Kalipayan Beach Resort** ( (38) 411-3060 is a newly opened bed and breakfast which also has a great cliff-side pool. A gem just waiting to be discovered is **Jul Resort** ( (38) 411-4999 located about 15 minutes from Alona Beach, away from the huddle of the resorts. Everything about this resort says serenity. The main house is perfect for large groups, with its kitchen, stereo system, rustic charm, and five spacious bedrooms. The cottages are all furnished in beautiful antiques. **Balicasag Dive Resort** ( (912) 516-2675, Balicasag Island, is home to some of the best reefs in Bohol, and the resort attracts serious divers. Accommodations are comfortable but basic.

Considered one of the best resorts on Bohol, **Bohol Beach Club** ( (38) 411-5222 or ( MANILA (2) 522-2301 FAX (2) 522-2304, Suite 1401, Victoria Building, United Nations

**Pyramid Resort, Alonaville Beach Resort,** and **Aquatica Resort** all charge less than US$20 for a cottage, and provide mosquito nets. **Bohol Divers Lodge** offers a variety of rooms, some air-conditioned, and some simpler rooms with common bath. It's a good place to meet other divers. The charming **Alona Tropical** offers perfect location and accommodations for a budget price. It's at the far north end of the beach, where it's quiet and less crowded, and the food here is the best on the beach. Behind Kalipayan Beach Resort, **TGH Casa Nova Garden** has a pool

Avenue, Ermita, Manila, is a sister property of the Tambuli Beach Club in Cebu and is accessible by a 20-minute transfer from Tagbilaran. It has the advantage of being far more private, with pleasantly furnished, native-style bungalows with fans and private verandahs. A pool, Jacuzzi and saunas, a tennis court and a range of water sports facilities make up the resort complex. The island itself is pretty, with a three-kilometer (two-mile) ring of sand.

### Inexpensive

Along Alona Beach, numerous native-style resorts offer comfortable, convenient cottages, and most have restaurants. Don't expect hot water, air-conditioning, or phones though.

and an overgrown tennis court. Rooms are basic but cozy here, and it's off the main drag, for peace and quiet — although it is surrounded by chickens and goats.

Practically every dining option along Alona Beach is inexpensive. All the restaurants dish up pretty good seafood dishes as well as local cuisine. With its open air bamboo pavilion, **Alona Kew** is an excellent place to sit and watch the beach and surf. Their specialties are sizzling platters — shrimp or squid to tenderloin tips. **Bohol Divers Lodge** imports Australian beef, while the nearby **Flying Dog** and **Kamilag** offer German and Italian cuisine — not to mention a funky

Living up to their name, the ever-changing brown hues of the Chocolate Hills.

atmosphere. A favorite among tourists and locals alike is **Alona Tropical**. The spot is gorgeous — on the southern end of Alona beach with the surf crashing literally at the door of the open-air cabana restaurant. Their fruit shakes are the best around and the popularity of their food is obvious, with crowds forming after 7 PM.

## How to Get There

Asian Spirit has flights leaving Tuesdays, Thursdays, Saturdays and Sundays from

**WG&A Superferry** ( (2) 894-3211 makes trips from Manila to Bohol twice a week for less than US$20. The trip takes 26 hours.

## NEGROS

Across the Guimaras Strait from Cebu is the lushly beautiful island of Negros, with its cloud-wreathed purple mountains, fertile forests and volcanoes, hot springs and paradisiacal beaches. Yet, more than any other island, Negros symbolizes the feudal and economic rifts and struggles that have

Manila to Tagbilaran City. The flight takes one hour and 55 minutes. Tricycles from the airport to Alona Beach on Panglao Island should cost no more than US$5 for the ride. Otherwise, you can flag down an air-conditioned taxi that can take you the short distance to Panglao Island.

Another option is to fly into Cebu City, where there are more airline and flight times to choose from. Air Philippines, Cebu Pacific and Philippine Airlines all have direct daily flights. You can take a taxi to the pier for the two-hour ferry to Bohol. The **Supercat** ( (32) 232-3455 is the fastest and most reputable of the ferries. The **Bullet Express** ( (32) 255-1384 departs numerous times a day as well, for the same price.

plagued the Philippines. The fourth-largest island in the archipelago (some 215 km or 133 miles in length) most of the sugar plantations in the Philippines are concentrated on Negros. Once one of the richest islands in the archipelago, until the 1980s collapse of world sugar prices, it has now become one of the poorest. The plummeting price of sugar plunged the future of some two million migrant workers on the island into turmoil. It has been calculated that five million Filipinos were affected adversely, albeit sometimes indirectly, by the crash. Worst hit were the 300,000 sugar workers and their families. Their existence was perilous at the best of times, but they were suddenly exposed to destitution and starvation on such a scale as to put Negros on the world poverty map and send economic shockwaves throughout the Philippines.

Until the nineteenth century, Negros was almost uninhabited, but by 1893 it had become an ant-like hive of industry, devoted almost entirely to sugar production; with 274 steam-operated sugar mills surrounded by hundreds of thousands of hectares of sugarcane fields to supply them and an enormous migrant worker population, most of whom had swarmed from outlying islands in search of wages. In response to the island's

economic suffering, Negros has also witnessed a communist insurgency, in a way that has been described both on Negros and throughout parts of the Philippines as *ningas cogon* (literally, "sudden brushfire"). Turbulence is traditional here.

In the Spanish-style churches, tropical expanses of cane, violently beautiful sunsets, and resplendent sumptuous *haciendas* — airy ranch houses on stately plantation estates — there are strong echoes in Negros of the American antebellum South. In some settings, you half expect to see a Filipina version of Scarlett O'Hara calling out for her maid from a polished, antique-filled mansion. The Spanish called the island after its predominantly Negrito population.

*Cebu and the Visayas*

Steam and smoke still belch out from the chimneys of the **Victorias Milling Company**, one of the largest sugar refineries in the world. Antique steam engines still ply the tracks along with their modern brethren, carrying endless loads of sugar cane from the fields to the mills. Yet now Negros both hopes and actively anticipates that its future may improve with the increase of another and new industry — tourism, as the many recently constructed hotels and facilities attest. With its location between Cebu and Panay, the island of Negros — both Occidental and Oriental — makes a perfect stopover if you have time to spend in the region.

## BACOLOD

Surrounded by plantations, Bacolod — capital of Negros Occidental — exudes all the peculiarities of a formerly feudal society. A relatively modern city, it has its share of wealthy landowners' mansions and elaborate churches. Bacolod is interesting to pass through, especially during the **Masskara Festival** in October, but rather than stay in overnight, opt for the island's beach resorts. In recent years, Bacolod has been striving to become the convention capital of the Philippines.

### General Information
The **Department of Tourism** office ( (34) 29021 FAX (34) 433-2853 is located at the Bacolod Seawall.

### What to See and Do
Start your explorations in the **Plaza**, which draws multitudes each Sunday and on fiesta days. It is flanked by the **San Sebastian Cathedral**, built in 1882. Aside from some fine regional government buildings and city mansions, try to see some of Bacolod's antique collections, often private museums that are family run. The **Torres Antique Collection**, near the Airport Subdivision, with its Ming dynasty porcelain and Hispanic and native santos is worth seeing, as is the **Vega Antique Collection** at No. 4, 19th Street, with

OPPOSITE: Sunlight filters through the canopy of trees in a Bohol rainforest. ABOVE: In Baclayon harbor, in front of the Philippines' oldest stone church, a small flotilla of bright *bancas*.

its fine collection of wooden and ivory votive statues, Indochinese furniture and pottery and the **Buglas Collection** on Lizares Avenue. In **Santa Clara**, near Bangao Wharf, is a little chapel with an extraordinary mosaic mural fashioned from thousands upon thousands of shells. You may need to book your visit in advance.

In Bacolod's **markets**, look for the sugar-laden delicacies Negros is famous for: *dulce gatas* (sweetened carabao milk), *pinsasugbo* (sticky, sugar-coated banana) and *pi-aya* (a flaky, sugar-filled pancake).

Bacolod is known throughout the Philippines for its fine ceramics and hand-painted porcelain, but you'll also see curious creations of colorful artificial flowers made out of wood shavings. Places to shop include **Philippine Antiques and Artwares** on Mandalagan Street, **Goldenfield Commercial Complex** and **Recuerdos de Bacoclod** on Rizal Street near the Plaza and **Samodal Woodshave Shop** on Second Street, Banahaw, in Villamonte.

Tours of the **Victorias Milling Company** are given throughout the day. You can take the Rainbow minibus from Bacolod which makes the 34-km (21-mile) trip out to the town of Victorias, then catch a jeepney to the mill compound, which functions as a mini-township. Like exploring the shipyards of Poland, there is a certain political frisson to visiting the mills in Negros. The **Saint Joseph the Worker Chapel**, built in 1948, has on display a remarkable mosaic made of broken beer and soft drink bottles by the American artist Ade de Bethune, which featured in a *Life* magazine report. It depicts Christ as a brown-skinned Filipino in native dress, and for this the chapel is more commonly known as the "Chapel of the Angry Christ."

As you drive out to Victorias, stop by at **Silay**, which lies 18 km (11 miles) north of Bacolod. It is a pretty coastal city of languid plantation estates and Spanish-era mansions quietly moldering away like that of Dickens' Miss Haversham. Make sure you stop to see **Hofilena Art Collection**, 5 de Noviembre Street, which has an eclectic and serious collection of painting. It also houses the country's oldest printmaking workshop.

**Patag**, 25 km (16 miles) inland from Silay, is notable as the last Japanese stronghold in World War II, and has a memorial marker.

### Excursions from Bacolod

Endowed with bubbling sulfur springs, **Mambucal** is a popular Negros beauty spot, yet it remains a tranquil place to visit, an hour's drive from Bacolod. The **Mambucal Mountain Resort** is a base for exploring the area's hot springs and mountain trails. Within the region, there are some dramatic climbing and walking trails in and around **Mount Canlaon** (also known as Canloan Volcano), with challenging climbs that encounter a white sand bank called Marghaha Valley, its twin craters rising 2,465 m (8,087 feet) above sea level. The bridge between the two craters of Balinsayao and Danao draws speculating vulcanologists who monitor the volcano's geological pulse.

## Where to Stay and Eat

**Bacolod Convention Plaza Hotel** ( (34) 434-4551 FAX (34) 433-3757, Magsaysay Avenue, is the best hotel in Negros, designed to soothe away the cares of weary conference goers. Amenities include a fine swimming pool and the best restaurant in town. **L'Fisher Hotel** ( (34) 433-3731 FAX (34) 433-0951, at the corner of 14th and Lacson streets, is a secluded hotel in the northern part of town, with attractively furnished, comfortable rooms that have most modern conveniences. Near the airport, **Goldenfield Garden Hotel** ( (34) 433-3111 FAX (34) 433-1234, Goldenfield Complex, is noted by locals for its good swimming pool and lively disco. All three are moderately priced.

*Cebu and the Visayas*

**Sugarland Hotel** ( (34) 22462, San Juan Street, is popular for its inexpensive bar and café, and the **Sea Breeze Hotel** ( (34) 24571 is a friendly if basic place to stay.

## ILOCOON ISLAND

At the northern tip of Negros, shaped like a gibbous moon, Ilocoon Island is a haven for snorkeling and diving, rich in marine life and coral reefs, and strewn with exotic shells on its sands. Villagers will only know it by its colloquial name of "Lakawon," so be sure to ask about it using this name. Ilocoon is a lovely place to visit, and it's interesting as well to see the villages en route.

Thatched village home on Panglao Beach, Bohol.

## DUMAGUETE

The provincial capital of Negros Oriental, Dumaguete draws divers for the multitude of magnificent dive sites in its surrounding clear blue waters. The main destinations to seek out from here, rather than spending much time in the town, are **Apo Island**, **Sumilon Marine Park** and **Siquijor Island**.

### General Information

**JMC International Travel and Tours** ( (2) 873109 FAX (2) 817-5556, Santa Monica Beach Resort, Banilad, Dumaguete, and **Magnum Marine Corporation** ( (2) 813-1696 FAX (2) 818-5043, South Sea Hotel, Bantayan, can advise on diving trips.

The **City Tourism Office** ( (35) 225-0549 is in the City Hall.

### What to See and Do

In Dumaguete, both **Silliman University** and the university's **Anthropological Museum** are worth a stroll through, especially the latter for its painstaking collection gathered from throughout the province and beyond in archaeological digs, with such oddities as well-preserved human bones and relics, limestone burial jars, witchcraft accoutrements and ancient Chinese pottery shards. Silliman University was the first private American Protestant university in the Philippines and was built in 1901. It is known for its conservation-minded marine and ornithological research and programs. Within its extensive grounds is also a bird sanctuary.

If mountain trekking is on your list, then definitely head to **Mount Talinis**, where you can find verdant forests and lakes and rare wildlife such as the Philippine spotted deer. At 1,800 m (5,905 feet), tempatures run on the cool side, which is a nice reprieve from the intense heat.

On the slopes of Mount Talinis, **Casaroro Falls** plunges directly into a bathing basin. Another good place for a swim is **Banica Picnic Park** in the picturesque town of Valencia, where a river feeds two swimming pools.

### Apo Island

Located about five kilometers (three miles) off the southeast coast of Negros Island, Apo Island was declared a marine sanctuary to protect its unusual coral formations and fish. Apo Island is used as an offshore study center by the Silliman University. It is rated as one of the best dive sites in the country. It is popularly known as "Clown Fish City" with fabulous underwater gardens that vary from sloping sand with hidden springs to drop-offs with pelagic and schooling jacks. It's also popular for its drift dives at Mamsa Point, where the fierce current makes you feel like you are flying underwater. The island itself is a natural wonder — with its wide and vast rock formations that are popular with foreign and local rock climbers.

### Sumilon Island

With its magnificent marine life, Sumilon Island is a valuable laboratory base and scientific observation post for Philippine and visiting marine biologists. Developed as a marine sanctuary, largely through the efforts of Silliman University, Sumilon Island later became the source of much disputation between local fishermen, unwilling to give up their usual practices and some unscrupulous dive operators.

Despite local tensions, the **Sumilon Island Marine Sanctuary** has lovely beaches and excellent snorkeling and diving. Offshore, dolphins and whales are frequently sighted.

### Where to Stay

The small, inexpensive, **Santa Monica Beach Resort** ( (34) 3441, Banilad, four kilometers (two and a half miles) south of Dumaguete, is popular with divers.

### How to Get There

Philippine Airlines, Cebu Pacific and Air Philippines have daily flights to both Bacolod and Dumaguete from Manila (about one hour) and Cebu (about 30 minutes).

Cebu Pacific and Mindanao Express have flights from Cebu on various days of the week. Check with the airlines to confirm their schedules.

By boat, Negros has regular links with Manila and the main ports of all the neighboring islands — Bohol, Panay, Guimaras, Cebu, Mindanao and Siquijor. The super fast and luxurious *Saint Michael* ferry plies between Iloilo and Bacolod twice each day except Sunday. There are also direct Cebu–Bacolod buses that traverse the route in one day, a rather grueling experience.

Apo Island is 10 km (six miles) south of Dumaguete and Sumilon Island Marine Sanctuary is about 12 km (eight miles) northeast of Dumaguete. Both are reached by rented *banca*.

## SIQUIJOR ISLAND

Lightning laced the sky in white fire. The earth wailed in that painful, joyous sound of new life. The ground shuddered, the seas raged. The churning waters parted and from ocean's womb was birthed an island of rock and fire. Thus did, according to legend, the island of Siquijor emerge from the sea. The Spaniards called it Isla del Fuego, "the island of fire," referring to the eerie glow the island gave off as galleons passed in the night. Mystery permeates Siquijor Island, renowned as a destination for those in search of supernatural assistance. Filipinos will warn you of strange curses, wanton witches, macabre practices and unexplained mystic events that occur on this island.

Fewer than 100,000 people live on the island, most eking out a rustic existence that is deeply entwined with voodoo-like rituals. The donning of *anting-anting*, or amulets supposedly invested with specified powers, enjoys a special significance here.

It is a fascinating island to visit. The hills of Siquijor conceal caves — dark, ominous, and honeycombed with unknown passages. Grim, black cliffs made of jagged, craggy surfaces look suspiciously like underwater coral reefs. Fossilized mussels, snails and other undersea creatures have been found in the central highlands, lending credence to the stories that the island once lay beneath the waves.

### What to See and Do

The main towns of Siquijor are **Larena**, the sleepy port where ferries dock, the capital **Siquijor**, the mountainous hamlet of **San Antonio** and **Lazi**, a rustic wharf side settlement where the main entertainment is cock fighting. San Antonio is the epicenter of the archipelago's faith-healing community, which comes to life during Holy Week, when alleys

are strewn with dried herbs, strange wafts of noxious-smelling brews permeate the air, and healing rites are conducted behind closed doors. The special herbs and plants they use are found in the mountains surrounding San Antonio. On the southwestern side of the island, **Paliton Beach**, near **San Juan**, is one of the most attractive beaches, with a resort conveniently located on it.

The diving is spectacular here as well. It varies from wall drop-offs to beautiful gentle sloping terraces. Jacks, butterfly fish, trigger fish, grouper, spade fish, barracuda, lion fish, turtles and black tip sharks are found in the waters and there is even a Japanese ship, sunk in 1945, which lies under about 30 m (98 feet) of water.

### Where to Stay and Eat

Don't expect fine accommodation, varied cuisine, or phones here. And some visitors feel that the locals have less than a welcoming attitude. Nevertheless, **Larena** offers some opportunities for shelter and sustenance, with small guest houses and eating houses that open their doors when the ferries dock. The **Larena Pension House** and **Luisa and Son's Lodge** are both inexpensive and friendly places to stay.

Sandugan Beach, only six kilometers (three and three quarter miles) northeast of Larena, is a long, peaceful beach with decent sand, excellent diving, and almost a dozen inexpensively priced resorts. The new **Kiwi Dive Resort** ( (912) 504-0596 FAX (35) 424-0534 provides self-contained cottages right at the water's edge. There is also a full restaurant. **Islander's Paradise Beach** ( (918) 775-2384 at Sandugan, run by an Englishman and his Filipina wife, has a good restaurant, while the **Hidden Paradise** at Bitaog is run by an irrepressible hotelier who is also a tricycle driver and can escort you around the island for a reasonable fee. Booking is pot luck since — as with many of the more remote islands in the Philippines — telephones are scarce on Siquijor.

Paliton Beach, near San Juan, is another fine beach with a few simple bungalows such as **Sunset Beach Resort** and **Paliton Beach Resort**. Both have rooms for less than US$10. Two kilometers (one and a quarter miles) south of San Juan in Tubod you'll find the

**San Juan Coco Grove Beach Resort** with swimming pool, restaurant, jeepney rentals, and air-conditioned rooms with "private marble bath."

### How to Get There
Pacific Airways flies every Monday and Thursday from Dumaguete to Siquijor. The 15-minute flight costs P250-300. The same airline flies from Dipolog on Mindanao to Siquijor on Wednesdays, though this service is often cancelled during the low season months. The 30-minute flight costs P550-600.

The island is reached via fast ferry from Dumaguete to Larena. A Delta Line fast ferry leaves Dumaguete many times daily and takes 45 minutes to reach Larena on Siquijor. Large outriggers are only recommended when the seas are calm, they depart Dumaguete daily and take just over two hours to reach Tambisan at the western tip of Siquijor.

Supercat and Delta ferries leave for Larena from Cebu City's Pier 4 daily. The **MV Dona Cristina** can be boarded in Cebu every Saturday, but takes an uncomfortable 24 hours to reach Siquijor, due to its stop in Iligan in northern Mindanao.

## PANAY

Panay is one of the economically developed islands of the archipelago. This is mainly because of political events at the middle of the nineteenth century, when the British forced Spain to open the Philippines to the world market. Thereafter, scotch whiskey capitalist Nicolas Loney brought modern agribusiness to Panay and Negros with the installation of sugar plantations.

Panay is famous not only for its sugar production but for its beautiful beaches. Best known is Boracay, which has experienced a surge in tourism over the last two decades since its discovery by wandering backpackers seeking a slice of the paradise pie.

Kalibo, the city near Boracay, was the entry point of an earlier foreign invasion too. It was there, in 1214, that a big group of Bornean Malays landed to settle and stay. Panay, at that time, was widely populated by Negritos. The Bornean Malays, although superior fighters and better armed than the Negritos, chose not to take the island by force

but rather to buy it from the native inhabitants. A contract was made between Datu (chieftain) Puti of the Borneans and the Negritos' chief Marikudo.

As a concession to the Negritos, who were probably fleeced in the deal, the new Malay settlers in subsequent fiestas blackened their skin with coal to look more like the Negritos, or *Ati*, as they name themselves. In Panay, the tradition of with blackening of the skin to look like the Ati during fiestas is still very much alive today — with the Ati-Atihan festivities in Kalibo as the best example.

Panay has four provinces: Iloilo, Aklan, Antique and Capiz.

## ILOILO

One of the country's loveliest Spanish colonial settlements, Iloilo is a charming place with white stone, sixteenth-century churches, aristocratic ancestral mansions, plentiful gardens, unspoiled beaches and bustling markets. If you choose a more elaborate route through the Visayas and want to see some of its sleepy backwaters, this is a good place to start. From here, you can explore the rest of Panay, visit the offshore islands of Guimaras and Sicogon, idle away time at the nearby resort of Isla Naburot and travel to Caticlan bound for Boracay. From Iloilo, flights leave for regional islands.

## General Information
The **Department of Tourism** Office ( (33) 75411 or (33) 78874 FAX (33) 50245 is within the Western Visayas Tourism Center, Capitol Ground, Bonifacio Drive, Iloilo.

## What to See and Do
The **Miag-ao Church**, declared a World Heritage Site by UNESCO, is the centerpiece of Iloilo's architectural tradition. Built

Guimaras Island, a scarcely damaged array of Victorian china and bottles of port wine and Glasgwegian beer.

There are a number of rather unusual churches in Iloilo province; many are musty and quietly redolent of an impassioned Catholicism left behind by the departing Spaniards. The Gothic-Renaissance-style **Molo Church**, just outside Iliolo city, dates from the 1800s and was built in solid coral. The **Jaro Church** is an impressive Gothic-style cathedral and the red-stone Renaissance-style **Pavia Church**, 13 km (eight miles)

in 1786, the Spanish colonial church has an unusual façade that bursts with botanical motifs in carved naive-style motifs that bear a likeness to Aztec designs. Its unconventional shape and pillared columns give it a playful, unique charm. The fascinating **Museo Iloilo** should not be missed. It is a well-presented repository of prehistoric artifacts dug up from Panay burial grounds and offers a detailed impression of the early lives of the island's tribes. Among its exhibits are gold-leaf death masks, antique seashell jewelry and other decorative ornaments worn by Panay islanders. The museum also displays some of the recovered treasure from a nineteenth-century British cargo ship that was wrecked off

northwest of Iloilo City has unusual window frames made of coral pieces. In San Joaquin, 53 km (32 miles) southwest of Iloilo city proper, the **San Joaquin Church**, built in 1869, sports a bas-relief of the historic battle between Spanish Christians and Moors of Morocco in Tetuan in 1859, while the **Cabatuan Cemetery**, its entrance flanked by Gothic-style gates and chapel, is filled with elaborate ancestral tombs and graves dating from 1875. Six kilometers (three and three quarter miles) west of Iloilo, **Arevalo** has some fine nineteenth-century mansions.

OPPOSITE and ABOVE: Party time during the annual Ati-Atihan Festival held each January in Kalibo, Aklan Province, on Panay Island.

In the main **markets**, look for the unique fabrics from this region, *piña* and *jusi*, made from pineapple and banana fibers and then hand-embroidered and fashioned into Filipino clothes, such as the *barong tagalog*. It's interesting to browse for handicrafts, *nata de coco* or native-made soap and baskets.

### Where to Stay

The best place to stay if you are making an overnight stay in Iloilo City is the **Sarabia Manor Hotel and Convention Center** ( (33) 335-1021 FAX (33) 337-9127 on General Luna Street. It's located outside of the city center and has an Olympic-size pool, seven restaurants, and the BASE Discotheque. Also, **La Fiesta Hotel** ( (33) 338-0044 FAX (33) 79508, M. H. del Pilar Street, Molo District, with its wrought-iron banisters that spiral all the way up the three-story inn, is spacious and comfortable.

### How to Get There

Air Philippines, Cebu Pacific, and Philippine Airlines have daily flights to Iloilo from Manila and Cebu.

Ferry services ply between Iloilo and Bacolod on Negros. Contact WG&A Ferries (see TRAVELERS' TIPS, page 247) to check their schedule from Manila to link with Visayan destinations. Within Panay, a range of jeepneys, buses and bus coaches make connections daily between Caticlan and San José de Buenavista in Antique province and Roxas in Capiz province, but be prepared for a long and bumpy trip.

## GUIMARAS ISLAND

Located 15 minutes from Iloilo, this pretty island offers rich marine life and many beaches, waterfalls, and springs.

Guimaras Island's **Tiniguiban Puland Payasan Beach** will appeal to divers with its quantities of rare red shrimps that breed in a nearby lake and emerge at high tide.

On Good Friday, hundreds of devotees clamber through the **Catilaran Cave**—a half-kilometer-long (one-third-mile) cave-tunnel — reciting Latin prayers, hopeful that this will ensure protection from evil spirits. Priceless Ming jars have been unearthed here. The curious summer house known as the **Roca**

**Encantada** is perched on a promontory overlooking the Guimaras Strait. It was built by the distinguished Lopez clan.

### Where to Stay

Most of the accommodation on Guimaras Island is in the moderate price range.

Run by the Saldena family, the secluded and gloriously situated **Isla Naburot Resort** ( (33) 76616 or (33) 75867, Sinapsapan, Jordan, Guimaras Island, is a special place to stay, despite its lack of electricity. Surrounded by such natural beauty, candlelight only adds to the ambiance. The resort is simply but attractively designed, with thatched bungalows set amongst palm trees, some built for two people, others for as many as eight, all under airy lofts and full of unusual features such as carved wooden doors. The coral island itself is rimmed with soft white sand and blue waters, with a lush interior of prolific vegetation. With its peaceful coves, this is a perfect place to come for a few days of snorkeling and relaxing by the beach.

With spacious, attractively decorated bungalows and good facilities, **Costa Aguada Island Resort** ( (33) 831-2261 MANILA (2) 895-8624 FAX (33) 833-0357, Inampulugan Island, Guimaras, is well recommended, although it lacks the fabulous scenery offered at Isla Naburot. **Nagarao Island Resort** ( (36) 337-8613, Nagarao Island, Jordan, Guimaras, is another getaway beach resort, with a restaurant and swimming pool overlooking the bay.

## MARBUENA ISLAND

On the western side of Panay, **Marbuena Island Resort** ( (33) 337-2574 is worth going out of your way to find. Its owners run this moderately priced hideaway along environment-friendly lines and it sits within its own forested coral island, home to wild parrots and fruit bats. Its pretty beaches feel secluded and the trail that runs across the island was created so that guests can experience the stillness and beauty of its exotic vegetation. Nipa-walled rooms are simple but comfortable and there are facilities for snorkeling, canoeing and scuba diving. To reach the resort, rent a taxi from Iloilo to **Culasi**, where a 15-minute pump boat ride will take you to Marbuena.

## KALIBO

Kalibo, the provincial capital of Aklan, is most famous for its raucously festive and exuberant **Ati-Atihan Festival**, held on the third week of January (FESTIVE FLINGS, page 51 in YOUR CHOICE). Otherwise, it is merely a place to pass through en route to the island of Boracay.

## BORACAY

Washed by the South China and Sulu seas and rimmed with legendary sugar-textured white sands, Boracay is one of the Philippines' best known and loved islands. This butterfly-shaped island lies just off the northwest tip of Panay, south of the island of Romblon and southeast of Mindoro. The superlatives uttered about its silky sands and clear blue water remain accurate, yet this delicate little island is suffering from the onslaught of careless development and too many visitors.

Boracay was considered a well-kept secret by cognoscenti travelers when it was first discovered as an idyllic haven in the early 1970s. Back then, visitors to the island stayed with villagers, or in tiny, makeshift huts, temporarily experiencing the lifestyle of a remote, clannish island, which depended almost entirely on subsistence fishing and agriculture. Local Boracayans are a mixture of races, primarily of Negrito descent.

Today, however, life in Boracay is almost entirely dedicated to accommodating and entertaining droves of tourists. Some of these visitors are hardy travelers making their way through the region, while others have flown in from Hong Kong or Australia for an uncomplicated beach holiday in blissful surroundings. The tiny island — 1,000 ha (2,500 acres) — hums with beachfront hotels, cafés, restaurants and shops. Village boys rove the beaches in search of customers to take around the island on their outrigger *banca* canoes; groups of middle-aged women — usually well-versed in the art of massage — offer to rub tired shoulders and limbs under a tree; children sell shells on the sandy pathway that passes as Boracay's main street on White Beach.

There is concern that the impact of tourism is not only disturbing the island's ecological balance but also causing social rifts within the lives of the native Boracayans, who have had to adjust sharply to keep pace with the mushrooming tourist-based economy. Yet the islanders are proud of their idyllic home and its old traditions, and are eager to preserve them. Tourists, who outnumber residents, are considered "guests" and should take care to respect the mores of the locals — who look askance upon public nudity, brawling and displays of loud, bad manners.

Since the pre-electricity days of the 1970s, when the nearby airfield in neighboring Caticlan, Panay, was merely a tin shack and a grass strip, the island has been transformed. Neon lights and disco strobes have replaced flickering kerosene lamps in the tourist havens, and the new airstrip has been slightly upgraded. The main mode of getting to the island is still by *banca* outrigger.

Dotted with hotels, the main attraction is White Beach, which, despite the large numbers of visitors to the island, remains lovely. As you walk along the beach, you will see the pretty puka shells that are part of Boracay's charm. They used to be exported from here, but islanders now worry that they will all disappear.

### GENERAL INFORMATION

The usual (and more effective) way to make reservations and get information for Boracay's

Good winds have earned Boracay a reputation as a windsurfing and sailing center. Here a *banca* competes in a Boracay Regatta.

resorts and hotels is to contact their Manila representative office, rather than calling them on the island directly, which can be difficult to impossible.

On White Beach, close to Angol Beach, the **Boracay Tourist Center (** (36) 288-3689 or (36) 288-3705 offers a reasonably efficient service and deals with most arbitrary business needs such as telephone calls, sending mail and faxes and changing currency. It has a travel desk where you can arrange onward ticketing and make bookings. It's also the place to get up-to-date local information. Next door is a well-stocked shop.

The **Boracay Medical Clinic and Drugstore (** (36) 288-3147 is along Boat Station 2, off the main road.

Most hotels will send e-mail for their guests. **Nigi Nigi Nu Noos** (see WHERE TO STAY, below) has an Internet Café — with one computer. Otherwise there's the Computer Center at the Boracay Imperial Beach Resort, popular because of its central location. Prices for Internet use is higher on Boracay than in most places in the country. You'll be charged between P90 to P150 per hour.

## WHAT TO SEE AND DO

There are three main villages on Boracay: **Balabag**, **Manoc-Manoc** and **Yapak**, each of which bustles with stalls, little shops and impromptu outdoor cafés. White Beach, facing the Sulu Sea, is lined with shops, cafés and hotels. Near its south end, the *talipapa*, or **flea market**, is a good place to shop for beach clothes, hats, cotton bags and cheap jewelry. Tie-dyed shirts and sarongs are especially popular, along with perishable flour-sack clothing.

The widest, longest and most sheltered beach on the island is **White Beach**, which stretches from **Diniwid Beach** at its tip to **Angol Beach** and has relatively safe (currentless) swimming as far as 50 m (55 yds) out. At the northern tip, **Yapak** and **Puka beaches** are both beautiful, with sheltered sandy coves and inviting water with a deep ocean floor, good for scuba diving and snorkeling close to shore.

When you tire of lazing ashore, rent a *banca* and cruise around the island, either for snorkeling, scuba diving, or to choose a

secluded bay in which to swim. This is the Philippine version of renting a gondolier and rates are negotiable, usually by the hour. Ask around and at your hotel for the going price. The Boracayan sailors who offer their services know their island's currents and swells — they and their ancestors have been plying these waters for centuries in similar boats. There are several relatively serious-looking scuba diving outfits along White Beach, all offering diving lessons and daily expeditions to surrounding dive sites, including nearby **Laurel Island**.

The more expensive resorts, such as Friday's and Lorenzo's, have various watersports facilities. Otherwise you can browse for **windsurf** board rentals along White Beach. Boardsailing (as windsurfing is known here) is an entrenched fad in Boracay, which hosts the **Boracay International Funboard Cup** — touted as Asia's best boardsailing event — each January. The untamed eastern side of the island facing the Sibuyan Sea is popular with windsurfers. Inquire at Green Yard Beach Resort and Seasport Center **(** (36) 288-3208 or (36) 288-3748.

As well as walking trails across the island, there is a **horseback riding** stable **(** (36) 288-3311 at the end of White Beach, near Friday's Resort. You can cross the rocky routes either from north or south of Balabag and head for the caves in Yapak, from which bats fly out regularly in search of fruit.

**Bicycles and motorbikes** are easily rented throughout the island. There are also tennis courts and equipment available for rent, north and south of White Beach. And for the only spot in the entire country where **parasailing** is available, head to Skyrider Parasail, next to the Bazzura Disco. For 10 minutes you can soar above the crystal waters, with breathtaking arial views of the island.

out the selection of souvenirs, carvings, T-shirts, and sarongs at the **Talipapa Flea Market** at the southern end of Boat Station 2. Another excellent shop along the main strip near Boat Station 2 is **NoyJinji**, where a husband and wife team sells unique hand-painted shirts, postcards, and world music recordings.

The island's pace is somewhat quickened with the advent of the **Fiesta Sa Bora-Boracay-Cay** festival, held variably between November and December, with parades, regattas, food, art contests and sporting events.

With good reason, sunset watching is regarded as a sacred activity along White Beach. Whether you are strolling along the sands, watching from a bar tucked away in a forested hillside, or have made the expedition out to the Kon-Tiki floating bar, it is an event. On a full moon, gazing at the heavens is equally awe inspiring.

**Fairways and Bluewater Resort Golf and Country Club**, north of White Beach, has an 18-hole, par- 72, Graham Marsh-designed golf course. It's normally for members only, but occasionally it's open to non-members — check with your resort to find out. A tricycle can take you there.

If the many vendors that wander the beaches don't have what you want, check

## WHERE TO STAY

There are about 200 hotels, resorts and guesthouses here to choose from — accommodation ranges from full-service resorts to the simple cottages clustered around White Beach. You can choose to stay on the island with the luxury of most modern conveniences, including CNN on the television, or rough it by candlelight or kerosene lamp. The most pleasant cottages are made of native materials, palms and grasses and slatted with bamboo poles, a variation on the theme of the typical Boracayan cottages.

Dresses OPPOSITE and sunhats ABOVE LEFT make a colorful display at Boracay. ABOVE RIGHT: Vacation cottages on Punta Bungo Beach.

At the opposite end of the island, on the northwest, the more private coves of Diniwid, Balinghai and Punta Bunga offer secluded and simple accommodations.

### Expensive

One of the first resorts and probably still the best is **Friday's** ( (36) 288-6200 FAX (36) 288-6222 WEB SITE www.fridaysboracay.com, located at the far end of White Beach away from the bustle along the main strip. It exudes an intimate, relaxed atmosphere, with thatched cottages made of polished bamboo, and with air conditioning and good facilities. Make sure you reserve in advance and request a room or villa near the beachfront, rather than the rear villas where water pressure can be weak and the walk to the white sands can be far. The alfresco, sand-floor restaurant and bar is a pleasant place to linger throughout the day, and it serves great breakfasts, with a range of fresh seafood barbecues for lunch and dinner — although a bit overpriced. They also have the island's best wine list.

Next to Friday's is the contemporary **Pearl of the Pacific Beach Resort** ( (36) 288-3962 FAX (36) 288-3220, MANILA (2) 924-4480 FAX (2) 924-4482 WEB SITE www.pearlpacific.com.ph. The design of the resort is the most original of all here — the furnishings were created by a famous Filipino designer. You can choose from beach-level rooms or hillside cottages, connected to the main pavilion by a funky zigzag metal bridge. Further along White Beach is **Waling Waling Beach Hotel** ( (36) 288-5555 to 5560 FAX (36) 288-4555, MANILA (2) 724-2089 FAX (2) 721-4927, where every room's private terrace looks out onto probably the best portion of White Beach. Unlike the traditional nipa cottage style, the Mediterranean-style façade and interior have large, spacious rooms, thick mattresses, dresser drawers, and large televisions. They can also arrange for seafood barbecues on the beach at sunset. Right across from Boracay's most photographed landmark, Willy's Rock, is **Willy's Beach Resort** ( (36) 288-3151 or 288-3395 FAX (36) 288-3016. Willy's offers the best value of all along this strip, with its Mediterranean-style villa shaded by lofty coconut and palm trees, and amenities include air conditioning and hot showers.

### Mid-range

The three Lorenzo Resorts, Main, South, and Grand Villas, all offer guests comfortable accommodations, and no matter which one you choose, you can use any of the other resorts' facilities. **Lorenzo Main** is located in the heart of White Beach and can be a bit loud. The rooms are traditionally decorated and there are two swimming pools, a games room, a disco, and a Filipino restaurant. **Lorenzo Grand Villas**, the newest of the family, is situated at the far south end of the island on a cliff that commands beautiful views of the passage between Boracay and Panay. This is the best place for families. There is a pool here also. **Lorenzo South** is probably the most convenient. It is not as loud as Lorenzo Main and not as far away as Lorenzo Villas, where transportation can be a problem. The beachfront here can be secluded and the snorkeling is excellent. All are booked through their Manila office ( MANILA (2) 812-9551.

In Balabag, not far from White Beach, is this fairly new and modern resort — the **Boracay Regency Beach Resort** ( (36) 288-6111 FAX (36) 288-6777. It's the only place with a pool on the front beach, using fresh water from a natural underground spring on the property. No more salty showers! Further along, **La Reserve Resort and Hotel** ( (36) 288-3020 FAX (36) 288-3017 provides creatively painted traditional bungalows right on the beach It is also home to one of the best restaurants on the strip.

### Inexpensive

**Nigi Nigi Nu Noos** ( (36) 288-3101 FAX (36) 288-3112 is recommended for its well-maintained, thatched pagoda-style, cottages furnished with traditional native materials, woven palm leafs, rattan grasses and tropical hardwoods and set in a jungle-like garden. This resort seems especially popular with Australians and has a good restaurant and bar area. **Pink Patio** ( (2) 812-9551 FAX (2) 810-8282 is a modern apartment-style hotel with a clean, efficient feel. Air-conditioned rooms are cozy; some bathrooms even have a bathtub as well as shower — a rarity in Boracay — and some

---

Many of Boracay's resorts and beachfront nightspots mimic traditional island bungalows.

have a private garden. The Patio Café serves good breakfasts with excellent coffee. Managed by an Austrian family, **Mona Lisa White Sands** ( (36) 288-3205 FAX (2) 924-7052 is a pleasant, small bungalow complex. **Jony's Jony's Place** ( (36) 288-6119 has simple, native nipa-style, rattan furnished bungalows with the basic amenities, including mosquito nets.

**Diniwid Beach** is an idyllic secluded part of Boracay and is in many ways the loveliest and most private part of the island. A number of foreigners have bought land here and some of the dwellings can be seen tucked into the hillside and above the rocks. You can stay here in simplistic seclusion at **Mika's Place**, which has 12 bungalow rooms for extremely reasonable prices, starting from about US$15, with clean shower and bathroom facilities. There is a non-fussy family-style café, serving fresh grilled fish and simple, appetizing dishes. You can have dinner here and the owner will help make arrangements to get you back to your resort by boat if the tide is in. It is a magnificent place to enjoy the sunset. **Boracay Rainforest Resort** ( (36) 621-1772 is the place to come if you want to be away from the strip of resorts and have a truly personal, independent vacation. It's like a Robinson Crusoe island getaway tucked high up on a cliff among the trees with views of the waters crashing below. Despite its rustic and basic appearance, the rooms are handsomely equipped with CD/radio, refrigerator, bathroom (no hot water), desk, queen-size bed, alarm clock, coffeemaker, and intercom to the main house, where the restaurant is located.

To come here directly from Caticlan, just tell the boatman you want to go to Diniwid Beach, rather than White Beach. There may be a nominal surcharge. You can also reach Diniwid by tricycle from White Beach, or walk to the end of the White Beach, past Friday's (at low tide). An alternative route (by foot, bicycle, tricycle, motorbike or horse) is to follow the main road until you reach the Diniwid road, and then follow it to the beach.

## WHERE TO EAT

Boracay is a culinary melting pot. For such a small and intimate island, the array of

dining options is quite overwhelming; ranging from French, German, Italian, or Swiss to Thai and Indian. A stroll along the sandy strip of White Beach will awaken your tastebuds — practically every restaurant is situated here. Not surprisingly, you can have seafood for every meal if you wish and Filipino flavors are available in abundance. The ingredients, especially the fruit and fish, are fresh, the dress code non existent and the rush, well, you will be on "island time" so settle in, relax, and let things come to you!

All of the following restaurants are in the moderate price range.

Among the must-try specialties of the island are the soft freshly baked bread from the **English Bakery**, the rich and creamy gelati from **Ice Rock Café**, and the fruit crepes from Duo and Gorio's **Café Breton**. Dinner at **True Blue** ( (36) 288-3142, at Boat Station 2, is heartily recommended. There is something exotic about eating spicy dishes while sitting Indian-style on huge pillows in a spacious alfresco hut. It feeds on the romantic fantasy of being on a faraway island.

The restaurant and bar at **Friday's** is worth visiting. They serve the best breakfasts on the island and have a good menu, with daily specialties and a decent (for the island) wine list. Another favorite that boasts quite an extensive wine list is **La Reserve**, which serves French cuisine and, if you are up for it, Cuban cigars. Nearby on White Beach, **Mango Ray** ( (36) 288-6129 has a cozy garden restaurant with a tropical flair and pretty good local and international cuisine. For European fare, try **El Toro** (no phone) for Spanish or **Gorio's Restaurant** (no phone) for French and Italian. **Chez Deparis** (no phone), serves up excellent French food also. Frenchman Roger Deparis and wife, Lani will make sure your palette is pleased. **Sulu Thai** ( (36) 288-3400, Boat Station 3, is a great place to people watch on the "beach expressway." It's nothing much to look at but they serve great Thai food.

A stop at Boracay would not be complete without trying its classic fruit shakes. Mango, avocado, melon, watermelon, strawberry, pineapple, banana, papaya and more, or any combination of these, can be mixed for a refreshing cold drink. **Jonah's Fruit Shake and Snack Bar** (no phone) tends to stand out for its gigantic shakes. Also try **Avenhja's Fruitshakes** (no phone). They serve shake variations of sweet mango, tart green mango, cantaloupe, coco-banana, choco-peanut, with or without the addition of the infamous Philippine rum.

What makes Boracay so fantastic is that with a little effort you can steer away from the strip of European restaurants and do as the locals do, and at inexpensive prices. Check out the local market for the color (great photography opportunities) and for fruit on a stick, dried squid, or roasted piglet. Crack open a coconut and try *buko*, a mixture of coconut juice and tart *calamansi* juice, a local fruit similar to a lime. Other local dishes to look for on menus include squid with mango sauce, *rellenong bangus*, milkfish stuffed with raisins and pork, and *tapa*, or salted beef.

## NIGHTLIFE

Aside from moon watching and drinking long into the night, there are a number of bars and beach discos to suit more hyperactive tastes. Dance the night away at one of the island's discos on White Beach: **Beachcomber** (Boat Station 1), **Bazura** (Boat Station 2), or **Sulo Bar** (at Boat Station 3). **Moondogs** (Boat Station 1) offers a commemorative T-shirt to anyone still standing after 15 shots. **Titay Main Garden Theater Restaurant and Bar** (Boat Station 3) hosts regular performances of ethnic dance and music. You'll need to take a tricycle to get here. The floating **Kon-Tiki Bar**, some meters off White Beach and reached by boat, is worth sampling day or night and a good place to watch the sun go down. The most quirky bar is the **Music Garden**, tucked into the hillside at Angol Beach, with its murals of rock stars of bygone years and repertoire of old rock-and-roll classics.

## HOW TO GET THERE

Philippine Airlines flies twice daily from Manila to Kalibo City in Aklan province on Panay Island, southeast of Boracay. Air Philippines, Asian Spirit, and Cebu Pacific also have daily flights from Manila to Kalibo. The onward journey from Kalibo takes about two hours by bus or jeepney overland to the coastal town of Caticlan — a pleasant ride flanked by winding paddy fields. As there is no jetty on Boracay, you'll have to wade ashore from the boat, so wear something suitable!

Asian Spirit has three direct daily flights from Manila to Caticlan. Connecting motorized outriggers then ply between Caticlan Point and across the Tablon Strait to Boracay, 15 minutes away. Be prepared for both yourself and your luggage to get wet on this journey, and possibly to wade thigh deep to board or disembark.

During the summer season, it is also possible to reach Boracay from Manila via the once-weekly Aboitiz Super Ferry. Bear in mind that transportation from Kalibo to Caticlan can be prearranged with your chosen resort or hotel. Boracay can also be reached from Tablas in Romblon by boat.

Cebu Pacific and Mindanao Express have limited flights from Cebu to Kalibo City — usually twice a week.

## LEYTE

A densely forested, fertile island, Leyte was where General Douglas MacArthur fulfilled his pledge and returned to the Philippines, landing on the island with four American invasion divisions at midnight on October 19, 1944. As Stanley Karnow wrote in *In Our Image*, his book about the American empire in the Philippines: "Leyte, a grim tropical battlefield, presaged Vietnam." It was to be the largest naval engagement in history, with four months of "bitter, exhausting, rugged fighting, physically the most terrible we were ever to know," as a United States Army historian has described it.

In the events leading up to the battle of Leyte, some 28,000 American men had been lost in the Pacific; MacArthur had to convince Roosevelt and his joint chiefs to pledge more lives, promising quick, dramatic results in the stepped-up battle against Japan. Some 7,000 American craft — from warships to transports — bearing 200,000 troops were sent streaming to Leyte. General Yamashita then had 200,000 troops to defend the entire archipelago, most of which were concentrated on defending Luzon at the expense of the other islands. He ordered only 20,000 men to Leyte, giving them instructions to bedevil potential United States invaders from their mountain roosts, rather than along the shores. But this miscalculation proved to be the Japanese general's undoing. It was not until 11 months after MacArthur landed on Leyte that the Japanese finally capitulated, brought down by the bombing of Hiroshima.

The evening before the Leyte landing, MacArthur wrote in his diary: "Men lined the rails or paced the decks, peering into darkness and wondering what stood out there beyond the night. There is a universal sameness in the emotion of men, whether they be admiral or sailor, general or private, at such a time as this." Before the American fleet opened fire on Leyte at dawn, MacArthur spoke through a radio transmitter, stoking the emotions of the pious Filipinos whose support he was counting on: "People of the Philippines, I have returned. Rally to me! The guidance of divine God points the way. Follow in His name to the Holy Grail of righteous victory!"

The months that followed saw fearsome casualties and battles, with the Japanese unleashing scores of kamikaze pilots and both sides repeatedly strafed and bombed. Yet by December, as Karnow writes: "Despite his initial opposition to the venture, Yamashita had by Christmas squandered 60,000 troops, nearly his total force, on Leyte. He now elected to abandon the island, knowing that the bloodbath had already sapped his strength to defend Luzon, his main priority. The Japanese soldiers left behind to fend for themselves suffered agonies of betrayal.

"Thus the Americans were able to advance in the Philippines and edge closer to Japan. The critical United States victory at sea, however, hinged as much on luck as it did on skill and courage."

A Japanese veteran, Shohei Ooko, recounted his experience in his remarkable novel, *Fires on the Plain*, which vividly describes the horrific scale of the carnage — as land battles, often hand-to-hand, commenced across the island's coastal towns,

steamy jungles, and mountain caves — and the realization that his starving fugitive comrades were turning to cannibalism as they roamed the island. Though starving himself, he managed to survive on insects before being captured by Filipino guerrillas, who turned him over to the United States Army. About 60,000 Japanese died on Leyte. The United States Army lost 4,000 men there, with 15,000 wounded.

Anyone whose life has been touched by the experience at Leyte will need no exhorting to realize the dramatic resonance this island has, and both Americans and Japanese have returned to visit, remember and grieve. In preparation for your visit to Leyte, you may find it interesting to watch the film *MacArthur*, in which Gregory Peck plays the general, characteristic pipe cocked in mouth and face set in a scowl of determination.

## TACLOBAN

Capital of Leyte, Tacloban is the main township of the province, with a bustling port set around a deep-water harbor. Two personalities have thrown larger-than-life shadows across Tacloban, albeit in entirely different ways, yet their lives briefly collided: MacArthur and Imelda Marcos.

Imelda grew up in the nearby town of Tolosa as a beautiful yet impoverished daughter of one of the province's old but not powerful aristocratic families — the Romualdez family. After winning beauty competitions and becoming the country's First Lady, much of Imelda's life and identity was filtered to the Philippine people through her powerful need to expunge the memories of her early years as the "Rose of Tacloban."

When MacArthur and his troops landed in Leyte, "Meldy" was a budding beauty of 16. She stepped into an early spotlight of stardom when she sang for the battle-weary American GIs. Barely a town fiesta, civic parade or fundraising benefit would pass by without her being asked to sing a few songs. Today, Imelda Avenue and numerous buildings, including her reconstructed ancestral mansion, bear her name.

### General Information
The **Department of Tourism** ( (53) 321-4333 is within Tacloban's Children's Park. They have published an interesting tourist map of Tacloban that includes visits to village relief projects, memorial sites and religious icons, as well as battle sites.

### What to See and Do
For veterans and war historians, the entire island of Leyte has a significance that could be lost on many tourists; its beautiful forests and coasts are laced with memories of wartime massacres.

It's possible to see most of Tacloban's historic sites within a day's visit. Palo's **Red Beach** is the best-known tourist site, 12 km (seven miles) away from Tacloban, and the scene of MacArthur's landing. Larger-than-life statues commemorate the event at the **MacArthur Landing Memorial**, depicting the general striding through the waves, flanked by Sergio Osmena (who became president of the Philippine commonwealth) and General Carlos Romulo. Each October 20, "Liberation Day" is held at Red Beach.

In Palo town, the imposing **Neo-Gothic cathedral**, built in 1596 and with an additional seventeenth-century gold altar, served as a sanctuary for local people during the Leyte battle and later as an evacuation hospital for wounded American soldiers. In the vicinity, **Guinhangdan Hill**, or Hill 522 in military parlance, was a notorious battlefield and is now covered with commemorative white crosses. Visitors can walk to the summit, survey the hillside views out to sea, and view the bunkers and foxholes used by the Japanese. Another infamous battlefield, **Breakneck Ridge**, lies 72 km (45 miles) west of Tacloban, near Limon.

The **Santo Niño Church** on Plaza Rizal in Tacloban contains an ivory image of the child Jesus, patron saint of Tacloban and Leyte. Referred to as the "Capitan," the image was lost on a sea voyage in 1889, only to mysteriously resurface some months later. A sudden outbreak of cholera that allegedly ceased as soon as the statue reappeared increased its miraculous powers in the eyes of the town. This event is celebrated with great color and gusto during the annual city fiesta (worth timing your visit to witness) on June 30. At Easter, a similar frenzy of devotion surrounds Palo, when hooded flagellants make bloody parades re-enacting the Passion of Christ. Notice the grand house nearby that was built as a guest residence for the Marcos family, its design personally supervised by Imelda. Both the **Heritage Museum** and the **People's Center and Library** are interesting to visit, the latter for its dioramas on ethnic tribes. The **Madonna of Japan Shrine**, set in a small park along Magsaysay Boulevard, was presented to the town by the people of Japan as a peace symbol.

Notable for its role during World War II, the **Price Mansion** is two blocks from Plaza Rizal. Now the Governor's Guesthouse, it was used as a Japanese officer's club during the occupation, and later acted as MacArthur's headquarters in Leyte. Close by, the **Divine Word University** has a quirky museum that provides insights into the ancient history of the region, with 6,000-year-old Stone Age relics unearthed around the Sohoton Caves, antique Chinese ceramics and tribal burial jars.

Tacloban is also the jumping-off point for a visit to the Sohoton Natural Bridge National Park, on nearby Samar Island (see SAMAR, below).

### Where to Stay and Eat

**Ormoc Days Hotel** ( (53) 561-9745 FAX (32) 254-6584 on Obrero Street, Ormoc City, is a deluxe hotel not too far from Tacloban City. Major golf courses surround the hotel and its facilities are of a very high standard. A modern, functional hotel with an enormous stone swimming pool, **Leyte Park Hotel** ( (53) 321-2444, Magsaysay Boulevard, Tacloban City, is a comfortable and serene place to stay. Both are moderately priced.

Nestled into spacious grounds along the historic Red Beach, the inexpensive **MacArthur Park Beach Resort** ( (53) 323-3015 or 3016, Government Center, Candahug, is located near the site of perhaps the most dramatic World War II naval battle in the Pacific. Small and friendly, situated on an island just offshore from Tacloban, **Dio Island Resort** ( (53) 321-2811, San José, Tacloban City, has good facilities, and is the least expensive option.

### How to Get There

Philippine Airlines, Air Philippines and Cebu Pacific fly to Tacloban from Manila daily, with a flight time of one hour and 10 minutes. Asian Spirit used to have daily flights from Cebu to Tacloban until quite recently, when service was suspended until further notice. Check with the airline to see if service has resumed.

Several shipping lines operate regular services to Tacloban, linking the town with Manila, Cebu and Samar. WG&A ferries offer a luxurious and efficient service between Manila and Tacloban.

As Leyte is linked by road to Samar, across the San Juanico Bridge, it is possible to make the journey from Manila by bus or car, with a break for the car ferry service from Luzon to Samar.

## SAMAR

The second largest island in the Visayas, Samar is considered rather off the typical tourist track in the Philippines, even though the island is peppered with alluring offshore islands and has much natural beauty. The people of Samar are of Visayan extraction and speak Waray-Waray, a strictly local dialect. Periodically, central and eastern Samar townships become stages for new incidents in the NPA insurgency, which means that if you are determined to travel throughout the island you should inquire about the political status quo before you set off.

**San Juanico Bridge** connects Samar to Leyte. This is the longest bridge in Southeast Asia, more than two kilometers (one and a quarter miles) long and quite a remarkable feat of construction.

Off the northeastern tip of Samar, **Biri Island** is favored by divers for its untouched beauty and coral reefs, exotic scenery scattered with large boulders. Off the northwest coast, **Capul Island**'s history is interwoven with the early Spanish galleon trade, hence the name Capul, a corruption of Acapulco. This legacy is evidenced by the town's seventeenth-century church and tower. A network of caves marks the other side of the island, of which **Bito Cave** is the best known, some 20 m (66 feet) deep.

One of the most dramatic stretches of scenery in Samar lies along the coastal road from Allen — the small port town at the island's northern tip — and Calbayog, a journey of about an hour and a half each way. The most beautiful scenery is that approaching **Viriata**, as the road skims mountains and steep cliff faces and looks out across offshore islands and curving bays. The town itself is pretty enough, with a large waterfall and walks through surrounding forest, but the drive rather than the destination is the real highlight of this trip. From Calbayog, the main highway south passes through the provincial capital, **Catbalogan**, before continuing down to Basey, the jumping-off point for the **Sohoton Natural Bridge National Park**.

The eight-square-kilometer (three-square-mile) park is the province's main attraction, with its beautiful native forests, marbled caves and birds, monkeys and butterflies. It is best reached from Tacloban in Leyte.

## GENERAL INFORMATION

The Department of Tourism office and the **Community Environment and Natural Resources Office** in Basey ( (55) 321-2048 or 321-4333 can provide guides, gear and information on exploring the caves of Sohoton National Park.

## SOHOTON NATURAL BRIDGE NATIONAL PARK

Reached by water, the Sohoton Natural Bridge National Park is an awe-inspiring place. Rich in archaeological finds, it has a steamy, almost fearful beauty, and its primeval landscape can be explored for hours.

Although the park is located on Samar Island, it is more convenient to reach it from Tacloban, Leyte. Whether you get there from within Samar Island or from Tacloban, though, you enter the park by *banca* via **Basey**, on Samar. The boat journey upriver from Basey takes about 90 minutes and is in many ways as spectacular as the destination. The only time it is possible to visit the park — with its underground cave chambers and waterfalls — is between March and July, when the river level is relatively low. The caves deserve a two-day trip, although it is possible to visit in a day. Check with the Department of Tourism office and the Community Environment and Natural Resources Office in Basey, which can also help with transport and provide a guided tour of the park, including equipping you with such all-important items as kerosene lamps to see the wondrous cave interiors.

There are many caves in the area, most relatively unexplored. Three that are most familiar to local guides are **Upper Sohoton**, **Lower Sohoton** and **Panhulugan Cave**. Upper Sohoton cave looks like a very large tunnel with a depth of about 100 m (328 feet), and a diameter of about 25 m (82 feet). It contains several large limestone formations and a soft, cold wind constantly blows inside. At one end of the cave a balcony about 70 m (230 feet) above the ground overlooks a river. Lower Sohoton is about 50 m (164 feet) long and can be easily traversed with

a little help from a guide. Panhulugan Cave has many of the best limestone formations in the area, with figures ranging from chairs to human shapes and prominent Philippine landscapes (like the Banaue Rice Terraces). It is multi-chambered and may seem like a difficult maze to the uninitiated.

### Where to Stay

In Calbayog, the best place to stay is the **Seaside Drive Inn** ( (57-41) 234, in the outlying suburb of Rawis, while in Catbalogan, the best option is the **Fortune Lodging House**

( (57-41) 680, on Del Rosario Street. Both are inexpensive. Neither destination justifies a stay beyond recuperating from the drive.

### How to Get There

Asian Spirit runs flights from Manila to Calbayog on Tuesday, Thursday, and Saturday each week. Or you can fly Philippine Airlines on their twice-daily flights to Tacloban City in Leyte and take a car to Basey. Taxis cost about P15 for the 30-minute trip across the 2.16-km (one-mile) San Juanico Bridge that connects Tacloban City with Basey in Samar.

A weekly ferry connects Manila with Catbalogan. The Pan Philippine Highway, links Samar and Leyte with the southern tip of Luzon (a ferry takes vehicles across the narrow San Bernardino Strait).

The journey to Basey from Tacloban, 27 km (17 miles) — either by jeepney or by rented car — takes about an hour.

A large monitor lizard making an appearance out of the thick forest. These mostly harmless reptiles are common in most forested parts of the Philippines.

# Mindanao

DESPITE ITS REPUTATION as a somewhat turbulent hotbed of insurgency, Mindanao should not be missed by adventurous travelers. The region is rich in extraordinary natural scenery — promiscuous splashes of exotic plants and blossoms, exquisite beaches and pristine waters and a fascinating amalgam of Muslim and tribal cultures. With its striking mulong-clad women, the geometrical, colorful, sails of the local *vintas*, or boats, and the presence of the Badjaos, or sea gypsies, amongst many of the fiercely independent tribes native to this region still clinging to the beliefs and traditions of their ancestors, Mindanao is a world away from the heavily touristed and somewhat anodyne pleasures to be found in beach resorts of, for example, Cebu.

Located northeast of Borneo, Mindanao is the second largest and southernmost principal island in the Philippines and has a complicated medley of tribes, only a small proportion of which are mentioned in any detail here. The Christian majority and the Muslim minority, along with the main Muslim coastal tribes — Samal, Tausug and Yakan — have until recently lived together peacefully for years.

Although most of the Philippines was converted to Roman Catholicism by the Spanish missionaries in the sixteenth century, many of the southernmost islands remained staunchly Islamic. Ethnically, the Philippine Muslims (who number about 1.5 million) are slightly less Malay than the rest of the island's population, and their features suggest their Arab ancestry. During the 1970s, Mindanao became the center of a Muslim rebellion led by the Moro National Liberation Front (MNLF), the largest Muslim organization in the country, which waged a bloody insurgency against the dictatorship of President Marcos. Moros in general have always been resistant to the idea of centralized government and their insurgency has paralleled that of the New People's Army (NPA) in Northern Luzon. In 1976, under considerable pressure, Marcos agreed to bestow upon the Moros a large amount of regional autonomy, including a separate judiciary and security force, yet little was actually done to achieve this. In 1989, the MNLF declared a cease-fire after the Aquino-led government pledged to

honor some of its demands. The same issues have remained unresolved in real terms and sectarian strife continued. Nevertheless, in August 1996, President Ramos and the head of the MNLF, Nur Misuari, brokered a complex agreement that was supposed to be the key to lasting peace in the region. But both the Christian majority and some Muslim factions have denounced this agreement, and fighting has broken out sporadically since it was signed. More than 150,000 people have been killed in the secessionist rebellion in the past 30 years.

Today, as the government negotiates with the moderate leadership of the MNLF for a limited regional autonomy, another rebel movement has emerged from Mindanao as the frontline disrupter of peace. The Abu Sayyaf organization reflects the younger, increasingly radical generation of Filipino Muslims, whose ideology has been influenced by Saudi Arabia and Libya. Their strident call for a *jihad*, or holy war, against the government and what they refer to as the "Christian settlers" on southern Mindanao make them the Hizbollah of the Philippines.

Operating from their main jungle camp base in the densely forested island of Basilan, about 27 km (17 miles) off the coast of Mindanao's Zamboanga del Norte, the Abu Sayyaf rebels are believed to be responsible for many bombings, grenade attacks, kidnappings and murders in the southern Philippines. Many of its numbers are Muslim

OPPOSITE : Young girls of the T'boli tribe, from South Catabato Province, don their traditional beaded finery for fiesta days and for occasional visits to town while ABOVE a boys group has a giggle.

Filipinos who initially fought alongside mujahidin rebels in Afghanistan, and some disgruntled Moro Front members. What used to be a loosely affiliated group has become the nation's most violent rebel movement. Their presence is especially strong in Basilan, and for this reason it's not safe to travel there.

Yet despite these rather alarming hazards, Mindanao remains well worth visiting and fairly safe if you keep to the main tourist resort areas, such as Davao and Dakak, and avoid the autonomous zones of Basilan Island and the Sulu Archipelago. Zamboanga City itself is somewhat unstable and periodically suffers random bomb attacks and shootouts. Foreign journalists often brave this region, yet bear in mind that even if you are not an American Christian missionary, as a foreigner you may still be a likely target if you stray off the beaten track.

Diverse mixtures of tribes inhabit Mindanao and the Sulu Archipelago. Among the Muslims, the Moros were so named by the Spanish because of their perceived resemblance to the Moors of North Africa, even though, at that time, they were an amalgam of distinct ethnic groups, each under the leadership of a sultan or *datu* (chieftain). Photographs dating back to 1898 give an impression of the extraordinary appearance of Mindanao's aristocracy; dressed in exotic, gaudy silk costumes, elaborate sarongs, turbans and headdresses, with curving swords tucked jauntily at the waist. Headdress was indicative of a strictly observed social hierarchy between tribes, functioning as a prestige ornament. Only those who had killed many enemies could wear the most elaborate variety, ranging from scarlet and gold silk to bark or rattan matched with cock feathers. High-ranking women traditionally wore their hair in Chinese style and painted their faces. Perhaps the most fashion conscious were the Bagobos, who wore cloths made of heavily beaded, woven tinalak or abaca fiber lined with brass bell trimmings, which tinkled with their movements, and who had their teeth cut to spiky triangles. The Bagobos were — and still are — considered among the most elaborately dressed and adorned tribal people in the Philippine Archipelago.

MINDANAO

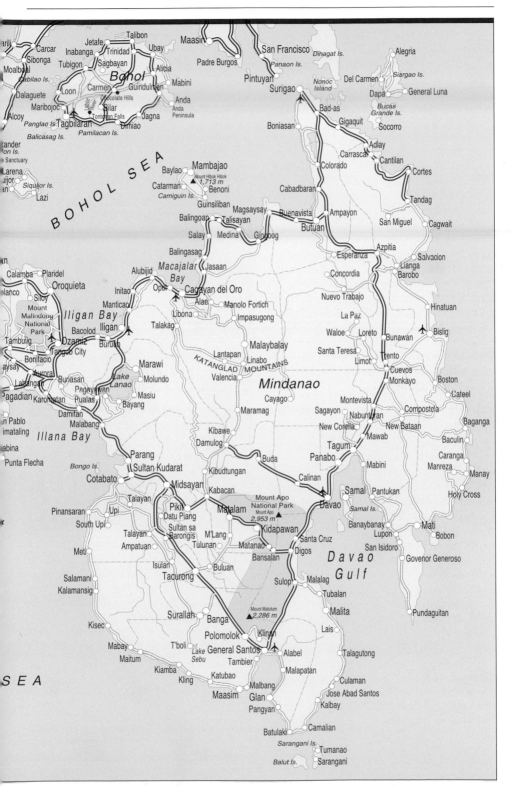

The Samal, a group of Islamic traders, seafarers and fishermen, are famous for their villages built on stilts around the shallows of Mindanao's shores. For a tribe adept at sea, the watery expanses offered protection against intruders. Linked together by plank walkways, these land and sea villages near Zamboanga are a remarkable sight. With a similar way of life, the Tausug dominate the most attenuated part of the Sulu Archipelago. Some 30,000 Badjaos also live a water-borne lifestyle up and down these coasts, and at Sitangkai they have constructed entire floating villages; their lives are completely at the whim of tides and typhoons.

It would be interesting to speculate what these sea dwellers — who only come ashore to visit markets and ultimately to be buried — would think of the Hollywood movie, *Waterworld*, with aspects of the movie's futuristic vision resembling their daily life.

The Sulu Archipelago has been and continues to be regarded as a dangerous area, with its notorious Moro pirates and smugglers.

## DAVAO CITY

An introduction to the cultural diversity and vastness of Davao begins upon touchdown at Davao Airport. Muslim motifs draw attention to the spacious terminal building, with its dark wood paneling and dangling *capiz* shell chandeliers. From the tarmac, the 244,000-ha (603,000-acre) expanse that is Davao City stretches toward the horizon, where the impressive cloud-covered Mount Apo looms in solemn majesty.

From the airport to downtown is a mere 25-minute ride along J.P. Laurel Avenue, past burgeoning industrial and commercial districts, golf courses, the casino, hotels and inns, manufacturing plants and government offices. Downtown is a bustling grid of shopping arcades, market places, movie and shop houses, restaurants, modern office building and apartment rows.

Today, Davao is a melting pot of people from all over the archipelago. This diversity extends itself to all aspects of society, from cultural and traditional practices to religious and political affiliations. In spite of these differences, the people of Davao

thrive in peaceful co-existence, and provide an excellent example of the well-known Filipino hospitality.

Aside from its people, Davao is also a land of many natural attractions. Outside Davao city proper are agricultural plains planted with exotic flowers and fruit. Outlying islands harbor beaches and coral reefs teeming with marine life. Within its forests are sanctuaries of rare animal and plant species, and the surrounding hills and mountain ranges beckon with the promise of adventure.

### GENERAL INFORMATION

The **Department of Tourism** ( (82) 221-6798 FAX (82) 221-0070, No. 7, Magsaysay Park Complex, Santa Ana District 8000, Davao City, is located beside the Apo View Hotel. The office is very helpful and is well stocked with information about local tours, guided walks, inland resorts and city lodgings. They can also let you know if your visit has coincided with any festivals, parades or other special events.

ABOVE: Davao is famous throughout the archipelago for its tropical fruit and splendid orchids. The blossoms are at their most beautiful from April to September. RIGHT: Mount Apo, southwest of Davao City rises to 2,953 m (9,685 ft), making it the country's highest peak.

## WHAT TO SEE AND DO

Davao City's **San Pedro Cathedral** rests solidly like the boat of Saint Peter at the corner of San Pedro Street and C.M. Recto Avenue. It is unusual for its blend of Moorish and traditional Christian influences.

The **Dabaw Etnica** at the Mandaya Weaving Center is a fascinating display of traditional craftwork. Members of the indigenous Mandaya tribe from the east coast of Mindanao carry on their ancient weaving tradition on the airy nipa and bamboo verandah of their new home behind the Davao Insular Hotel (see below). Women in tribal dress sit at their looms, deft fingers moving in and out of root-and bard-dyed abaca fibers as they weave the intricate patterns of the *dagmay* fabric. The men then fashion the material into bags, wallets, purses, shoes, rugs, and wall decor accented with bells, beads, and embroidery. The tribal artifacts, costumes and native fabrics at the **Dabaw Museum** ( (82) 25-1876, in Insular Village, Lanang District, are similar to the work created today. The museum also has fascinating dioramas, musical instruments, ethnological maps, weavings and burial, wedding and war implements.

A traditional gate shields the well-kept grounds of the **Lon Wa Buddhist Temple** from the traffic on J.P. Cabaguio Avenue. Amidst candle trees and rustling bamboo, the temple is built of black-veined marble, with carved wood ornamentation depicting the life of Buddah. A carp-filled lily pond aids in meditation, while within the high-ceilinged halls, saffron-robed monks chant the sutras to an Italian marble Buddha, or light incense to a golden Kuanyin.

On the other side of the ecumenical coin is the **Shrine of the Holy Infant Jesus of Prague** in Matina, seven kilometers (four miles) from the city center. The shrine features an open-air replica of the holy image of Prague that the owner was said to have built after seeing it in a dream. She later made a pilgrimage to Prague and found that her shrine was an exact replica. Aside from devotees who visit the reputedly miraculous image and donate clothes, the shrine buzzes with excursionists who troop in to picnic under the shady fruit trees: students on retreat, bikers, joggers, and those who simply come up to get the best panoramic view of Mount Apo and Davao City. The Santo Niño de Praga Festival is held here every January 14 and 15.

Davao is a rewarding destination for those interested in flowers, especially orchids. The **MINFLO market** (Mindanao Federation of Cut Flower and Orchid Grower's Association) has a wide selection, ranging from the indigenous waling-waling to colorful hybrids like vanda, mokara, and kagawara. Outside the city, it is glorious to visit the orchid plantations, especially from April to September, when the ethereal and delicate blossoms are at their most beautiful, before being plucked, packaged and flown off to some far-flung, flower-starved destination. The well-known plantations are the **Yuhico Orchid Gardens** in Greenhills, **Derling Worldwide Orchid Corporation** in Dumoy, and the **Puentespina Orchid Gardens** along J.P. Cabaguio Avenue.

Davao is also famous for its tropical fruits, especially the durian, which is said to "smell like hell but taste like heaven." The **Madrazo fruit district**, near downtown, is an excellent place to get to know these unusual and exotic fruits. Elsewhere, fruit orchards bulge with export produce, including Cavendish bananas, the small Davao papaya, hairy rambutan, mangosteen, prickly durian, sweet pomelo, green mandarins and other citrus fruits.

Outside the city are the beaches of **Talomo**, **Talisay**, **Salakot** and **Guino-O**, all with small fishing villages alongside them. The Japanese landed their vessels at Talomo Beach in 1942, followed by the Americans in 1945, and wartime shipwrecks are submerged at various points around the bay.

## SHOPPING

Davao has over a dozen malls, with the five branches of the **Datu Complex** open until 10 PM daily. **Gaisano Mall** on Malvar and Bolton Streets is the latest mall to open up in Davao and the biggest, with endless department stores, boutiques, restaurants and a cinema. **JS Gaisano Citimall** is a multi-level modern shopping mall on Ilustre Street, with an airline and shipping ticketing office, supermarket, a number of food shops and jewelry stores, and the most modern movie theater in Mindanao.

The best place in the region to sample tribal wares is the **Aldevinco Shopping Center**, which has neat rows of small stores that sell Mindanao tribal crafts, woven mats, brassware, antiques, batik cloth, and wood carvings. Across the road from the airport, **Nieva's Arts and Crafts** is an excellent, comprehensive showcase of the work by local and regional craftspeople, and certainly worth visiting.

PO Box 144, Lanang, is the city's top resort, with well-furnished rooms, good facilities and various restaurants. Its views across the Davao Gulf to Samal Island are stunning. The swimming pool, with coconut trees set all about it, is paticularly attractive. Back in town, the **Marco Polo** ( (82) 221-0888 FAX (82) 225-0111, M. Recto Street, is conveniently located in Davao's bustling business center.

### Mid-range
The **Apo View Hotel** ( (82) 221-6430 or (82)

The reclusive and artistic T'boli tribe live in a settlement along the shores of **Lake Sebu**, in the shadow of Mount Matutum in South Cotabato. Isolated and somewhat at the mercy of encroaching civilization (like other indigenous tribal people of the Philippines), they weave the unusual *t'nalak abaca* cloth and forge brass utensils you might see for sale in Davao.

### WHERE TO STAY

#### Expensive
The **Insular Century Hotel Davao** ( (82) 234-3050 FAX (82) 235-0902 or ( MANILA (2) 751-5555 FAX (2) 751-1155 WEB SITE www.century-hotel.com/insularcentury/v5.html,

893-1288 FAX (82) 221-0748, at the corner of J. Camus and Bonifacio Streets, is a sizeable, upmarket hotel with a large swimming pool, decadent poolside bar and a very popular discotheque. The hotel's Zugba Restaurant serves delicious local seafood dishes. The Apo also offers a sushi bar, and its Café Josefina serves good espresso coffee. **Mercure Grand Hotel** ( (82) 235-0888 FAX (82) 234-3858, on J.P. Laurel Avenue, and **Hotel Galleria Davao** ( (82) 221-2480 or (82) 221-2657 FAX (82) 221-8162, on Governor Duterte Street, are both in the heart of town — and a stone's throw away from one of Davao's largest superstores.

Endless rows of rare and exotic orchids are grown in Davao City.

## Inexpensive

Many inexpensive options within the city center are surprisingly loaded with amenities. **Regency Inn (** (82) 222-5819 FAX (82) 227-4333, on Villa Abrille Street, and **Hotel Maguindanao (** (82) 227-8401 or (82) 221-1699 FAX (82) 221-8121, on C.M. Recto Avenue, are good value and well-maintained. **Casa Leticia (** (82) 224-0501, at the corner of J. Camus and Palma Gil Streets, is a small but friendly hotel with clean, well-kept rooms. The top floor Toto's Bar and Café — with old albums and pictures of rock stars, cranks out loud tunes

almost every night. This may or may not sound like your ideal place to stay, but it is a great place to meet other travelers. The owner is the DJ every now and then.

## WHERE TO EAT

Davao is a place where you can eat simply and well, with its abundance of fresh fish, fruits and exotic culinary crosscurrents.

## Expensive

**Tsuru Japanese Restaurant (** (82) 227-2896, Don R. Castillo Building, Legaspi Street, is well known to be the best place in town for Japanese food. If you have an itching for rabbit or frog legs, **Claude's Café (** (82) 222-4287, Habana Compound, J. Rizal Street, serves authentic French cuisine from an authentic French chef.

## Mid-range

There are a number of good Asian restaurants throughout Davao City. **China Royale (** (82) 227-5962, R. Magsaysay Avenue, is

probably one of the city's most popular for its Szechuan-style cooking. **Mandarin Tea Garden (** (82) 227-3912 has several locations, but the one at Uptown Plaza, J. Rizal Street, is the most frequented. They have dim sum at very affordable prices. **Davao Korea Town Restaurant (** (82) 224-1671 or 224-1672, on Villa Abrille Street, is Korean spicy at its best.

**Ramen Tei (** (82) 235-1613, on Airport Road, has good quality sushi and noodle dishes. **Annie's (** (82) 221-2564 or (82) 221-8566, at the corner of Ilustre and General Luna Streets, is ideal for a dose of Americana — burgers, hot dogs and apple pie. **Pescadero Seafood (** (82) 222-6018 and **Sarung Banggi Steak (** (82) 221-5615, on F. Torres Street, are both popular with the twenty-something crowd, as is **Hagar's Place (** (82) 233-1018, Insular Village I, which is open later than most in Davao — until midnight — and serves European cuisine, with particularly good Austrian wursts. The **Down Under Inn and Restaurant (** (82) 298-0214, JMC Building, McArthur Highway, has thick and juicy steaks imported from Australia.

Locals followed **Davao Dencia's (** (82) 227-6777 to its new location on General Luna Street, keeping it a Davao institution serving excellent Chinese-Filipino cuisine. **Banok's Garden Barbikyu (** (82) 235-2338, on Washington Street, offers barbecued chicken in a welcoming outdoor setting.

Local delicacies abound in Mindanao, and Davao's restaurants do an excellent job of representing them. Probably the most off-beat place to sample them is **Sana's Kabuwan Carenderia** (Carabao Eatery). Owner and chef Porferia Jales, also known as "Sana," serves her famous spicy and steaming hot Carabao soup to a regular crowd of devotees. Give it a try yourself.

## Inexpensive

The seaside cafés at **Luz Kimilaw Place (** (82) 226-4612 on the Santa Ana Wharf have a good reputation for their sizzling, freshly caught and freshly cooked fish dishes. Rows of *bariles* (yellowfin tuna) are grilled over hot coals at the back of the restaurant. Also excellent are the *sugpo* (large prawns) and *pusit* (squid), served with steamed rice and *toyomansi* (lemon soy sauce). The delicious Chinese food at **Tai Huat Clay Pot** ( (82) 226-4576, on Magsaysay Avenue, is popular with Davao's Chinese community.

For pizza, pasta, and chicken, there are a number of **Giacomino's** in town, and of course the golden arches of **McDonald's** for that Big Mac craving. **Daba Java Espresso Bar** ( (82) 227-8401, in the Hotel Galleria, serves excellent coffee, brewed as only a true *barrista* knows how. The spiked coffee of **Silvercup** ( (82) 224-3361 is a must try. They also offer Internet access.

### HOW TO GET THERE

Davao City is the international gateway to the southern Philippines. Philippine Airlines runs flights to Davao several times each day from both Manila and Cebu, with the flight from Manila taking one hour and 35 minutes, or 55 minutes from Cebu.

Philippine Airlines also connects Davao with Cagayan de Oro and Zamboanga, and Bouraq Indonesia Airlines runs twice-weekly flights to Davao and Cagayan de Oro from Manado in Indonesia, and flies between Hong Kong and Davao via Cebu.

If you've the time and want a more scenic route, **Philtranco Bus Lines** ( (2) 833-1369, EDSA and Apelo Cruz Street, Pasay City, have

a 20-day overland trip along the Pan Philippine Highway from Manila to Davao.

## SAMAL ISLAND

Despite its relative remoteness from Manila, **Pearl Farm Beach Resort** ( MANILA (2) 526-1555 FAX (2) 832-0022; ( DAVAO (82) 235-0876 or (82) 235-2159 on Samal Island is, for some, the entire point of coming to Mindanao. This extraordinary resort is, at around US$150 a night (US$200 for suites), significantly less expensive than Cuyo's famous Amanpulo

resort, but it is comparable in many ways. Formerly a pearl farm, the resort's design incorporates native materials like bamboo, rope, stone, coral and native wood, along with arts and crafts of the tribes of Mindanao. The stilt cottages and suites are built over the water, in a luxury version of the stilted houses found in the region, and they meld seamlessly with the surroundings. Cottages have unforgettable vistas as do the restaurant and sea pavilion bar. The resort lies within some 14 ha (35 acres) of gardens and is now developing a recreation center.

OPPOSITE: Bukidnon tribespeople. ABOVE LEFT: Tropical fruits, and coconuts, abound in Mindanao. RIGHT: The Philippines' exotic orchids are in great demand throughout the world.

Following a breakfast of tropical fruit and Western-style cereals, resort guests devote most of their day to serious hedonism, with plenty of opportunity to windsurf, sail, scuba dive, snorkel or work on their tans. The restaurants are good and the swimming pool is sublime, with views of the surrounding sea. Make sure you reserve waterside accommodation, as the longhouse on the hillside (US$125), while comfortable, lacks the atmosphere of the waterside cottages and suites. All the resort's rooms have air conditioning, and all have views over the ocean.

Pearl Farm is connected to the rest of the world by radio only, so you will have to reserve through either its Manila or Davao office (see above).

Samal Island offers many other enticing beaches and diving possibilities, as well as Christian and Muslim fishing settlements to explore.

**Samal Casino Resort** ( (82) 222-5201 to 5204 FAX (82) 222-5200 MANILA (2) 813-2732, Kaputian, Samal Island, has spacious rooms at a little less than Pearl Farm. Its casino is popular with Asian businessmen.

## THE DAVAO PROVINCES

The face of the booming metropolis bears little resemblance to the Davao that was, and still is further into the three Davao provinces. Davao Oriental, Davao del Sur and Davao del Norte provinces are home to ethnic tribes like the Bagobo, the Manobo, the Mandaya, the Mansaka, the B'laan, and the T'boli. These early inhabitants gave the land her name — from daba-daba — meaning fire — conjuring images of tribal wars and ritual fires along the banks of the Davao River. Other tribes like the Maguindanaos from the adjacent provinces of Cotabato, Zamboanga, and Jolo also settled in the fertile basin of the river. It was not until the mid-nineteenth century that the Spaniards were able to overcome the stronghold of the Muslim chieftains. With this conquest came Christian settlers from Luzon and the Visayas.

### WHAT TO SEE AND DO

There is much in the Davao region to explore. The Philippines' highest mountain,

**Mount Apo** ("grandfather of mountains") is 2,954 m high (98,400 feet) and straddles the borders of Davao del Sur and North Cotabato, 25 km (miles) out of Davao City. Mount Apo is the centerpiece of **Mount Apo National Park**. Its 72,796-ha (180,000-acre) extent goes as far north as the provinces of Agusan del Sur and Misamis Oriental. A good way to explore the park's environs is to take a Department of Tourism organized climb (see below).

In a large forest reserve of rare plants and birds, the **Philippine Eagle Research and Nature Center** ( (82) 298-2663, open daily from 8AM to 5 PM, is a nurturing base for the endangered Philippine eagle. The Philippine eagle is endemic to the archipelago's forests, but have been adversely affected by the widespread destruction of their habitat. At the center, a 30-minute film introduces *Pag-sa* (which means "hope"), the first Philippine eagle to be born and bred in captivity. With its unusual crested feathers and quizzical face, the Philippine eagle is almost irresistible. The center is located in Calinan, about 36 km (22 miles) northwest of Davao City. Ask at the Department of Tourism office for details of how to visit — they sometimes run tours. Another interesting bird sanctuary, **Caroland Farms**, in Bago, 13 km (eight miles) south of Davao City, is home to wild native ducks known as "whistling ducks" for their strange shrill calls.

The unusual practice of **horse fighting** can be witnessed from November to May in Malita, 150 km (93 miles) south of Davao City. The fighting stallions are trained by Tagakaolo and B'laan tribesmen and transported down from their villages to the Malita arena. One of the more fiesta-style events connected with horse fighting occurs on January 28, with a celebration including ethnic dance and music performances staged by the Tagakaolo, B'laan and Manobo associations.

Sagada in northern Luzon isn't the only place for excellent **caving** opportunities. You can explore deep caves and hike to hidden waterfalls in Epol and surrounding areas, high up in the mountain ranges that surround Davao. Check with the Department of Tourism for guides and equipment.

For adventure seekers the area has many adrenaline-inducing experiences as well. Eco adventours (82) 226-3418 E-MAIL ecoadventours@yahoo.com, Esparanza Arcade, F. Torres Street, Davao, specializes in **inner tubing adventures** on some of the more powerful rivers in mountainous Davao del Sur.

**Apo Golf and Country Club** is the first ever course outside Luzon to host the prestigious Philippines Open. Aside from being labeled as a tough course, it is one of the more scenic ones — the tenth hole and fairway sit right smack at the foot of Mount

sulphur pillars, rainwater lakes, three swift-flowing rivers (including **Marbel River**, a milky river flowing from Mount Apo's crater), steaming **Agko Blue Lake** and **Lake Vanado**, thundering falls and cascade showers. If all goes well you'll reach Mount Apo Crater. Kidapawan trail, for which you must register at Davao's Department of Tourism, is one of the most manageable of the park's longer scenic trails. For current and more local information on the trails and guide hire contact the Kidapawan Tourism Council ( (64) 238-1831.

Apo. Lanang Golf and Country Club, Davao City Golf Club, and Ma-a Driving Range are also nearby.

## Climbing Mount Apo

Challenge your mountaineering skills while communing with nature as you conquer the roof of the Philippines — mighty Mount Apo, the country's highest peak at 2,953 m (10, 311 feet). It can take three to five days, depending on the trail you take. There are several from the Davao side, like Calinan and Tamayong (said to be the most scenic but also the hardest). Other jump-off points, include Kidapawan, South Cotabato, which is best for beginners. On its forested slopes you'll come face-to-face with geysers and

### SURIGAO DEL NORTE

Mindanao's northern province of Surigao del Norte incorporates the islands of Siargo, Dinagat, Nonoc, and Bucas Grande, as well as some 950 smaller islands. This isolated region is becoming known on the backtracker trail, particularly among surfers for the "Cloud Nine" break off the coast of Siargao Island.

### SURIGAO CITY

Surigao City is the capital of the province of Surigao del Norte, and serves as the point

The odd practice of horse fighting attracts locals and visitors alike to Malita.

of entry to the province. There isn't much to see here, however it is the place to refuel your pesos or organize excursions to the surrounding islands or surfing on nearby Siargao. If you find yourself here for a day or two, there are some good **beaches** around the city as well as the **Silop Cave** only seven kilometers (four and a half miles) away.

Off the shores of the city of Surigao is a group of islands that provide excellent day trips. **Hikdop Island**, a 45-minute boat ride from town, has refreshing beaches and **Buenavista Cave**. Probably the most popular

**way Hotel (** (86) 826-1283 FAX (86) 826-1285, along the airport road, which has large rooms, air conditioning, and cable television. The Gateway has a good restaurant. The **Tavern Hotel** nearby on Borromeo Street, has a restaurant that overlooks the ocean. There are also **barbecue stalls** scattered throughout the city, with some particularly good ones on the wharf.

### How to Get There
Generally, travelers fly to Cagayan de Oro (see page 212, below) and then bus their

of Surigao's day excursions is **Nonoc Island**, where a 400-m (1,335-foot) footbridge links Nonoc to neighboring Sibale Island. The walk across is fantastic — if heights aren't a bother to you. Most of the pumpboats to these surrounding islands leave daily in the morning.

The local tourist office is across from City Hall in Surigao City, and a main branch of the Department of Tourism, which can advise on travel throughout the entire northern Mindanao region, is by the city grandstand on Rizal Street.

### Where to Stay and Eat
The only place worthy of resting your head in Surigao City is the recently opened **Gate-**

way to Surigao. Buses run quite often and the trip takes about six hours.

### SIARGAO ISLAND

Not to be confused with nearby Surigao City, Siargao Island is a Mecca for extreme surfers who want to slice their boards through the infamous "Cloud Nine" surf break about six kilometers (three and three quarter miles) north of General Luna, a small town on the southeast coast. The Siargao Cup surfing competition is held in late September or early October every year — the best months to catch some great surf here. For those who have never put foot to the board, Siargao also offers beautiful and tranquil beaches, mangrove swamps, forests to hike through, waterfalls to indulge in, and offshore islands to explore.

Siargao Island is reached by several high-speed ferries that leave Surigao daily. The trip takes less than two hours and the boats usually leave in the mornings. Be sure to check the times at the wharf on Borromeo Street in Surigao.

For those seeking a ride on Cloud Nine, there are a few places to stay facing the prized surf. The budget **Cloud 9 Resort** (no phone) has small cottages on the beach, perfect for

in trails leading through tropical forest, touches of Spanish colonialism and ancient archaeological treasures make this an idyllic island to visit, and tourists are still rare. Most of the island inhabitants survive on farming and fishing and live in bamboo stilt homes built over mangroves. Camiguin is especially fun to visit in October, when the islanders celebrate the **Lanzones Festival** for two ornately costumed, fiesta-filled days (see FESTIVE FLINGS, page 51 of YOUR CHOICE). Stay at least a few days in Camiguin, longer if you can.

spectators who would rather watch the surf madness than be pounded by it. Run by two surfers, **Tuason Point Resort** (no phone) is another budget option near Cloud Nine. They also have a popular restaurant.

## CAMIGUIN

Camiguin is a tranquil island lush with vegetation and blessed with a plenitude of springs and waterfalls. The island's seven volcanoes are all active, yet relatively peaceful at present, aside from the occasional distant rumble.

Empty curves of alternating white and black sandy beaches, clear seas, solidified lava flows, hot and cold springs tucked away

### WHAT TO SEE AND DO

It is possible to explore the island from tip to tip within several hours by jeepney, bus and tricycle, but you could linger on its beaches or walk its forested tracks for hours. **Mount Hibok-Hibok** dominates the skyline, with its 1,250-m-high (4,100-foot) summit. In the Philippines, this is regarded as one of the more challenging mountains to climb. It is also the most active of the volcanoes here. Trails around its perimeter allow you to appreciate its low-lying scenery.

OPPOSITE: The luxurious Pearl Farm Resort, Samal Island. ABOVE LEFT: The Katibawsan Falls drop 50 m (170 feet) into a beautiful natural pool. ABOVE RIGHT: Fishing is the chief occupation for the Camiguin islanders.

About four kilometers (two and a half miles) from the main town of **Mambajao** (which has some pretty Spanish colonial mansions and a church), the **Katibawasan Falls** are impressive, cascading 50 m (164 feet) to a natural pool surrounded by wild orchids and ferns, boulders and forest. Other beautiful scenic places within the island are the **Santo Niño Cold Spring** in Caterman and the **Esperanza Ardent Spring**, a free-flowing hot spring that is heated by geothermal activity from Mount Hibok Hibok, nestled amongst trees and boulders. If you manage to be here alone, it is heavenly. Elsewhere on the island, **White Island** is the main beach strip, an uninhabited sandbar, reached by *banca* from Barangay Agohay. Evidence of the destructive power of the volcano is suggested by the huge white cross out in the bay, marking what was once a small town that collapsed into the sea when Mount Hibok Hibok erupted in 1871.

## WHERE TO STAY AND EAT

By and large, making reservations is not easy in Camiguin. The island doesn't yet have much of a tourist infrastructure, let alone an efficient telephone network. On the upside of this lack of tourism are the inexpensive options that are available.

**Turtle Nest Beach Cottages** ( (6388) 387-9056, on the coast west of Mambajao, have simple cottages facing the sea and decent food served in a beachside restaurant. It is geared to divers who are keen to explore the coral reefs that ring the island. To get here, ask the *motorella*, or tricycle, driver for Turtle's Nest Beach, close to Mahayahay Beach.

In Mambajao itself, **Tia's Beach Cottages** ( (6388) 387-1045 is inexpensive and friendly. At Bolokbolok, one kilometer (half a mile) west of Mambajao, you can stay in a novel "tree hotel" at the **Tree-House**, which has a café and tennis court. If you are seeking something a bit more modern, try **Caves Beach Resort** ( (6388) 387-9040 FAX (6388) 387-0077 at Agoho, also near Mambajao, which has more conventional bungalows, a dive shop, and a reasonable beach.

In Manila, **Blue Horizons Travel and Tours** (see TRAVELERS' TIPS, page 246) can reserve accommodation on Camiguin.

## HOW TO GET THERE

Philippine Airlines and Cebu Pacific have daily flights to Cagayan de Oro City from Manila, and Asian Spirit, Cebu Pacific and Mindanao Express fly to Cagayan de Oro from Cebu City. From Cagayan de Oro you have to go by boat to Benoni, Camiguin.

The 10-km (six-mile) journey takes a long, long time and Mabuhay class is the best option (although the air conditioner is permanently set to "blizzard"). Alternatively, you can travel by land to Balingoan, about one hour, then catch a slow ferry to Benoni.

Ferries operate regularly from Cebu, Dumaguete, Tagbileran, and other points in the Visayas. These options are not the new, fast ferries.

## CAGAYAN DE ORO

The city of Cagayan de Oro is the provincial capital of Misamis Oriental. It is a friendly, hospitable town, prettily arranged around Macajalar Bay, with a backdrop of pineapple plantations and green mountains. It is, after all, home to the Del Monte processing plant. The proximity to some remarkable beaches, caves, springs and dive locations make this an understated, but special place. In the city, see the **Xavier University's Museo de Oro**, which has a collection detailing the tribes of Mindanao. Within the outlying Tubigan Hills, near the village of Initao, caves shelter a highly unusual species of bat, with odd, cauliflower-shaped noses. A good time to visit Cagayan de Oro is during the **Kagayhaan Festival**, when the Cagayanons throw a colorful Mardi Gras-style street fiesta to honor their patron saint, Augustine.

A branch of the Department of Tourism is located at the front of the Pelaez Sports Center on Velez Street.

## WHERE TO STAY AND EAT

**Pryce Plaza Hotel** ( (88) 858-4536 is probably the best hotel in town. Its swimming pool, is open to non-guests as well for a

Ingenious treehouse, complete with moored boat, in Camiguin.

minimal fee, and a local band plays in the bar every night. For beachside slumber **Lauremar Beach Hotel (**/FAX (88) 858-7506 has comfortably rooms on gorgeous grounds that lead down to the beach. They also have an outdoor dining area and pool. Both are moderately priced.

## How to Get There

Cebu Pacific, Philippine Airlines and Air Philippines have daily flights to Cagayan de Oro from Manila.

WG&A has ferries leaving for Manila on Tuesdays, Fridays and Saturdays, and Negros Navigation have boats leaving twice a week, usually on Sunday and Wednesday evenings. The trip takes a whopping 48 hours.

## THE LANAO PROVINCES

The hilly provinces of Lanao have much natural beauty, with their profusion of forested lakes, springs and natural falls. **Iligan** is the provincial capital of Lanao del Norte. Close by, the legendary **Maria Cristina Falls** — 30 m (100 feet) higher than the more famous Niagara Falls of North America — are breathtaking.

Lanao del Sur province, ranged around the beautiful and gigantic **Lake Lanao**, is considered the Islamic cultural capital of the Philippines. This is where you'll find the **King Faisal Center for Arabic Studies**, the **Aga Khan Museum**, and the **Mindanao State University**.

Since there has been an advisory warning from the United States State Department that traveling in this inland region can be risky, you may wish to check the situation out with your embassy while you are in Manila before setting out.

## THE ZAMBOANGA PROVINCES

Farther across the northwestern coast, Dipolog, in the far north of Zamboanga del Norte, is the main gateway to western Mindanao's provinces of Zamboanga del Norte and Zamboanga del Sud. These two provinces stretch down the Zamboanga Peninsula, with Zamboanga City sitting at its southern tip.

### Dipalog

The capital of Zamboanga del Norte, Dipalog is best known for the series of exquisite sheltered beaches along the coastline between here and Dapitan, and around the tip of this small northern peninsula. This coastline is the location of the exceptional **Dakak Beach Resort**. The lush surrounding forest is a haven for native birds and deer, and has some spectacular walking trails for energetic hikers.

The nearby town of **Dapitan** remains largely untouched since the days when José Rizal lived in exile here for four years from 1892, banished from Manila for founding the *Liga Filipina* — the Philippine League. With ancestral houses and shady plazas

fringed by acacia trees, it was described then by Rizal as "especially made for isolation from the vulgar world," which remains an accurate description. During his stay here, Rizal set up a medical clinic and a school, showed the local fishermen how to use modern equipment, and experimented with growing fruit and coffee. He painted, sculpted and even sent rare plant and insect specimens to naturalists in Europe. He also met Josephine Bracken, the American woman who became his common-law wife, then 18 years old and accompanying her blind father on a tour of the archipelago. A **shrine** in memory of Rizal lies along the seashore of the town of Talisay.

Dapitan is also the site of the annual **Kinbayo Festival**, held in July, a flamboyant re-enactment of the Battle of Covadonga fought between the Spanish and Moors (see FESTIVE FLINGS, page 51 in YOUR CHOICE).

The **Dapitan Homestay Association** is quite active, and has a number of welcoming homes on its books. The town is small enough that it is possible to make inquiries once you arrive.

### Dakak Park Beach Resort

An elegant and secluded hillside hideaway, Dakak Park Beach Resort (/FAX (65) 212-5932, on the ruggedly beautiful northwestern tip of Mindanao, a short drive from Dapitan, has 80 air-conditioned, marble-floored, thatched nipa cottages in a lush,

Access to the stilted Taluksangay Muslim Village, in Zamboanga.

50-ha (120-acre), tropical forest setting of palms, frangipani and fruit trees. The huts face the 700-m-long (766-yard) sandy beach cove, with views across Dapitan Bay. Dakak is owned by flamboyant Filipino television producer Romie Jalosjos and thus popular with the country's glitterati — with a seaside restaurant and bar, water sports, tennis, horseback riding and wonderful sunset views from each bungalow's private verandah. Dakak has the sort of modern conveniences that make rustic isolation that much more comfortable, such as satellite

television, a large swimming pool, a Jacuzzi and sauna and a discotheque, as well as simple hammocks strung up under trees. It is reached by a 20-minute boat ride from Dapitan. They have a well-equipped diving center and offer scuba instruction. Encircled by large islands, Dakak manages to avoid the otherwise stormy winds of the typhoon season.

### How to Get There

Philippine Airlines flies to Dipolog via Cebu every day except Sunday, taking two hours from Manila (45 minutes from Cebu). They also have a 70-minute direct flight from Manila five days a week. Dapitan is 10 minutes further by bus.

## ZAMBOANGA CITY

With its sixteenth-century Spanish fortress, pink-tinged sand beaches and ethnically-mixed population, bustling Zamboanga City, on the tip of the Zamboanga Peninsula, is distinctly exotic. Zamboanga is an important regional fishing and trading port town and is also the gateway to the Sulu Archipelago and Basilan Island.

Like the city's main language, Chabacano, which is a babel of pidgin Spanish, Visayan and tribal dialects, Zamboangans are also an unusual blend of Christians, Muslims and some five tribal groups, including the Samal, Tausug, Yakan, Badjao and Subanon.

Arabic and Muslim influences are clearly reflected in the city's architecture, with its qutab-topped mosques and curvilinear roofs. The Moro men put on their traditional best for special occasions — sarongs with braided waistcoats and cummerbunds, with a fez or a turban, many armed with a decorative dagger tucked at the hip — while the women wear harem-type trousers with colorful silk brocade jackets.

Spanish influences preside here in the widespread Christianity, with smatterings of Spanish in the local dialect and in a diaspora of Spanish colonial forts, watchtowers and buildings.

The **Department of Tourism** office ( (62) 991-0217 is within the Lantaka Hotel, on Valderosa Street.

### What to See and Do

In the somewhat bland, modern city center, there are several places to see before you venture out to the more traditional stilt villages lying on Zamboanga's perimeters.

A good place to start exploring the city center is Plaza Pershing, the town square named after "Blackjack" Pershing, the first American governor of the region, which was formerly known as Moroland and was said to have spurred the development of the .45 pistol. **Fort del Pilar**, east of city hall on Valderrosa Street, is an old Spanish fortress which dates from 1635. Reeking of early

ABOVE: Elaborate beaded T'boli headdress. RIGHT: A Yakan tribeswoman demonstrates traditional weaving in Zamboanga.

imperial power, with its sturdy one-meter-thick walls and its cannons, this was the southernmost outpost for the Spanish, who made their capital around this fort. It was occupied by the Americans in 1899 and then by the Japanese in World War II. On the outside of the eastern wall, the shrine of **Nuestra Señora del Pilar**, the city's patron saint, draws devotees to pray and light candles here, especially on Saturday evening and Sunday services.

In the curious **Salakot House**, which is built in the shape of a large, wide-brimmed

nected by bamboo and wooden causeways, dominated by a mosque with ochre-tinted minarets. The arched bridge near the village is a good place to view the villages from a polite distance. The residents aren't impressed with amateur anthropologists or curious foreigners wandering around their living space clicking away with cameras, but will respect you if you respect them.

At the harbor near the Lantaka Hotel (see below), the beach and the sea are the site of a **floating market**, with the local boatmen operating *vintas* laden with reed mats, hand-

salakot hat, an extensive collection of Moro brassware is on display, giving you the chance to see the evolution in design of many beautiful but functional utensils used throughout the centuries. Other buildings in the compound are intriguing, such as the vinta-shaped cabin and a house built from shells. At the time of writing, the house was closed, but it may reopen in the near future. Leafy **Pansonaca Park** has beautiful botanical gardens and is where Zamboangans come to picnic.

A trip to see the unique stilt villages of **Rio Hondo** and **Taluksangay**, approximately 19 km (12 miles) east of Zamboanga, is also worthwhile. A mixture of Samal, Tausug and Badjao live here, with the settlements con-

woven textiles, wood carvings, Muslim brassware, unusual ceramics, and coral and shell trinkets — some of which are locally made and some of which are imported from China, Indonesia and Malaysia.

Keep an eye out especially for the colorful, geometric, hand-woven Samal and Yakan mats and cloth, as well as the famous T'boli *nalak* woven patterned cloths. Zamboanga's **city market** is the place to find such handicrafts. The market is open from dawn to dusk. **Yakan Weaving Village**, about three miles from the city, is another excellent place to find tribal weavings. And for shells, **San Luis Shell Industries** ( (62) 991-1044 on San Jose Road or **Zamboanga Home Products** ( (62) 991-1717 also on Jan Jose

Street, both have good selections. Those still in a bazaar mood should take a visit to the fish market near the wharves to see the fabulous daily array of ocean creatures and the adjacent public market. Zamboanga is proud of its unusual seafood delicacy, locally grown in fish farms, called *curacha*, a hybrid cross between a crab and a lobster. Another local dish is a salad of fresh lotus leaves.

The **Zamboanga Golf and Country Club** ( (62) 991-6817 FAX (62) 991-1796 is an attractive course just out of the town center.

Great Santa Cruz Island and Little Santa Cruz Island, which make up the **Santa Cruz Islands National Park** — only a 25-minute boat ride from the city — are popular for swimming, diving and snorkeling. Their beaches have remarkable pink sands, a result of the centuries-long erosion of pink coral in the surrounding reefs. There is a cemetery on Great Santa Cruz with small smiling figures and miniature wooden boats marking the gravesites of the Badjaos.

### Where to Stay and Eat

The moderately priced **Garden Orchid Hotel** ( (62) 991-0031 to 0033, on Governor Camins Road, is the most luxurious hotel in Zamboanga, with a decent restaurant, travel agency, shop, swimming pool and well-equipped health club. The drawback is that it's located out by the airport and thus not overly convenient to the town itself.

The **Lantaka Hotel** ( (62) 991-2033 to 2035, FAX (62) 991-1626, on Valderosa Street, is perhaps the most popular in town: the old queen of Zamboagan hotels, it is right on the waterfront. If somewhat worn, it has charm, friendly staff and reasonable facilities at inexpensive prices. The outdoor bar here is a great spot for sundowners. Another inexpensive option is the **Grand Astoria Hotel** (/FAX (62) 991-2510, close to the airport on Mayor Jaldon Street, which has clean, sunny rooms with friendly and knowledgeable staff.

**Alavar's Restaurant** ( (62) 991-2483, on Don Alfaro Street, is famous for its freshly caught local seafood dishes. The specialty is *curacha*, crabs in a creamy, sweet-spicy sauce. **Lotus Restaurant** ( (62) 991-2510, on Mayor Jaldon Street, is a recommended spot for Chinese and Filipino meals, while

**Palmeras** ( (62) 991-3284, Santa Maria Road, specializes in Spanish-style barbecued meats and fish.

### How to Get There

Philippine Airlines, Air Philippines, Asian Spirit, and Cebu Pacific all have daily flights from Manila to Zamboanga, with a flight time to Pagadian Airport of 90 minutes.

Flights are also available from Cebu and other regional airports in the Visayas and Mindanao, including Dumaguete, Davao,

Bacolod, Iloilo and Cagayan de Oro. Inter-island ferries connect with both provincial and regional ports. There are also boats to and from Sandakan, in Borneo.

OPPOSITE LEFT: A scarecrow on guard in a rice paddy. OPPOSITE RIGHT: Red snapper and other fish at the Zamboanga Fish Market. ABOVE: A Philippine hawk eagle.

# Palawan

REGARDLESS OF HOW MUCH I TRAVEL, or how many spectacular visions of nature I encounter, I cannot fail to be awed by the scale and beauty of Palawan. Majestic black limestone and marble caves with deep secretive forests arouse wonder, while marvelous seascapes beneath the waves were described by the late diving guru Jacques Cousteau as the most beautiful he had ever seen.

The least developed of all the large Philippine islands, Palawan defies superlatives. Here, more than on any other part of the Philippine archipelago, nature appears at peace with itself and man merely a temporary witness. In some of the island's remotest reaches it is easy to imagine, as your boat slides past giant crags rimmed with white sand and emerald sea, how early explorers felt when they saw this vision of undisturbed nature for the first time. Ashore, there are birds, animals and plants seen nowhere else in the Philippines. These include the rare parrots, peacock pheasant, Palawan mongoose, mouse deer, and king cobra. Palawan has wondrous butterflies — over 600 species — including the country's largest, the black and green papilo trojano.

The 400-km-long (248-mile), 40-km-wide (25-mile) ribbon-shaped island is the largest province in the Philippines, making up some five percent of the country's total land area. It has islands scattered around both its tips, with the best-known island groups being the Calamian islands in the north, the Balabac-Bugsuk group in the southeast and the Cuyo islands in the northwest. There are 1,768 islands within its perimeters, among them are Busuanga, Culion, Coron, Cuyo, Dumaran, Balabac and Bugsuk.

Inland, gigantic mountain crags make much of central Palawan almost impossible to explore, and traveling to different parts of the island can be difficult. In some cases, the journey by coast-hugging boat proves to be less time-consuming than the hard-going overland routes. Travelers have been known to arrive in Puerto Princesa, the island's capital in central Palawan, and, impressed by the natural beauty of that area, to decide to explore the remote north — for which they have returned to Manila to pick up the charter flight back to El Nido, the airstrip in the north.

Palawan hit the world's headlines in 1978 when anthropologists discovered a small kinship-based community of cave dwellers thought to have lived this way for many thousands of years, without outside contact — the Tau't Batu, or "People of the Rock" in Singnapan Basin, close to Ransang, in the Quezon area of the island. The Tau't Batu live along labyrinthine limestone ledges, some linked by wooden catwalks, and survive by hunting bats, frogs and birds with huge swats (made out of bamboo and woven palm fronds, laced with rattan thorns) and by gathering fruit, insects and crabs. When a creature has died or is killed, they make a wood or stone representation of it, apparently in compensation to nature. Their caves have been decorated with charcoal drawings of many kinds of anthropomorphic figures, thought to be representations of animals, birds and ghosts. This entire region is off-limits to visitors and, traveler beware, this ruling is heartily enforced by Palawan's military authorities.

Elsewhere, Palawan is sparsely populated. Many of its inhabitants originate from the Visayas. Among Palawan's indigenous tribal communities are the Pala'wan — who are quite shy and (perhaps understandably) wary of foreigners — and the Batuk. Nomadic Negrito tribes, who survive by hunting in the jungle, have resisted most attempts to coerce them to attend schools or to use more modern agricultural techniques. On Palawan's northern tip, the Tagbanua live in settled coastal villages. They fascinate anthropologists and linguists with their syllabic writing system, which is similar to that of the Hanunoo of Mindoro.

Palawan's natural wonders include the Tubbataha Reefs, which lie 150 km (93 miles) east of the island in the Sulu Sea, where you'll find one of the most spectacular marine reserve areas in the world. In southern Palawan, Saint Paul Subterranean National Park contains the world's longest underground river, eight kilometers (five miles) long, about half of which is navigable by boat. The experience of witnessing these glowing stalactites and stalagmites, deep under the earth, is impossible to convey. All who visit

El Nido: despite the luxury of the resorts, simple boats are de rigueur.

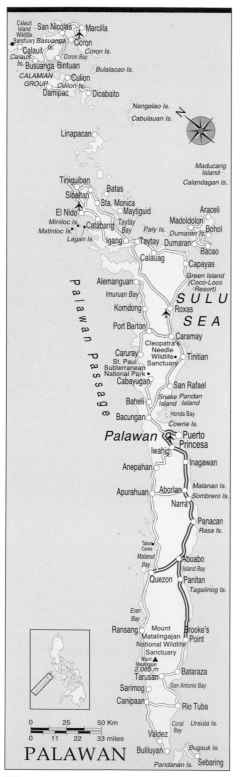

Calauit Island Wildlife Sanctuary
San Nicolas
Marcilla
Basuanga
Coron
Calauit Is.
Coron Is.
Calauit Is.
Busuanga
Bintuan
Coron Bay
Bulalacao Is.
CALAMIAN GROUP
Culion
Culion Is.
Damipac
Dicabaito
Nangalao Is.
Cabulauan Is.
Linapacan
Maducang Island
Calandagan Is.
Tiniquiban
Batas
Sibaltan
Sta. Monica
El Nido
Maytiguid
Araceli
Miniloc Is.
Catabang
Taytay Bay
Madoldolon
Matinloc Is.
Paly Is.
Bohol
Lagan Is.
Igang
Dumaran Is.
Taytay
Dumaran
Bacao
Calauag
Capayas
Green Island (Coco-Loco Resort)
Alemanguan
Imuruan Bay
SULU
Komdong
Roxas
Port Barton
SEA
Caramay
Caruray
Cleopatra's Needle Wildlife Sanctuary
Tinitian
St. Paul Subterranean
National Park
Cabayugan
San Rafael
Baheli
Snake Pandan Island Island
Bacungan
Honda Bay
Cowrie Is.
Palawan
Puerto Princesa
Iwahig
Inagawan
Anepahan
Apurahuan
Aborlan
Malanao Is.
Sombrero Is.
Narra
Panacan
Rasa Is.
Tabon Caves
Malanut Bay
Aboabo Island Bay
Quezon
Panitan
Tagalinog Is.
Eran Bay
Ransang
Mount Matalingajan National Wildlife Sanctuary
Brooke's Point
Mount Matalingajan 2,085 m
Bataraza
Tarusan
San Antonio Bay
Sarimog
Canipaan
Rio Tuba
Coral Bay
Ursula Is.
Valdez
Buliluyan
Bugsuk Is.
Pandanan Is.
Sebaring

0  25  50 Km
0  11  22  33 miles

**PALAWAN**

come away in amazement at the glorious complexity of nature. In the north, El Nido and its surrounding limestone caves offer magnificent scenery both above and below the sea, and two well-run resorts, which are perfect as diving or snorkeling bases.

The central and northern islands of Palawan are home to some of the finest resorts in the Philippines. Amanpulo, on Pamalican Island in the Cuyo Group, the El Nido resorts on the islands of Miniloc and Lagan, and Club Paradise on Dimakya Island in the Calamian group are all havens of comfort, providing a very high standard — in Amanpulo's case, exceptional standard — of comfort and relaxation.

Palawan's southernmost point reaches out towards Malaysia and is bounded to the west by the Kalayaan Islands within the South China Sea, a cluster of 53 tiny coral islands, islets, reefs, shoals, and cays better known as the Spratleys. Scattered over a vast area of sea, these islands, said to be rich in oil and other mineral deposits, are hotly contested by China, Vietnam, Taiwan, Malaysia, Brunei and the Philippines. The Philippines today occupies a handful of these isles.

The future for Palawan is uncertain. Will the Philippine government be able to preserve this spellbinding sanctuary from the many environmental depredations that have proved so devastating elsewhere in the archipelago? Since oil was discovered off Palawan's northwestern coast, the imminent development of this industry looks almost certain. Widespread logging has already devastated much of Palawan's precious forest — at least 20,000 sq km (7,700 sq miles) so far — and with their habitat gone, many endemic species have been lost. The environmental effects of any more industrial development may spell disaster for this fragile island paradise.

"The tragedy of the oceanic islands lies in their uniqueness, the irreplaceability of the species they have developed by the slow process of the ages. In a reasonable world, men would have treated these islands as precious possessions, as natural museums filled with beautiful and curious works of creation beyond price because nowhere in the world are they duplicated." When the prescient Rachel Carson wrote this 30 years ago, she could well have been writing specifically about Palawan.

Yet, many Philippine environmentalists, and the Palawanese themselves, are determined not to see their home altered for the worse, and there is a high level of awareness of these issues even in remote villages.

Malaria is known in the Palawan region, especially during the monsoon season between July and August. Malarial mosquitoes tend to decline in numbers during the dry season, reducing the risk. The malaria-carrying breed of mosquito, known as anopheles, is the culprit.

Make sure you are well-prepared, by covering up legs and arms after dark and by following antimalarial medication dosages carefully. Larium, for example, requires that you begin treatment a week before arriving in a malaria-prone region, that you continue taking tablets throughout, and then for four weeks after you leave. Resochin and Fansidar are commonly prescribed, yet the mosquitoes in Palawan seem to have developed a resistance to Resochin. If you do suspect you might be coming down with malaria, with its telltale signs of persistent fever and chills, go straight to the hospital at Puerto Princesa, where local doctors are familiar with both symptoms and treatment. Mosquito repellent and nets are clearly useful.

## PUERTO PRINCESA

Palawan's provincial capital is the most convenient destination from which to start your trip to other parts of central Palawan. If, however, you plan to visit some of the more remote parts of the archipelago, then it is often more practical to charter an aircraft from Manila.

### GENERAL INFORMATION

The information counter at the airport can help with immediate queries. The **City Tourist Office** ( (48) 433-2154 on Rizal Avenue near the Roxas Street corner is more helpful though. The **Provincial Tourist Office** ( (48) 433-2983 in the Provincial Capitol Building on Rizal Avenue, is useful to visit for more regional information.

Both of these organizations are independent of the government tourist offices found on other Philippine islands. Visiting in person is advised.

You should clear your travel plans to protected or remote areas with the **Conservation and Resources Management Foundation** ( (4821) 705-5001. The monthly newsletter *Bandillo ng Palawan*, which is published by local environmentalists, is a good introduction to the preoccupations of the island.

In Puerto Princesa, the **Metrobank** and the **Philippine National Bank** ( (48) 433-2321

will cash travelers' checks and foreign exchange; elsewhere on the island you won't find this service easily.

The private **Adventist Hospital** ( (48) 433-2156 is located on San Pedro Street. And for any emergencies, Puerto Princesa's **Police Station** ( (48) 433-2818 or (48) 433-2101 is on Peneyra Road.

There is ample reason for civic pride in Puerto Princesa. This relatively modern city of a little over 100,000 residents has won much praise. In 1993, Puerto Princesa won the Earth Day Award for "World Wildlife and Protected Area Management." In 1994, it was given the Philippines' National Distinction Award for being the "Best-Governed Local Government Unit," the First Macliing Dulag Environmental Achievement Award, and was cited as the "Cleanest and Greenest City in the Philippines." Recently the city captured the Philippines Development Award, the first time that a local government was elevated to the elite circle of management award winners.

Fun at the Puerto Princesa Foundation Day Festival.

Much of this acclaim is a result of the efforts of concerned local officials who have headed a drive to protect their island by keeping out polluting industries, developing "green" tourism, and replanting forests. They initially launched the Bantay Puerto Program, a campaign against forest environmental degradation. One of its offshoots was the *Pista Y Ang Kageban*, or "Feast of the Forest," initiatives, that mobilized thousands of Palawanese to plant some 700,000 trees throughout the island. Another was the establishment of a sort of guardian angels volunteer network on the sea, the Bantay Dagat, whose efforts led to the arrest of more than 7,100 vessels for violation of fishing laws such as illegal dynamite fishing and cyanide poisoning. In addition, local officials are seeking alternatives for islanders who endanger the forests through slash-and-burn farming — and encouraging Palawan farmers to grow seaweed instead.

It is impossible not to be impressed by these efforts. Yet smokers beware! Puerto Princesa is positively Singaporean in its non-tolerance of those who attempt to throw away their cigarette butts in the street — and stiff and immediate fines apply to offenders.

Puerto Princesa was founded by the Spanish in 1872 and named after the Queen of Spain's daughter, Asunción. After her early death, the town's name was changed to Puerto de la Princesa, which soon shortened to the present name.

## WHAT TO SEE AND DO

Most visitors come to Puerto Princesa with the intention of seeing **Saint Paul Subterranean National Park** as ecotourists. While in the capital, however, there are a few intriguing places to visit, not to mention some amusing signs along the main Rizal Avenue: the "**Infant Jesus Learning Center**," and "**Tecson's Derm Center** (We Take Care of Your Skin)" to start with. The twin-spired **Puerto Princesa Cathedral** looms over the center, which includes a number of modest Spanish colonial buildings, including the Governor's General's Residence and the Holy Trinity College. The **Palawan State College Museum** has some ethnological treasures culled from prehistoric dig sites, including fossils and crude implements.

Located near the airport, the **Vietnamese Refugee Center** seems an unlikely subject to mention in a guide book, yet visitors may otherwise be baffled by the large population of Vietnamese in Puerto Princesa. Nicknamed "Little Saigon" it was opened in 1979. The camp, staffed by foreign aid workers, is essentially an orientation camp for refugees who have been admitted into the Philippines for resettlement, and its inhabitants are freely allowed to visit the city. It is worth sampling Vietnamese snacks and soups at the cafés just outside the camp.

The **Irawan Crocodile Farming Institute**, located between Puerto Princesa and Iwahig,

is a Japanese-financed crocodile farm that aims to preserve and advance international research studies on the endangered Philippine crocodile. Somewhat alarmingly, this farm has allegedly exported some of the beasts in the inanimate form of shoes, belts and handbags. The farm is open Monday to Friday from 1 PM to 4 PM and on Saturday and public holidays from 8 AM to noon.

## Iwahig

In Iwahig, which lies 23 km (14 miles) south of Puerto Princesa at the foot of Mount Stavely, there is an unusual prison "commune," in which inmates live in relatively unguarded villages without walls — tending crops, orchards and coconut plantations set in 386 sq km (149 sq miles). It was established in 1904 and is perhaps the only prison without bars in the world. Tourists are welcome at the prison shop, which sells handicrafts made by the prisoners, who are called "colonists." Palawan has a remarkably low incidence of repeat offenders — perhaps this experiment in criminal psychology is one of the reasons. The penal colony is entirely self-sufficient and is not funded by the state. You can hire a tricycle from Puerto Princesa for a half day to visit both of these destinations, which are about a half hour's journey from Puerto Princesa. Otherwise ask about buses at the City Tourist Office.

Large outriggers, used commercially and as passenger boats, in the harbor at Puerto Princesa.

*Palawan*

## Honda Bay

The islands that pepper Honda Bay, about 12 km (seven miles) from Puerto Princesa, are rewarding to visit, and it is possible to stay overnight on some of them. While divers wax lyrical about the underwater panoramas, less ambitious activities — such as snorkeling, lazing on the beach, or exploring coastal tracks — are equally sublime. Majestic mountain scenes dominate the horizon — in the distance, Mount Cleopatra's Needle rises 1,590 m (5,220 feet).

The Honda Bay islands include the following: **Pandan**, **Snake**, **Cowrie**, **Starfish**, **Bat**, **Meara Marina** and **Loli**. Most of these islands have inviting, shallow reefs and good beaches for picnics. Pandan Island is the best known, yet Snake Island, despite its name, is probably the most pleasant for a day's visit. There is a small resort on Meara Marina Island. Bat Island is home to more than a thousand bats, which hang off the mangroves by day, and by night flap off in search of fodder.

## WHERE TO STAY

### Mid-range

**Asiaworld Resort Hotel (** (48) 433-2022 FAX (48) 433-2515 **(** MANILA (2) 242-6546 or **(** (2) 834-1354, National Highway, Barangay San Miguel, is Puerto Princesa's largest and most modern hotel, formerly part of the Hyatt chain. It has a good swimming pool and both Chinese and Japanese restaurants, as well as nightly live entertainment at its disco.

### Inexpensive

**Badjao Inn (** (48) 433-2761 on Rizal Avenue, is very popular with divers and has either fan-cooled or more expensive air-conditioned rooms, with refrigerator and television. The hotel has a pleasant garden and restaurant. **The Casalinda (** (48) 433-2606, on Trinidad Road and Rizal Avenue, is similar in style to the Badjao Inn, with a verandah as well as a courtyard garden and parrots. It's a great place to just lounge around and meet other travelers. American Pat Murray and his Filipina wife, Gina will be around to answer any questions you might have.

The new kid on the Puerto Princesa block is **Hotel Fleuris (** (48) 233-3380, on Lacao Street. The three-story building has an impressive atrium and lobby and the rooms are large and comfortably furnished. If you are looking for something resembling a native nipa-hut getaway but don't want to be far from your e-mail, check out **Trattoria Inn and Swiss Bistro (** (48) 433-2719 on Rizal Avenue. Each room has an individual Internet connection. Swiss owner Claudio Schoch is good at providing the finer details, like individual sandals for each room and a bar bell for appreciative drinkers. His travel agency on the property is very helpful at arranging transport to the underground river in Sabang and providing accommodation once there at Mr. Schoch's other property, Panaguman Beach Resort.

## WHERE TO EAT

Puerto Princesa has a good reputation for its seafood specialties, as well it should, with access to so many varieties of fresh fish. For a traditional experience **Ka Lui's (** (48) 433-2580, opposite the Badjao Inn on Rizal Avenue is considered to be the city's best restaurant. They specialize in seafood and vegetable entrees. The delicious food and the open-air bamboo verandah make for a very relaxing experience. There is even live music on various nights, when adults and children come together with handmade instruments. Inexpensive to moderate.

**AsiaWorld (** (48) 433-2022 has quite a variety of regional cuisines to choose from at moderate prices. A culinary mix of Japanese, Chinese, and international dishes awaits at its Tagpuan Garden Grill, for tasty steaks and seafood, Seven Dragon, for Chinese, or Yoko for Japanese. They also scoop out homemade ice cream in the lobby.

## HOW TO GET THERE

Philippine Airlines has daily flights from Manila, which take 70 minutes to reach Puerto Princesa.

Pacific Airways Corporation and Aerolift also have flights to and from Cuyo and Coron in Palawan. Inter-island boats ply regularly from Manila to Puerto Princesa and make stops along the route via the Cuyo islands and Panay, in the Visayas.

Around the island, boats are used to make coast-hugging journeys to regions inaccessible by jeepney, bus or car, such as the Saint Paul Subterranean National Park.

## EXCURSIONS FROM PUERTO PRINCESA

**Saint Paul Subterranean National Park** Also known as the "Underground River," Saint Paul Subterranean National Park encompasses 39 sq km (15 sq miles), with

growl of the boat's motor as it glides through, past awesome glistening, marble-like colorful stalagmite and pillared stalactite formations. The way is lit by the boatman guide, who carries a carbide or kerosene lamp. About halfway into the cave, the boats disembark on a small muddy underground beach, which is usually a cue to turn around and return. It is possible to go farther, as the river extends another two kilometers (one and one quarter miles). The local guides have sound instincts about current conditions within the caves, and it is best to defer to their wisdom.

spectacular mountains, limestone caves, white sand beaches and lush forest. The river itself flows through the underground cave for about eight kilometers (five miles), emerging into the sunlight where it meets the South China Sea at Saint Paul Bay. The majestic **Saint Paul Mountain** soars for 108 m (354 feet) above the cave's entrance.

Visitors can either board a boat at Sabang or walk along marked paths through the wilderness for almost an hour to the cave's entrance. Once the boat enters the pitch-black passageway, your eyes take a while to get used to the darkness. Strange sounds break the otherwise uncanny silence: bats mewing and flapping, drips of moisture from the ceiling some 15 m (49 feet) above, and the

WHERE TO STAY
There are several inexpensive places to stay overnight in Sabang, including the **Villa Sabang**, **Mary's Cottages**, or the **Bambua Jungles Cottages**. Camping facilities are also available at the **park ranger station** ( (48) 433-2409 itself.

**Panaguman Beach Resort** ( (48) 433-2719 is situated on its own island not far from the cave. If you book with them they will arrange to have a boat waiting for you at the cave to take you the short distance to the sleepy, cozy island getaway. It is a great value and truly captures the nature of the area.

There is much to smile about in Puerto Princesa. The city has won awards for its orderliness and policies towards development.

**HOW TO GET THERE**

Before entering the park you must secure an entry permit, which you can get at the **Saint Paul Subterranean National Park office** ( (48) 433-2409, on Manalo Street in Puerto Princesa. The minimal price includes boat and guide. The permit is also sold at the park's entrance in Sabang.

The park is reached most easily from the township of Sabang, by four-wheel-drive vehicle along the relatively new road from Puerto Princesa It's an effortless 90-minute-or-so journey in the dry season, but takes longer during the monsoon season.

The whole trip can be arranged through the Provincial Tourist Office in Puerto Princesa. **Go Palawan Travel and Tours** ( (48) 433-4570, based at the Trattoria Inn on Rizal

Avenue, makes the journey a cinch. They offer the cheapest, most comfortable and reliable means of getting to Sabang and the Underground River. From Sabang, pump-boats (included in your permit fee) can take you the 20 minutes to the cave entrance, or you can start at the wilderness trails and hike by foot.

Another route is to travel to **Baheli**, also about 90 minutes' drive from Puerto Princesa, where outrigger *bancas* make the three-hour voyage to the river's starting point. This option is only recommended during the dry season, as heavy rains during the monsoon can create treacherous conditions. Generally, you'll be discouraged from visiting the park during rough weather or storms, which tend to occur from June to November.

and spectacular drop-offs make this a stunning place to explore.

Tubbataha Reefs are home to some 300 species of coral and nearly 400 species of fish (including six shark species), the two main reef sites are frequently visited by hawksbill and green turtles. Black-tip and white-tip sharks, small jacks, barracudas, mackerel and schools of vibrantly colored tropical pelagic fish are easily sighted, as well as the unusual dugong. Vast communities of migrating seabird colonies also visit the nesting sites within the Tubbataha Reefs National Marine Park, with more than 1,000 brown boobies nesting here every season. Giant turtles lay their eggs on the reefs' shores and baby sharks often doze on their rocky shallows.

Yet sadly, since the marine park was established the reefs have noticeably deteriorated. An estimated quarter of the coral is now damaged, in part because of illegal dynamite fishing, but mostly because of the regular visits by dive boats. Dive boats often anchor directly on reefs, a problem that becomes compounded by repeated visits to the same sites.

In 1989, a controversy over the management of this precious marine resource erupted when a group of divers observed that a large-scale seaweed farm was being set up with government permission within the Tubbahata Reefs. The seaweed entrepreneur behind the venture was in the throes of constructing an entire stilt-house village, to which he planned to bring some 6,000 families to work as his employees. Finally, months later, after the Philippine conservation groups rallied to prevent the farm, President Aquino ordered its removal.

Although the protest was ultimately successful, the incident jaundiced Philippine and international conservationists, who realized the extent to which industry could take priority over the protection of what was an apparently shielded environment. The UNESCO World Heritage Fund has provided funding since 1996 to initiate monitoring of activities and to provide information and education campaigns to protect the park from further negative impacts.

## Tubbataha Reefs National Marine Park

Lying in the middle of the Sulu Sea, about 150 km (93 miles) from Palawan, the Tubbataha Reefs are world famous. The best known of all Philippine dive locations, the reefs were declared a marine park in 1988. Despite the region's isolation, dive boats are frequently booked up for months in advance by avid Japanese, European and American divers. This is partly because diving is only possible between mid-March to mid-June when the monsoon winds no longer blow.

The eight-kilometer-long (five-mile) and one-kilometer-wide (half-mile) reefs are bounded by a pair of rocks, their deep blue lagoon ringed with shallower light green waters, which vary in depth from knee-deep to waist-high. Many varieties of coral, fish

Part of the spectacular Saint Paul Subterranean National Park.

The marine reserve is managed with the assistance of the Tubbahata Foundation, a collection of conservationists and dive operators, and only diving and sustainable fishing practices by the nearby Cayancillo islanders are permitted. **Queen Ann Divers** E-MAIL trattori@pal-onl.com in Puerto Princesa can arrange diving trips to the reef aboard their live-aboard boat. The **MY** *Nautika* E-MAIL inquiries@divephil.com also makes seasonal luxury dive cruise trips to the reef. The vessel accommodates sixteen divers in four twin-berth and two four-berth cabins.

Each one is furnished like a holiday suite and equipped with individual toilet and shower with hot and cold water, sink and vanity.

## TRAVELING SOUTH

Traveling farther south, the region around the city of **Quezon**, 157 km (97 miles) southwest of Puerto Princesa, reveals another of Palawan's remarkable natural gems: the network of 200 or so warrens that make up the **Tabon Caves**. Since their discovery in 1962, only 29 have been explored and only seven are open to the public. The caves have been a rich site for finds of fossilized prehistoric remains — called "Tabon Man," carbon-dated to 50,000 years, the oldest trace of Homo sapiens in the Philippines. **Diwata Cave** is the most beautiful, 30 m (100 feet) above the sea. The best way to arrange to visit is to ask at Quezon's small and interesting **National Museum** for a guide to the caves — the tour takes about half an hour. From Puerto Princesa, it is a five-hour jeepney ride to reach the caves.

Quezon is the venue for a colorful annual festival: the **Feast of our Lady of Lourdes** (see FESTIVE FLINGS, page 51 in YOUR CHOICE).

About four kilometers (two and a half miles) northwest of Tabon, the **Tabon Village Resort** has simple, inexpensive and comfortable cottages and is a good base from which to explore the surrounding waterfalls and dense jungle. Located on Tabon Beach, it is managed by a Belgian called Theo. Tabon Village is a beautiful place, although the rocky shore can make swimming difficult. The resort's restaurant, **Mutya ng Dagak**, "Pearl of the Sea," is on an artificial island, connected to the mainland by bridge. It's an unusual place to dine.

On the southeastern point of Palawan, British explorer Sir James Brooke once lived on **Brooke's Point**, and the watchtower he built still stands. The small township of Brooke's Point has a backdrop of gigantic ranges dominated by **Mount Matalingajan**, at 2,086 m (6,843 feet), it's the island's largest mountain, which lies 25 km (16 miles) away. If you have come this far, you must go to **Mainit Hot Springs**, 10 km (six miles) northwest of Brooke's Point. Near forest and mangroves, the waist-deep hot sulfuric springs look onto a waterfall. Heavenly.

The nearby, uninhabited **Ursula Island** used to attract thousands of nesting birds, but it seems many have been frightened away to far-off Tubbataha Reefs by the presence of shotgun-toting hunters. It is still home to the rare *sieste colores* ("seven colored") bird, unfortunately prey to poachers. At sunset, there is a spectacular display as birds swoop and wheel to their nests. You can reach Ursula Island by hiring a pumpboat from Brooke's Point or **Bataraza**. Another notable destination is **Balabac Island**, off the southern tip of Palawan. This isolated island is home to the Muslim tribal Molbogs and has rare conus seashells. From here, vintas make frequent excursions across to the Malaysian islands.

## TRAVELING NORTH

From Puerto Princesa, if you have already reached Saint Paul Subterranean National Park and wish to travel farther, you will have to pass through **San Rafael**, a settlement that is close to an area populated by the nomadic Batak tribes. Reluctant to have much contact with outsiders, the Batak have unfortunately had to contend with the incursions of determined tourists, sometimes led by Philippine-organized tour groups. As in

many situations throughout the Philippines, the issue of whether or not to encroach on the private lives and customs of many tribal groups is an extremely sensitive one.

The Bataks are considered the most "primitive" and colorful of Palawan's tribal people, with trinket adornments, flying squirrel tails on their backs and flowers in their hair. Traditionally, men wear G-string-like garments and women are bare-breasted. To reach the Batak village involves a two-hour drive from Puerto Princesa to **Tanabao** and then a three-hour trek through jungle.

Farther north, the pleasant seaside village of **Roxas** looks out across a sweeping bay, ringed by a coral reef and a number of beautiful small islands, including **Pandan Island**,

*Palawan*

with the Coco-Loco resort. The coast-hugging road then passes vistas of breathtaking jungle, with hints of the exotic creatures — including crocodiles — found inland. **Taytay** was Palawan's original Spanish capital, with the ruins of a fort built in 1622. From Taytay, the rugged adventurer can explore by outrigger *banca* the many surrounding islands, some of which have small bungalows to rent. **Paly Island** is where giant hawksbill turtles come ashore to nest and lay their eggs from November to December.

### WHERE TO STAY AND EAT

The **Coco Loco Beach Resort** ( (48) 433-3877 FAX (48) 433-3554 WEB SITE www.palawan .net/peter/cocoloco.htm, Pandan Island, PO Box 18, Puerto Princesa, is a peaceful and beautiful getaway beckoning you to explore the surrounding island. The resort provides jungle river tours to a waterfall. The moderate-to-expensive prices include three meals a day. **Club Noah Isabelle** ( (918) 909-5582 or 909-5583 ( MANILA (2) 810-7291 to 7293 FAX (2) 818-2640, Apulit Island, Taytay, is popular with divers in search of a moderately priced base for exploring the beautiful Taytay Bay area. Hidden in a cove behind huge limestone formations, Club Noah's stilted cabanas perch over the water, with verandas that face the sea. It's one of the most eco-sensitive of the country's resorts, and binoculars are available to take advantage of the excellent bird-watching possibilities.

## EL NIDO

El Nido gets its name from *nido*, the prized *balinsasayaw,* or swiftlet's "nest," the essential ingredient for the region's famous, supposedly curative, bird's nest soup. Visiting ornithologist Paul Baker described, in 1927, the nests as "of pure white semi-translucent saliva half cups stuck against the sloping roots of small caves, like a half saucer of fine strings of glass, all matted together." Witnessing the dexterous Palawanese *boceadores*, as the nest gatherers are called, climb into the vertigi-

OPPOSITE and ABOVE: Palawan is still home to a number of primitive tribes, one of which, the cave-dwelling Tau't Batu, was only discovered in 1978.

nous heights of the limestone caves to harvest the swiftlet's nests is an impressive sight. Boceadores, who risk their lives each time they scale these jagged crags, acquire their right to gather nests by bidding for a concession granted by the municipal government and are always worried about opportunistic poachers: one kilogram (two and a quarter pounds) of top quality birds' nest can be sold for more than US$3,000.

Typical of a Southeast Asian village whose residents depend on the reefs for much of their food and income, El Nido town snuggles around a wide bay at the foot of a dazzling line of limestone mountains. Its residents are civic-minded and churchgoing, and the small but bustling **market** is the town's main focus. Signs dotted throughout the town point to an information campaign by the El Nido Foundation to raise environmental awareness, with instructions for "Zero Waste Management through Total Recycling of Domestic Wastes: You Can Adopt This Technology for Your Household Benefits." Notices pinned on trees advertise upcoming fiestas and band practices. Many of the men here make a living by fishing with fine nets on shallow reefs and seagrass beds and collecting sea urchins by hand. Spiky lobsters are a prized catch, relished by locals and visitors alike; recently their value has soared, so the bulk of the catch goes to restaurants.

## WHAT TO SEE AND DO

While many people come to El Nido to do nothing but relax and appreciate its beauty, other more strenuous activities are popular. Diving, snorkeling and windsurfing are all offered at the resorts and on El Nido beach.

The **El Nido Tourist Office** (no phone) on the main street is helpful for advising on local walks. They supply small maps of the town and the region, with suggestions for visiting ancient burial caves, adventurous hikes, marble cliffs and other spots for those in the know. Local fishermen often hire themselves out as guides, escorting you by *banca*. The Tourist Office likes for you to register in their visitor book, since visitors are still a novelty. This also allows them to keep track of guests while they are in the area.

Within the El Nido region, some of the more spectacular places to see include the **turtle sanctuary** at Inalula, the black marble **Pinasil Cave** at Bigan, and the **giant rock formations** at Dilumacad. **Matinloc Island** is one of the most beautiful islands, with its hard-to-find Secret Beach, which has to be reached by swimming through a wide rock crevice that only experienced guides will be able to bring you to.

## WHERE TO STAY AND EAT

### Expensive

**Miniloc Island Resort** lies in a tiny cove dwarfed by grand outcroppings of limestone. With stilted cottages and terraced bungalows, the resort is small enough to feel intimate — especially surrounded by so much rampant nature. Miniloc has also been devised to allow as much freedom as possible to explore outlying islands and dive sites, and guests are routinely ferried to their destination of choice for a stay of a few hours. Others opt to take kayaks on their own to explore the secret lagoons nearby, which teem with exotic fish. The resort is geared at serious divers, and diving packages include equipment and two dives a day, as well as all meals. When making reservations, ask for a stilted waterfront bungalow or a cliff-side cottage, either of which are more atmospheric than the beach cottages. Accommodations are pleasantly furnished, with ceiling fans and good hot-water pressure — almost a miracle in such a remote location. Service is friendly and the buffet-style food is good.

Built in 1997 to replace a resort that burned down on a nearby island, **Lagen Island Resort** is three times larger and more romantic than its neighbor Miniloc, and less expensive than the exclusive Amanpulo. Lagen is set within a pristine bay, in a rainforest surrounded by sheer limestone cliffs. Accommodation is in stilted cottages, and all marine sports are at your disposal, including the resorts's excellent diving facilities.

Reservations for both Miniloc Island and Lagen Island resorts should be made in Manila through **El Nido Resorts Reservations**

Arial view of North Palawan and its scores of islands.

( (2) 894-5644 FAX (2) 810-3620 WEB SITE www
.elnidoresorts.com, Second Floor, Builders
Center Building, 170 Salcedo Street, Legaspi
Village, Makati. Both resorts are run as a joint
venture between A. Soriano Corporation and
Nissin Sugar of Japan, with the stated aim of
developing awareness about conservation and
protection of the El Nido region, cooperating
with and employing the local community. The
company has initiated an environment education campaign, beach clean up and tree-
planting projects, and a mooring buoy project
to protect El Nido's coral reefs.

### Mid-range

I feel guilty writing up this resort — because
part of the beauty of it is that it has remained
a secret — an untouched, pure, affordable
paradise getaway. **Dolarog Resort** ( MANILA
(2) 365-9105 or (2) 365-2344 FAX (2) 365-2345
E-MAIL dolarog@cavite.com, located on its
own island just a short boat ride from El Nido
town, won't break the bank like neighboring El Nido resorts, but offers probably the
best views of the sunset and stunning rock
formations jutting dramatically from the sea.
Each private cabana comes with its own porch
hammock, and although there are no amenities like air conditioning or hot water, the
Italian marble bathrooms are sparkling clean.
Italian owner Edo and his Filipina wife have
created an unforgettable, peaceful retreat, and
the aura of the resort is simple and private.
Family-style meals are included in the rates
— usually a traditional Filipino meal.

For another Garden of Eden near El Nido
town, **Malapacao Island Resort** ( PUERTO
PRINCESA (918) 530-9116, ask for Wilma
( EL NIDO (918) 909-5573 or (919) 555-3176,
ask for Zoraida or Fritzie, is a harmonious
eco-conscious resort situated in its own cove
alongside El Nido's Bacuit Bay Marine Sanctuary. No meat-eating or smoking is allowed
in the simple, airy cottages — where communal living is the rule of the house. There
are opportunities to hike to waterfalls,
mountain climb, snorkel and island-hop, and
the food is always homemade and organic.

### Inexpensive

There are several small and inexpensive
bungalow-style cottages in El Nido town.
**Mariana Cottages** (no phone), at the quiet

end of the town's beach, is peaceful and
pleasantly decorated, and handy to the
town's restaurants.

## How to Get There

Tucked in the northern reaches of Palawan,
El Nido is difficult to reach from the southern part of the island, unless you are prepared
for a long land and boat journey. Many visitors to El Nido come to stay at one of the two
Ten Knots Development Corporation resorts
located here — the El Nido Miniloc Island Resort and the El Nido Lagen Island Resort —
and so arrive by charter aircraft. As the small
plane circles to land on the grass strip near
El Nido township, passengers glimpse the
majesty of the landscape they are about to enter.
The airport is charming and tiny, with iced
tea and snacks served to guests of the resorts,
who are ferried by outrigger boat across to
either island, past hovering giants of stone,
craggy coves and slivers of white sand.

For others, access to El Nido is normally
via a a 19-seater Dornier 228 aircraft, which
leaves from the **A. Soriano Aviation Terminal** ( (2) 804-0760 in Manila twice daily from
October to May, and once a day from June
to September. The trip takes about one hour.
If there are more than 19 reservations for the
flight, additional types of light aircraft are
made available. In most cases, the flight is
smooth, although slight turbulence is felt
during heavy rains, in which case, traveling
time may take longer. If you have arrived in
El Nido Town by another means and want
to fly back, you can check on the availability of seats at **Ten Knots Office** (known as
the White House) in El Nido.

The other alternative is to fly to Puerto
Princesa and take a jeepney to Roxas, which
takes seven hours, then a pumpboat from
Taytay to El Nido. Local boat owners in
Sabang (near the Underground River) also
take tourists on the seven-hour trip to El Nido
in their small pumpboats. The prices can get
hefty, but split between a group of people,
it's not so bad. It's a beautiful ride along the
white beaches on the South China Sea.

Or you'll be truly roughing it if you
choose to bus the Puerto Princesa route to
El Nido. Expect 10 hours of bumpy, tire-
busting, packed travel. Buses usually leave

early in the morning from the Malvar Street bus depot in Puerto Princesa.

## THE CALAMIAN ISLANDS

There are several smaller, wonderful strings of islands to explore near Palawan, including the Calamian group, with its main islands of **Busuanga**, **Culion** and tiny **Coron**. The largest port town and diver's base is on Coron Island. Spectacular coral gardens and submerged vessels sunk during World War II are some of the rewards to those who venture into the depths here. The names of some of the islands' towns are the same as those of the islands themselves, and so confusion often occurs. Note that Busuanga Island has both a Busuanga town and a Coron town, while Coron Island lies to the south.

Some 24 Japanese naval wrecks, of which 12 are charted, lie in the bay bordered by Culion, Basuanga and Coron Islands. This bay, called Coron Bay, is the Philippines' premier wreck-diving site.

### GENERAL INFORMATION

There are a dozen or so dive operators in Coron Town that have well-equipped boats and gear, as well as information on all the wrecks available for exploration. **Scubaventure** E-MAIL sventure@mozcom.com, has an excellent dive shop complete with bar, surround-sound stereo and television for movies after a day of diving. **Discovery Divers** E-MAIL info@ddivers.com is the oldest and most popular operator in the area.

### WHAT TO SEE AND DO

#### Wreck Diving

There are many secrets beneath the waters off the shores of Coron. For the advanced diver, the chance to explore the mulls, masts, and decks of over 14 World War II Japanese wrecks, each with its own character and story, is too great to pass up.

On September 24, 1944, after scouring the ground for a spot to place MacArthur and his troops, the United States Navy noticed that what was thought to be an island had shifted position. They were not islands, but a fleet of Japanese ships positioned for attack.

In retaliation, the United States Navy bombed the fleet and it was repositioned at the bottom of the sea from that day on.

From the Morozan, or Akitsushima sea plane that was once part of the Imperial Japanese Navy, to Nanshin Maru, an oiler, and Kyokuzan Maru, an almost-intact freighter, there are enough wrecks to keep any advanced diver occupied for a few days.

#### Calauit Island

Within the Calamian group is the very special Calauit Island. Founded in 1976, this unusual

wildlife island sanctuary is home to many African animals, a dramatic sight in such a radically tropical terrain. The island spans 3,700 ha (9,100 acres) and the animals roam free. There are giraffe, zebra, eland, impala, bushbuck, gazelle, and waterbuck from Kenya. From the original stock of 58, the population has increased some 400, of which most are island-born. Also, the island is home to several species endemic to Palawan, such as Calamian deer, scaly anteater, wild pigs, monkeys, monitor lizards, bear cats, squirrels, Palawan porcupines, mouse deer and the Palawan peacock pheasant, as well as other bird species. The seas surrounding the island abound with fish and coral, while giant turtles come ashore to lay their eggs, and the unusual *dugong*, or sea cow, grazes in its seaweed beds.

To visit Calauit Island, you need permission from the **Conservation and Resource Management Foundation** ( (2) 785081 to 89,

Fragile though it may appear, the outrigger *banca* is a most stable vessel, ideally suited for travel through the waters of the archipelago.

Ground Floor, IRC Building, No. 82 Epifanio de los Santos Avenue, Metro Manila. When calling, ask for Dr. Francisco Panol.

## WHERE TO STAY AND EAT

### Mid-range

**Club Paradise (** MANILA (2) 816-6871 to 6875 FAX (2) 818-2894, Dimakya Island, Coron, is located off the northern side of Busuanga Island, on Dimakya Island. The resort has 40 native-style comfortable, non-air-conditioned cottages with verandahs and tiled bathrooms, tucked into a palm-landscaped cove which is lovely for swimming. It is a good choice for action-seeking visitors who don't necessarily want to concentrate only on diving. It has a pleasant seaside lounge, a tennis court, swimming pool, and a games room, and arranges island-hopping excursions. There are a variety of water sports on offer, including fishing, and has full facilities for diving. Rates include all meals, an introductory dive and full use of all the sports facilities. It is reached from Busuanga via boat — a ride of an hour and 10 minutes. The luxurious resort of **Amanpulo** (see below) is located nearby on Pamalican Island, and can be reached from Manila by chartered plane. You can also visit Calauit Island from Busuanga.

**Sangat Island Reserve (** MANILA (2) 526-1295 FAX (2) 525-8041 E-MAIL reservations @sangat.com.ph, Sangat Island, Coron Bay, is a beautiful family-owned resort that has probably the best location in the area if you are planning to dive the wrecks, most of which are only a few minutes' boat ride away. The island has long been a traditional hunting ground for the Tagbanua tribe. It was recently declared a wildlife reserve, and the surrounding waters a marine sanctuary. The cottages are large and directly on the beach and blend into the surrounding wilderness, creating a natural, peaceful mood.

### Inexpensive

An inexpensive option popular with divers is the **Sea Breeze Guest House (** MANILA (2) 922-9750 in Busuanga. **Kalamayan Inn** (no phone) in Coron Town on Malvar and Don Pedro Streets, is a family-operated bed and breakfast with air-conditioned rooms and friendly staff. The bar and restaurant serve Filipino food and the coldest beer in town. **Kokosnuss** (no phone), in Coron Town, has always been a popular stop for divers, and **Dive Link** (no phone), the newest resort in Coron, is set on an island outside the town. It boasts an excellent restaurant, a swimming pool and comfortable cottages with fans.

## HOW TO GET THERE

There are daily flights between Manila and Coron on Pacific Air, Air ADS, and Asian Spirit. You can also take a ship to Coron on Viva Line,

Asuncion Line, or WG&A Superferry. Each has one departure a week, so be sure to check with them to confirm days. Trips range from 24 hours on the slower Asuncion Line to 12 hours on the speedy and more comfortable WG&A Superferry. If you're coming from El Nido you can charter a flight by inquiring at "The White House" in El Nido town.

## THE CUYO ISLANDS

Remote and scarcely touched, the pristine Cuyo Archipelago lies between the sea boundary of the Visayas and Luzon. Its islands are on the ancient trading routes from China to Borneo. They were explored by Miguel Lopez de Legaspi in 1568 and 1569 as he traveled the route that led to the conquest of Manila. The Spanish made the Cuyos part of their strategic defense against the Moro raiders during the seventeenth, eighteenth and early nineteenth centuries and built a string of forts that jut out along the eastern coast of Palawan and Cuyo. This was again repeated during World War II, with the incursions by the Japanese. The people of Cuyo have remained secluded, living mainly from fishing and seaweed gathering.

## AMANPULO

Amanpulo, or "peaceful island" is the best of the best in Philippine island resorts. Created for travelers seeking the idyllic beauty of a tropical island, it is set on a private island, Pamalican, part of the Quiniluban group of Cuyo Islands, within the Sulu Sea. Amanpulo, part of the Aman resort chain, is dreamlike, with a tropical perfection in every detail that cannot fail to soothe even the most finicky jetsetter. It is already a favorite with Hollywood movie stars and elite Asian travelers. But everyone is treated like royalty at Amanpulo.

### The Resort

Surrounded by white sand beaches, turquoise waters and a coral reef set 300 m (984 feet) from shore, Amanpulo ( MANILA (2) 759-4040 FAX (2) 759-4044 or ( UNITED STATES (212) 223-2848 or (800) 447-7462, provides a variety of water sports and beach activities.

There are 40 pavilions, 29 on the beachfront and 11 set amongst landscaped fragrant frangipani and bougainvillea plants. Gracefully and eclectically designed, with touches of Zen elegance, all of the 40 casitas are spacious, modern versions of the traditional Filipino bhay kubo house. Small carts are parked outside each pavilion if you can't be bothered to walk, although it is possible to jog and walk around coastal paths. It is the most sophisticated resort in the Philippines, with the added advantage of having expert diving tuition, facilities and equipment to explore several renowned dive sites in the surrounding reef.

All pavilions make the best possible use of natural light, and watching the constantly changing skyscape becomes addictive. Strategically placed hammocks and verandah deck chairs are poised for perfect sunset viewing. Each pavilion has air conditioning, a rather regal king-size bed, sliding glass panels that open out onto a wraparound wooden terrace, and hushed lighting that gives a lantern effect. Facilities include a telephone, a bar, a television and compact disc player. Bathrooms are splendid, accented by wooden slats and marble. Fresh flowers are placed throughout the pavilion daily. There is an enticing restaurant and bar, with all the sophistication you could want, but you can dine, if you prefer, on your own balcony overlooking the bay.

If all this perfection becomes a bit too much, you can patronize an establishment owned by an islander by the name of Gary, who has set up a small bar, the Amangary, which caters mostly to hotel staff. It is much cheaper and has equally lovely views of the sunset.

The rates for the beach and hillside casitas are US$650-$725 per night, and the treetop casitas cost US$575 per night. Deluxe Hillside Casitas are US$800 per night and the exclusive Nature Villa and West Villa go for a whopping US$2,500-$2,750 a night! An extra person charge of US$75 is applied for all casitas accommodating more than two people. Baby cots are provided free of charge, and as many as two children under 16 years old traveling with their parents stay free of charge. A four-day PADI diving course will cost US$400.

### How to Get There

Two charter flights a day service Pamalican Island from Manila airport. If you are transferring from an international flight, a car will meet your arriving flight and ferry you to the Amanpulo lounge, where you can leave any surplus luggage, should you wish. The cost is US$275 per person round trip and US$138 for children under six years. The aircraft is a 12-seat, pressurized Super Kingair 200; the flight takes 50 minutes. Space is on a first-come, first-served basis, but when the scheduled flight is full, additional flights are sometimes added.

In El Nido, award-winning resorts have been developed so that tourists can live as closely as possible to the environment while still enjoying a certain level of luxury.

# Travelers' Tips

## GETTING THERE

### BY AIR

Most visitors arrive in and depart from Manila's **Ninoy Aquino International Airport** (NAIA) ( (2) 877-1109. Increasingly too, Cebu's **Mactan International Airport** ( (32) 340-2486 or (32) 340-5522 is becoming a well-patronized hub for carriers such as Philippine Airlines and for international charter flights, notably from Sydney, Tokyo, Hong Kong and Singapore. In Luzon, Laoag International Airport is an alternative port of entry for travelers coming from Taipei.

**Philippine Airlines** ( (2) 816-6691 or (2) 832-3011, has seen its fair share of financial losses and uncertainties, and as a result flight service is unpredictable. It is advisable to check with the airline directly to confirm its schedule and services.

Other major airlines with service to Manila include: **Northwest** ( (2) 819-7341, **China Airlines** ( (2) 523-8021, **Cathay Pacific** ( (2) 848-2747, **Japan Airlines** ( (2) 810-9781, **Korean Air** ( (2) 815-8911, **Malaysian Airlines** ( (2) 525-9404, **Singapore Airlines** ( (2) 810-4951, and **Thai Airways** ( (2) 815-8421.

Manila is 16 hours from San Francisco; 15 from Los Angeles; and 22 hours from New York, Toronto, and Montreal. London is 16 hours; Sydney about nine hours.

Internal flights land at **Manila Domestic Airport** ( (2) 832-0991 or 0932.

### BY SEA

#### Freighters

Manila's busy port is served by legions of international vessels, yet few of these offer passenger services. Those that do include **American President Lines** ( (2) 530-0361, 530-0116, 1950 Franklin Street, Oakland, CA 94612, USA, and **Lykes Brothers Steamship Company** TOLL-FREE 008-343-0781, Lykes Center, 300 Poydras Street, New Orleans, LA 70130, USA. Both call in at Manila and other Far East ports between the United States, the Gulf Coast, and Singapore. Freighter passage is typically more expensive than airfare — not really surprising given that passengers spend many nights and take many meals aboard.

#### Sailboat

The Philippines is a popular destination for sailing and as a stop-off en route from Asia or Europe to Australia. If you are interested in joining a crew while in the Philippines, one of the best places to inquire is the **Manila Yacht Club** (2) 526-7868 FAX (2) 523-7183 E-MAIL mycrace@i-manila.com.ph, where a noticeboard solicits sailing partners and advertises boats for sale. The best time to set sail is from December through May, when the chance of a monsoon is less. One constant threat to boats on the open seas is piracy. The Philippines is listed as one of the world's most dangerous sailing regions (along with Indonesia, Somalia, Djibouti, Brazil, China, Hong Kong and Macao), particularly the waters off the coast of Mindanao towards Borneo. The area between Luzon, Hong Kong and China's Hainan Island is also risky. Increasing numbers of vessels are being hijacked; pirates are usually well armed with guns, pistols and knives.

### ARRIVING (AND LEAVING)

If you are coming from the United States, Australia, New Zealand, or Europe you need only have a valid passport and an onward ticket to a destination outside the Philippines. You will be given a visa valid for 21 days. To stay longer, you must apply for a visa extension either from a Philippine Embassy or Consulate in your home country prior to your departure, or from the Commission of Immigration and Deportation (CID), Magallanese Drive, Intramuros, Manila, after you arrive in the Philippines.

Any amount over US$3,000 brought into the country must be declared. You are allowed to bring in 400 cigarettes or two tins of tobacco, and two bottles of alcoholic beverages, not to exceed one liter each. When you leave the Philippines you have to pay a departure tax of P500 (US$20). If you are returning to the United States you may take back US$400 worth of goods purchased in the Philippines. Duty-free items include 200 cigarettes or 100 cigars (no Cuban cigars), a liter of alcohol, and most handicraft goods. Shells, coral, animals, or produce are not allowed.

## FOREIGN EMBASSIES AND CONSULATES IN MANILA

**Arab Republic of Egypt** ( (2) 843-9220, 229 Paraiso Street, Dasmarinas Village, Makati.

**Argentina** ( (2) 810-8301, Sixth Floor, ACT Tower, Señor Gil J. Puyat Avenue, Salcedo Village, Makati.

**Australia** ( (2) 750-2840 or 750-2850, Dona Salustiana S. Ty. Tower, 104 Paseo de Roxas, Makati.

**Brazil** ( (2) 892-8181 or 892-8182, Sixth Floor, RCI Building, 105 Rada Street, Legaspi Village, Makati.

**Canada** ( (2) 810-8861 or 810-8839, Ninth Floor, Allied Bank Center, 6754 Ayala Avenue, Makati.

**China** ( (2) 844-3148 or 843-7715, 4896 Pasay Road, Dasmarinas Village, Makati.

**Germany** ( (2) 892-4906 or 892-1001, Sixth Floor, Solid Bank Building, 777 Paseo de Roxas Street, Makati.

**Indonesia** ( (2) 892-5061, 185 Salcedo Street, Legaspi Village, Makati.

**Japan** ( (2) 551-5710, 2627 Roxas Boulevard, Pasay City.

**Netherlands** ( (2) 812-5981 to 5983, Ninth Floor, King's Court Building, 2129 Pasong Tomo, Makati.

**New Zealand** ( (2) 891-5358 to 5367, 23rd Floor, Far East Bank Center, Señor Gil J. Puyat Avenue, Makati.

**Norway** ( (2) 886-3245 to 3249, 21st Floor, Petron Mega Plaza Building, 358 Señor Gil J. Puyat Avenue, Makati.

**Russian Federation** ( (2) 893-0190 or 844-2460, 1245 Acacia Road, Dasmarinas Village, Makati.

**Singapore** ( (2) 816-1764, Sixth Floor, ODC International Plaza Building, 217-219 Salcedo Street, Legaspi Village, Makati.

**Sweden** ( (2) 819-1951, 16th Floor, PCI Bank Tower II, Makati Avenue, at the corner of De la Costa, Makati.

**Thailand** ( (2) 815-4220, 107 Rada Street, Legaspi Village, Makati.

**United Kingdom** ( (2) 816-7116, 15-17 Floors, LV Locsin Building, 6752 Ayala Avenue, at the corner of Makati Avenue, Makati.

**United States of America** ( (2) 523-1001, 1201 Roxas Boulevard, Ermita.

## PHILIPPINE EMBASSIES AND CONSULATES ABROAD

**Australia**: Philippine Embassy ( (2) 6273 2535, 1 Moonah Place, Yarralumla, ACT 2600. **Consulate** ( (2) 9299 6633, Level 7, Wynyard House, 301 George Stret, Sydney, NSW 2000.
**Canada**: Philippine Embassy ( (613) 233-1121, Suite 606, 103 Albert Street, Ottawa, Ont K1P5G4.
**United Kingdom**: Philippine Embassy ( (020) 7937 1600, 9a Palace Green, London W8 4QE.

**United States**: Philippine Embassy ( (202) 467-9300, 1600 Massachusetts Avenue NW, Washington, D.C. 20036.

## TOURIST INFORMATION

The Philippine Department of Tourism reaches many potential overseas visitors through its branch offices, which will provide brochures and booklets to plan your trip. In Manila, the main DOT office is very helpful, as are the computer printouts that outline accommodation, dining, and tourism attractions in various regions.

### PHILIPPINE DEPARTMENT OF TOURISM OFFICES

**Asia Pacific**
**Philippine Tourism** ( (612) 9299 6815 or 6506 FAX (612) 9299 6817 E-MAIL info@philtourism .com WEBSITE www.philtourism.com, Wynyard House, Suite 703, Level 7, 301 George Street, Sydney 2000 Australia.

Children returning home from a Bohol church.

**Manila Economic and Cultural Office** ( (886 2) 741599 FAX (886 2) 778-4969, Metrobank Plaza 107 Chung Hsioo E. Road Section 4, Taipei, Taiwan, ROC.

**Embassy of the Philippines** ( (816) 5355071 FAX (816) 5351235, 2F Dainan Building, 2-19-23 Shinmachi, Nishi-ku, Osaka 0013, Japan.

**Philippine Consulate-General** ( (852) 866-7643 or 866-6471 FAX (852) 866-6521, Room 6F United Centre, 95 Queensway, Hong Kong.

**Embassy of the Philippines** ( (65) 737-3977 or 235-2184 FAX (65) 733-9544, 20 Nassim Road, Singapore.

### In the United States

**Philippine Center** ( (212) 575-7915 FAX (212) 302-6759, 556 Fifth Avenue, New York, NY 10036.

**Philippine Consulate-General** ( (213) 487-4527 FAX (213) 386-4063, 3660 Wilshire Boulevard, Suite 825, Los Angeles, CA 90010.

**Philippine Consulate-General** ( (415) 956-4060 FAX (415) 956-2093, 447 Sutter Street, San Francisco, CA 94108.

### In Europe

**Philippine Department of Tourism** ( (49-69) 20893-95 FAX (49 69) 285127, Kaiserhof Strasse 7, D-60313 Frankfurt Am Main, Germany or ( (44-20) 7499-5443 or 7499-5652 FAX (44-20) 7499-5772, 17 Albermarle Street, London W1X 7HA, United Kingdom.

## DUTY-FREE SHOPPING

Duty-free shops are located at the departure and transit areas of the NAIA (Ninoy Aquino International Airport) in Manila and the MIA (Mactan International Airport) in Cebu. Just across from the NAIA is the **Duty-free Fiesta Shopping Center**. It is the country's largest duty-free outlet, and carries quality items ranging from international imports to selected Filipino export products.

## GETTING AROUND

Travel throughout the Philippines is generally easy and fairly cheap. Until recently, the air networks — which are extensive — have been dominated by Philippine Airlines. Overbooking used to be a major problem, especially in the peak season. However,

several new airlines have now stepped onto the scene, offering additional flights on popular routes, as well as creating new flights to more remote destinations.

Equally, the island nation's ferry infrastructure has seen dramatic improvements over the past year, as well as the launching of a luxury cruise ship service around the islands. With ferries, try to avoid traveling during inclement weather or if the vessel appears to be overcrowded. And also avoid taking small pump boats or *bancas* at night, when they risk being run down by larger vessels.

Because of the distances between islands, it is usually better to start and end most journeys by airplane. Long-distance buses are the main overland option, although there is a railway line from Manila to southern Luzon. A combination of bus and *banca* usually completes the journey to your destination. Car rental is also available and international agencies have offices in most major cities.

## FROM THE AIRPORT

Airport taxis (private companies that serve the airport) wait around the clock at Manila Airport. Rates are usually fixed; to Makati, the upscale business district, or Ermita, the tourist belt, expect to pay about P500 (US$12). This is much higher than regular taxis but you won't have to bargain with the driver or worry taking a roundabout route.

The major Manila hotels have shuttles; look around for one before using another means of transport. If you have made reservations, your name will appear on a list that the dispatcher has handy, and he will signal the taxi to take you to the hotel. The amount — usually from P450 to P600 (US$11.20–US$14) — will be charged to your bill. It's the easiest way to go, especially when you are jet-lagged.

## CAR RENTAL

From the traffic to thick pollution and exhaust, drivers must have the patience of a saint to venture on Manila's roads. If you must, however, the familiar rental car agencies are here, where you can either rent a car to drive yourself or hire the services of a driver. Hiring a driver is the best way to go, a cheap luxury used by most expatriates and many Filipinos. Hired drivers know the roads and the rules (or lack thereof).

Car-rental agencies in Manila include: **Ace** ( (2) 810-5147 **Avis** ( (2) 535-2206 or (2) 844-8498, **Budget** ( (2) 818-7363 **Dollar** ( (2) 896-9251, **Executive** ( (2) 832-5368, **Hertz** ( (2) 832-0520, and **National** ( (2) 897-9023.

## By Air

Manila's **domestic airport** ( (2) 832-0991 or (2) 832-0932 is the major hub for flights within

Schedules can change during peak seasons. It is best to call the airline and reconfirm your flight a day or two in advance.

Get to the airport early. If you are not there at least 45 minutes before takeoff, there is a possibility of getting bumped off the flight. This is also advisable to save stress, as airports are quite chaotic and crowded.

Airlines impose a "no show" fee for reservations that have not been cancelled.

**Domestic Carriers**
**Philippine Airlines** ( (2) 816-6691 FAX (2)

the Philippines, while Cebu also functions as a minor hub. Philippine Airlines (PAL), the nation's main domestic carrier, flies to 43 destinations within the archipelago, covering the major cities, but also servicing such remote points as Basco in the Batanes Islands and Jolo in the Sulu Archipelago.

Round-trip flights on Philippine Airlines can be booked from overseas, at about US$150. But PAL doesn't fly to the more remote outer islands, where many of the best resorts are located. To reach these resorts, you must travel on small charter planes — best booked through your travel agent or hotel — and their rates are much higher.

Here are some tips to remember when traveling by plane domestically:

816-6938, Fourth Floor, PAL II Building, Legaspi Village, Makati, Manila 1229.
**Aerolift Philippines** ( (2) 817-2369, Fourth Floor, JAKA II Building, 150 Legaspi Street, Legaspi Village, Makati, Manila.
**Air Philippines** ( (2) 843-7770, Seventh Floor, Ramon Magsaysay Building, Roxas Boulevard, Manila.
**Grand Airways** ( (2) 833-8090 FAX (2) 891-7667, Eighth Floor, Philippine Village, Airport Hotel, Airport Road, Pasay City 1301.
**Pacific Airways** ( (2) 832-2731 FAX (2) 832-7692, 3110 Domestic Airport Road, Pasay City 130.
**Asian Spirit** ( (2) 840-3811 to 3816 FAX (2) 813-0183, Ground Floor, LPL Towers, Legaspi Street, Legaspi Village, Makati, Manila.

A flotilla of Samal Boat People, Zamboanga.

**Cebu Pacific (**/FAX (2) 551-1218, Manila Domestic Airport, Pasay City.

**Mindanao Express (** (2) 832-1541 to 1545 FAX (2) 831-0959, Fourth Floor Cargohaus Building, MIA Road, NAIA Complex, Brgy. Vitalez, Paranaque.

Travelers with limited time can investigate the seven-day **Philippine Air Safari** "flightseeing" package offered through many tour organizers. This is an island hop around the country's major attractions, allowing you to see as much of the archipelago as possible within a limited amount of time. The voyage

## BY BOAT

More than ever before, island-hopping travelers are finding the Philippines' ferry system much to their liking. While in the past the country's ferries were more often than not rusty pieces of tin, often overcrowded and late (and with a bad reputation for sinking), in recent years a new breed of craft — super-ferries — has been sweeping the seas, zipping passengers along comfortably and safely.

is adventurous — with an itinerary that includes soaring over the active volcano of Mount Mayon, exploring Sohoton Caves National Park and Bohol's Chocolate Hills, staying overnight on the beautiful island of Camiguin and experiencing Palawan's El Nido, Busuanga Reefs and Calauit Island. Flights are seldom longer than 90 minutes — on twin-engine aircraft — and nights are spent in comfortable selected hotels. The package includes such activities as paddling outrigger canoes, sampling coconut wine and riding water buffalo. Contact **Blue Horizons Travel and Tours (** (2) 848-3901 FAX (2) 848-3909, 20th Floor, Trafalgar Plaza, Makati, an established company, that also offers a range of other tours.

Of the many inter-island shipping companies with scheduled trips to points within the archipelago, **WG&A SuperFerry** and **Suplicio Lines** (see below) have the largest networks and are the most intent on maintaining high standards of comfort and safety. Cabin accommodation ranges from deluxe to economy. Together, these two companies cover most popular destinations including Bohol, Cebu, Davao, Dipolog, Dumaguete, Iloilo, Leyte, Kalibo, Masbate, Surigao, Palawan and Zamboanga.

The voyage from Manila to the Visayas — the most popular trip — usually takes about 20 hours. The popular Cebu–Bohol WG&A SuperFerry trip, however, is considerably shorter, at two and a half-hours.

It is also possible to opt for the most luxurious alternative — the Philippine's first luxury cruise ship, the MV *Mabuhay Sunshine,* which offers four-day, three-night cruise packages from Manila to destinations such as El Nido, Sicogon Island, Iloilo and Cebu. A four-day cruise costs around US$480 per person, including all meals, entertainment activities, land transfers in Manila, service charges and taxes. For reservations contact WG&A Philippines, which also offers tour packages to Cebu, Iloilo and Puerto Princesa, along with participating hotels.

As in many parts of the world, dockyards and ports in the Philippines are not always the most savory places to be. The North Harbor in Manila in particular is infested with suspicious people. When heading to board an inter-island ferry it is wise to be alert — never leave any baggage unattended, and while making your way to your boat, be careful with your belongings. Take off all jewelry and carry backpacks in front of you.

Expect too to be hassled at the ports by swarms of hawkers as you disembark. They won't take no for an answer. To avoid them, simply linger on the ship for a little while longer, and you'll find that the troublemakers are washed away with the batch of people who exit first.

*Travelers' Tips*

Don't be surprised when you are asked to pay a small fee for the "porter," the nice old man you thought was simply volunteering to help you carry your bag to the airplane, boat, or taxi.

### Inter-island Ferries
**WG&A Superferry** ( MANILA (2) 894-3211, Fifth Level, Building B, SM Megamall, Mandaluyong City, Manila, has probably the best reputation of all the inter-island ferries available. Other ferry companies include:
**Sulpicio Lines** ( (2) 252-6271 to 6285, Pier 12, North Harbor, Tondo, Manila.
**Aboitiz** ( (2) 535-9303
**Negros Navigation** ( (2) 816-3481
**Sun Cruises** ( (2) 241-9701, PTA Cruise Terminal, Cultural Center of the Philippines Complex, Roxas Boulevard, Manila.

## By Rail

The service offered by **Philippine National Railways** (PNR) ( (2) 361-1125 is a mess. Trains no longer run north of Manila, traveling south only to Guinobatan in Luzon's Bicol region. There has been hope of a revival of service, particularly to Manila's south in Legazpi City, but as yet, nothing has been initiated to make this happen. You'll find the fares a bit lower than buses, however trips can take longer. Most people, even locals, avoid using the PNR.

## By Bus

Buses are a great way to see the Philippines. Most routes are no more than 10 hours, although a few longer routes run overnight schedules to Southern Luzon, for example.

Both air-conditioned and non-air-conditioned buses travel all the major routes in Metro Manila except Roxas Boulevard. On an air-conditioned bus, the fare starts at P6. Non-air-conditioned bus fares start at P1.50. Tell the conductor where you are going and he will tell you how much you owe. You should always keep your receipt as proof that you have paid. You should be able to tell which buses are reputable by scanning them at the bus stations; avoid the ones with lopsided axles that are dirty, rusty and dented.

Planting rice — the country's staple crop — in Bangaan.

There are about 20 major bus companies in the Philippines and almost as many terminals in Manila. Those closest to downtown Manila and Makati are at Plaza Lawton and along a portion of EDSA in Pasay City.

Some of the Philippines' more reputable and reliable bus companies include:

**BLTB** ( (2) 833-5501, EDSA at Aurora Street, Pasay City.

**Dangwa** ( (2) 731-2859, 1600 Dimasalang, Sampaloc.

**Pantranco** ( (2) 833-5061, Quezon Boulevard, Quezon City.

embellishments: fighting cocks on their hoods, horses prancing on the fenders, loud painted landscapes and scantily-clad women juxtaposed with depictions of Christ's bleeding heart and slogans redolent of Sunday School — "Sacred Heart," "God is Love" or "Praise the Lord" — and a plethora of patron saints.

Jeepneys crisscross Manila and are the cheapest form of travel for areas not served by the LRT, the light-rail system. Holding up to 20 people, they ply the city's secondary and even some major roads. Although there are regular stops, you can generally

**Philtranco** ( (2) 833-1369, EDSA and Apelo Cruz Street, Pasay City.

**Saulog Transit** ( (2) 827-2926 through 827-2930, Quirino Avenue, Paranaque.

**Victory Liner** ( (2) 833-0293, (2) 833-5020 or (2) 832-2456, EDSA, Aurora Street, Pasay City.

## BY JEEPNEY

In Manila and elsewhere, jeepneys are a way of life. Lovingly decorated, these elongated trucks are the principal mode of transport for most Filipinos. Successors to the United States Army jeeps converted into minibuses after World War II, these silver bullets live up to their epithet: "folk art on wheels." Jeepneys are festooned with a host of decorations and

flag one down and hop on just about anywhere — call out "Bayad!" and pay the driver as you embark. If you are too far back, pass your P1.50 down to him. When you are ready to get off, call out "Para!" then wait until he slows down for you to hop off.

The smaller, ubiquitous version of the jeepney is the other urban staple: the tricycle. These smoke-belching motorbike-powered taxis have gaudy oversize sidecar cabins, wide windshields, and vinyl-padded hoods and often have kamikaze drivers.

## BY LIGHT RAIL TRANSIT

The **Light Rail Transit** ( (2) 832-0423 is an elevated, modern railway, with 16 or so stops on its north-south axis. Another line extends along EDSA and continues all the way to Quezon City. The LRT provides the most painless, carbon monoxide-free, traffic-less way to cross the city. Tokens are P5. The LRT is open from 4 AM to 9 PM.

The LRT can be packed at rush hour, so minimize your load while riding.

## By Calesa

These horse-drawn carriages are seen all around **Binondo** (Manila's Chinatown), where they are used by schoolchildren, as well as at Intramuros and the entrance to Rizal Park, where tourists are solicited to experience the Old World charm of a horse-drawn carriage. Calesas are common too elsewhere in the Philippines, notably Cebu and Vigan. Sadly, the horses often look like they are on their last legs. They are mostly good for short excursions around a neighborhood and are cheap at about P30 for a ride.

## ACCOMMODATION

Whether you are looking to rough it and go native style with a squat toilet and a bucket of water, or be pampered with your own butler to open your doors and massage your feet, you can find it all in the Philippines. The major international chains such as the Shangri-La, Intercontinental, Peninsula, and the Holiday Inn are represented in Manila and the more upmarket resort areas. Further afield are the family-owned nipa-style cottages that frame the white sand shores of the country's islands and islets.

The peak season in the Philippines is from November to May. Make sure you have accommodation booked before arrival or be prepared to take your chances. On the more remote islands, such as Palawan, you generally won't have many problems though.

Check with your travel agent, and shop around for special package deals that may be offered — it is possible to find considerable discounts, particularly on the Internet. At some of the smaller beach resorts you can get as much as 40 percent off the advertised rate if bookings are slim.

In this book, accommodation categories are divided into **expensive** (US$120 and above),

mid-range (US$50 to $120) and inexpensive ($US50 and below).

Service is included in most hotels and restaurants (see TIPPING, page 250 below). Unless room rates are specified as a net price, calculate your total bill by adding on a 10 percent service charge and the government tax of between 13.7 percent and 14.6 percent.

## EATING OUT

Spanish, Japanese, Indonesian, Malaysian, and Chinese cooking are among the many

influences found in Filipino food. The result? An infusion of flavors so uniquely the Philippines. Whether you prefer the sour taste of *kinilaw*, the art of sour-cooking fish or meat, or the distinctive garlic and vinegar mix of *adobo* sauces, you'll find that even after your return from your journey here, you will crave that distinctive Filipino taste.

On a tight budget, you can spend as little as P300 (US$6) a day on food if you eat simple rice dishes, like *adobo* or *menudo* at market stalls. Even if you choose to splurge at a hotel restaurant, you won't feel that your wallet empties as your stomach fills. Vegetarians

OPPOSITE: A bus en route to the capital, Tagbilaran in Bohol. ABOVE: Dried fish on sale in Laoag, Ilocos Norte.

might have a tough time, however, as most of the local dishes are heavy on the pork or chicken. If fish is allowed in your diet, then you should be just fine.

Our price categories are based on the average cost of a standard Philippine-style one-course meal per person, excluding drinks:

**Expensive**: Over P500 (US$10)
**Mid-range**: Less than P500 (US$10)
**Inexpensive**: Less than P200 (US$4).

In some more rural areas, where there aren't as many varieties of dining options, the prices tend to be very cheap.

Drinking tap water is not recommended. They say the water in Manila and Cebu is potable, but bottled water is so cheap that it's better to be safe than sorry.

## BASICS

### CURRENCY EXCHANGE

The Philippine peso divides into 100 centavos. Bank notes are available in denominations of 5, 10, 20, 50, 100, 500 and 1000 pesos. Coins range from 25 centavos to P5.

Banks, hotels, foreign exchange dealers, private dealers and major department stores authorized by the Central Bank change most international currencies, generally including travelers' checks. Avoid unauthorized dealers. United States dollar transactions, as well as major credit cards, are widely accepted at larger stores and in more expensive hotels and restaurants in Manila and major cities.

ATMs (Automatic Teller Machine) are fairly easy to find throughout Manila and the major cities.

At press time, approximately P51 equals US$1; P34 to the Canadian dollar; P74 to the British pound, and P26 to the Australian dollar. To keep up-to-date on currency fluctuations check out CNN's interactive **currency conversions** at www.cnnfn.cnn.com/markets/currencies/.

### BUSINESS AND BANKING HOURS

Private and government offices are open either from 8 AM to 5 PM or from 9 AM to 6 PM, Monday through Friday. Some private companies are open on Saturday from 9 AM to noon. Most shopping centers, department stores and supermarkets are open from 10 AM to 7:30 PM daily.

Museums generally close for an hour or two at midday and are rarely open on Sundays and holidays.

Banks are open from 9 AM to 3 PM, Monday through Friday.

### TIPPING

Tipping is standard practice in the Philippines. Ten percent of the total bill is usual for waiters and hotel personnel. Most hotels and restaurants, however, automatically add this charge to your bill, in which case additional tips are optional. Five to ten pesos is sufficient for bell boys and porters, though if your luggage is difficult to handle, pay more. Taxi drivers are usually tipped.

### ELECTRICITY

Voltage is 220 AC, 60 cycles. Most hotels in Manila, and larger hotels throughout the Philippines, have 110- and 220-volt outlets.

### TIME

The Philippines clock is set at Greenwich Mean Time (GMT) plus eight hours.

## COMMUNICATION AND MEDIA

### TELEPHONE

The **country code** for the Philippines is 63. To place a **direct international call** from the Philippines, dial the Philippines' international access code (00), the international country code (for the United States and Canada 1, for the United Kingdom 44, for Australia 61, and for New Zealand 62), then the area or city code, then the number.

Most hotel rooms have IDD (International Direct Dialing) phones. USADirect is a 24-hour service for calls to the United States collect, without passing through a local operator. The international access code is 105-12 to reach an AT&T operator; 10515 for MCI; and 10517 for Sprint.

**Local phone calls** are untimed, except for pay phones, which cost P2 for three minutes. For **directory assistance** dial 114.

To make a call from one area to another within the Philippines, first dial the national access prefix 0, followed by the local area code.

## Area Codes within the Philippines

Angeles 455
Bacolod 34
Baguio 74
Banaue 73
Batangas 43
Bohol 38
Boracay 36
Cagayan de Oro 8822
Camiguin 88
Cebu 32
Davao 82
Dipilog 65
Manila 2
Mindoro 43
Pampanga 45
Puerto Princesa 48
Tagaytay 96
Zamboanga 62, 65

## NEWSPAPERS

Most newspapers published in the Philippines are in English: including the *Manila Bulletin, Philippine Daily Inquirer, Manila Chronicle, Manila Times* and *Philippine Daily Globe*. There is also a wide selection of magazines and major English-language newspapers and magazines — *Far Eastern Economic Review, International Herald Tribune, Newsweek, Asiaweek, Time* — at hotel bookshops and large stores.

## TELEVISION AND RADIO

Television programming runs from approximately noon to midnight, showing quantities of American-produced shows as well as Filipino. In some areas it is possible to receive CNN and ABC and other channels on the STAR satellite system.

Both AM and FM radio stations broadcast throughout the day and night, with primarily Tagalog on the AM stations and English on the FM stations.

## POSTAL SERVICES

Most hotels in Manila and other cities can send mail for you and provide stamps. The

Manila General Post Office ( (2) 527-8327 or (2) 527-0069, Plaza Lawton, Manila is best for sending packages, and has a poste restante desk.

The **American Express** office ( (2) 521-9492 Philam Life Building, Ground Floor, United Nations Avenue, Ermita, Manila, can also hold mail for you.

For letters to foreign countries, stamps cost P13, or P8 for a postcard or an aerogram.

## THE INTERNET

If the "Love Bug" virus, which originated in the Philippines and caused havoc to businesses and governments across the world in 2000, is any indication, the country is quite advanced when it comes to cyberspace. The many Internet cafés found throughout the country, even in rural areas, only proves this to be true. Connections may not be as fast as you are used to, but services are cheap and systems pretty current.

Wherever there are phone lines, you can bet someone is connected. Most of Manila's hotels and resorts have access to the Internet and there are cybercafés throughout Manila, Baguio, Cebu and other cities throughout the archipelago.

## ETIQUETTE

Filipino hospitality is legendary. However, in honoring that hospitality, being aware of the dos and don'ts is important.

Be cordial and patient when asking a question, and be sure to introduce your question by asking first, "May I ask a question?" Their hospitality is wonderful in one sense, but to many visitors the Filipino inability to say no or be direct when answering a question can be frustrating. And as with any sensitive issue in any country, be considerate when political or economic topics arise.

Filipinos are, though, generally proud to answer questions about their family, especially about their children, and will often politely inquire about your family.

Be aware of your voice volume and body gestures. Raising your voice, yelling, contradicting, and pointing at people are all shunned upon.

The Filipino's are pretty camera-friendly — ready to flash that classic smile. However, tribespeople in the highlands may expect payment of a few pesos to get a picture.

**A Few Tips:**
Elders are greatly respected in rural areas, greet them first when approaching a group. It is customary to take off your shoes before entering a Filipino home. Take a taste of food when offered, and remember to leave some food on your plate to show that you've had enough.

At business meetings, punctuality is valued (if not in social gatherings) — be sure to bring along your business cards, as Filipinos like to know who they are dealing with.

## HEALTH

The Philippines is not a high-risk destination, but like most tropical Asian countries, there are precautions to take. Vaccinations are only mandatory for visitors who have been to a cholera-infected or yellow fever region in the six days before arriving in the Philippines. It is wise, though, to have booster shots for cholera, typhoid, tetanus (especially for divers and snorkelers) and hepatitis. While not essential, it also a good idea to be immunized against smallpox, polio, diphtheria, and measles.

**Malaria** can be a problem in parts of the archipelago, such as Palawan, where the female anopheles mosquito is the culprit. Visitors are advised to protect themselves by covering up after dark and by taking antimalarial tablets. These days, with controversy over side effects, Larium is considered

the most effective choice. The malarial parasite has long become resistant to the historic antimalarial standby, quinine, and synthetic vaccines such as Chloroquine should be taken. Pregnant women especially should seek advice before taking antimalaria drugs.

If you thought you were safe in the day — think again. **Dengue fever**, another deadly disease transmitted through mosquitos, is found in female mosquitoes that are out in the early morning hours. There have been epidemics in the last few years, so be aware of symptoms — headache, fever and skin rashes — and see a doctor right away if you have any.

Next to mosquitoes, heat is the major health threat in the Philippines. The heat and humidity in Manila mixed with the lingering smog and pollution creates quite an unhospitable environment. Hydrate, hydrate, hydrate! That's the best preventative from heat exhaustion and sunstroke. When exposed to the sun on the beaches, definitely use sunscreen to prevent burns, and hats or umbrellas to avoid heat exposure.

Nothing can be worse than that sinking feeling one gets when **seasickness** begins to work its way from the stomach into the throat. Exploring an island nation will require many boat trips. If you are susceptible to seasickness be sure to pack motion-sickness medication. The tablets must be taken before setting sail — by the time you are feeling sick it's too late. Another tip: keep your eyes on the horizon and stay on top of the boat. Avoid going inside the bathroom until your body has had a chance to adjust to the movement.

Although tap water in the Philippines is generally suitable to drink, you may wish to stick to bottled water or use purification tablets. Sampling raw (unwashed and unpeeled) fruit and vegetables and unpasteurized dairy products, or patronizing insalubrious-looking restaurants, may be asking for trouble. Make sure you have antiseptic cream for treating cuts and scratches, especially from coral. Be wary of walking barefoot (except on the beach), since the Philippines has its share of microscopic parasites and worms that can burrow into the skin.

And a word on toilets — you won't find many toilet seats. The good old-fashioned squat toilets and a handy bucket of water are the norm in the more rural areas. You'll be surprised how efficient and easy this mode of toilet is!

Given the scale of the sex industry in the Philippines — which the government has been trying to crack down on — the grim statistics about the AIDS boom in Asia are worth bearing in mind. According to the World Heath Organization, the Philippines remains a low HIV-prevalent country. Epidemiologists think the estimate is too low, and health workers believe the Philippines could be headed for an AIDS disaster

Suite 400, Washington, DC 20005, or **Divers Alert Network** (DAN) ( us (800) 446-2671 or (919) 684-2948, which specilaizes in insuring scuba-divers.

The **International Association for Medical Assistance to Travelers** (IAMAT) ( (716) 754-4883 WEB SITE www.sentex.net/~iamat) offers tips on travel and health concerns in many countries, and lists local English-speaking doctors. **International SOS Assistance** ( us (800) 523-8930 or (215) 244-1500, PO Box 11568, Philadelphia, PA 11916, is an assistance company only.

because of rampant prostitution and the opposition of the Roman Catholic Church to educational programs about AIDS.

Medical facilities are fairly good for emergencies, diagnostic tests, and dispensing medication; most general hospitals are private. In Manila, the **Makati Medical Center** ( (2) 815-9911 or 892-5544 Legaspi Village is the best. Health insurance is best arranged before you depart your home country. Keep in mind though that many insurance companies don't cover injuries that result from "risky" activities like diving or hiking.

Of companies specializing in accident or medical care try **Travel Assistance International** ( us (800) 821-2828 or (202) 828-5894 FAX (202) 828-5896 1133 15th Street, NW,

## SECURITY

As a rule, crime in the Philippines is not directed at travelers. All the same, it is wise to be alert, especially in Manila.

Kidnappings and murders are not uncommon in certain parts of the Philippines. Travelers have recently been advised to stay away from portions of Mindanao, particularly the southern islands of the Sulu Archipelago, where rebels and pirates can pose a security threat. The Philippine government and the Moro National Liberation Front (MNLF) signed a peace agreement in 1996 to end the MNLF's 24-year military struggle for

OPPOSITE and ABOVE: Faces from Ilocos Sur Province.

autonomy in Mindanao. However, peace remains elusive following the rise of the militant Moro Islamic Liberation Front (MILF), which opposes the agreement. Considering the recent kidnappings of tourists and divers in that part of the country, its probably best to just stay away or at the very least proceed cautiously.

Gang thefts are the most common crimes reported by tourists to the police. The modus operandi is to befriend the potential theft victim with offers of hospitality in a bar, restaurant or other tourist spot, and then to drug

them with a strong sedative such as Ativan. Police say that victims are rarely harmed. Tourists should be on the lookout for thieves and tricksters (such as fake policeman and immigration officers wanting to impose on-the-spot fines), especially around Ermita and Malate.

Precautions are a matter of common sense. Obviously if you are flaunting cash or wearing expensive jewelry, or leave your room unlocked, you are asking for trouble. It is best to keep valuables and excess cash in your hotel's safe-deposit box until you need them. When walking around, keep your money, passports, and camera hidden. Consider wearing a money belt, or a small purse tucked into your pants with the straps well hidden under a shirt.

## WOMEN TRAVELERS

Women traveling together or alone will find touring the Philippines particularly pleasant. You will rarely, if ever, be approached or hassled by strangers. Feel free to start a conversation with a stranger without fear of misinterpretation, although it's still not advisable to take risks that you wouldn't normally take at home.

Locals may ask repeatedly where your husband or partner is. Don't feel threatened by this, as it is simply curiosity. You may have to take more care than your male counterpart does, however, to dress modestly, meaning no cleavage or midriff-baring tops, mini-skirts, or short shorts. Otherwise, you risk offending people on the grounds of either religious or local moral standards. Expect Filipinos to be warm, friendly people, who with even the slightest encouragement will go out of their way to be helpful.

## EMERGENCIES

Emergency services are pretty reliable in Manila. On remote islands such as Palawan, however, expect the grocer clerk to wear many hats (police chief, fire chief, judge, and doctor). For **immediate emergency assistance**, dial ( 166 or 168.

In Manila, the **Tourist Assistance Police** ( (2) 524-1660 or (2) 524-1724 can assist in cases of theft or other unfortunate incidents. They operate 24 hours a day.

The US State Department's **24-hour travel advisory service** ( (202) 627-5225 WEB SITE www.travel.state.gov/travel_warnings .html, lists the latest information on diseases or dangers affecting countries. Check to see if certain parts of the Philippines, particularly the southern region of Mindanao are unadvisable for travel.

## WHEN TO GO

The best time to go to the Philippines is between December and early May, during the dry season: January is the perfect month to visit. May can be hot, averaging 28°C (83°F). May is harvest — and fiesta — time. This peak time is also when you will find the most crowds and highest prices, so keep that in mind. The southwest monsoon brings on the rains from June to October, with July and August being the wettest month. If you're planning to head to the mountain provinces for hiking or caving during this season, expect roads to be muddy (sometimes impassable) and flights to these areas unpredictable. This is also the time when typhoons sweep through, although they are usually predicted far enough in advance to plan around them. Flexibility is the key if you arrive during this season. Keep in mind that Mindanao lies outside the typhoon belt, as does some of Palawan, so if you plan your trip well you can catch sunny dry weather at any time of year.

## NATIONAL HOLIDAYS

January 1    New Year's Day
April 9    Day of Valor
May 1    Labor Day
June 12    Independence Day
November 1    All Saint's Day
November 30    Bonifacio Day
December 25    Christmas Day
December 30    Rizal Day

During Holy Week, Maundy Thursday and Good Friday are holidays.

## WHAT TO BRING

The answer is — as little as possible. Light and loose clothes are the most practical and comfortable when walking or traveling. At an island resort, a shirt and shorts or a sarong over your swimwear will take you anywhere. Hats and sunglasses are essential as the tropical sun can be extremely hot. Bring a sweater, long trousers and socks if you are traveling into the mountains, and good waterproof walking shoes or sandals if you are planning to explore mountain trails or caves.

At formal gatherings, appropriate attire for women is a matter of personal discretion. If you plan on frequenting any of the well-to-do clubs and bars in the cities, be sure to bring or buy nice shoes. They don't accept any Teva-toting travelers. For men, if you attend any event that would normally require a jacket and tie (a curse in this weather) you can opt for a *barong tagalog* — an embroidered shirt that is considered

formal dress, usually worn with black trousers. They cost about P1,000.

Otherwise, general necessities include any prescription medications you may need (although department stores and pharmacies do stock patent medicines and prescription), sunscreen lotion, mosquito repellent and a first-aid kit. Depending on where you plan to go and how much yiou plan on roughing it, you may appreciate a raincoat or poncho, a flashlight, a Swiss Army knife, a travel alarm clock, a sleeping bag for overnight ferry trips and a padlock.

## PHOTOGRAPHY

There are many camera equipment shops in Manila. **One Stop Photo Center** ( (2) 633-5041, with branches in the SM Megamall and in the Shangri-La Plaza in Makati, provide developing and camera equipment. There are also photo labs for enthusiasts who want more specialized developing: **New City Studio Photography** ( (2) 636-4891 is one such lab, located at Robinson's Galleria on Ortigas Avenue.

Slide film and black-and-white film are hard to find, so be sure to bring enough from home. Also, if you want to be sure to get

OPPOSITE: Herbal medicine for sale outside Quiapo Church, Manila. ABOVE: Carbon Market, Cebu City.

fantastic shots of the rice terraces, chocolate hills, and other sites, a telephoto lens to 80mm is recommended. Be sure to bring protective cases for all lenses and cameras, as the humidity and rain can easily cause damage to your equipment.

## LANGUAGE

Although over 100 regional languages are spoken in the Philippines, the national language is Tagalog, with the second most widely spoken language being English. All business, governmental, and legal transactions are conducted in English. Although you can easily get by in the Philippines with English, you may wish to endear yourself by trying to speak Tagalog. Even if your accent is wrong, most Filipinos will be pleased that you are attempting to speak their language.

*Mabuhay*, the word tourists frequently encounter, means welcome, or long life. *Po* and *ho* are traditional expressions of respect still used widely, especially when addressing elders. *Salamat* or "thank-you," as in many cultures, is always appreciated. The Spanish influence is ever-present in the language of the Philippines, especially for basic words like *cuchara* (spoon), *ventana* (window) and *guapo* (handsome).

### BASIC EXPRESSIONS

yes   *opo*
no   *hindi po*
How are you?   *Kumusta po sila?*
I'm well, thank-you   *Mabuti po naman*
Good morning   *Magandang umaga po*
Good afternoon   *Magandang hapon po*
Good evening   *Magandang gabi po*
Good-bye   *Palaam na po*
Please come in   *Tuloy po kayo*
Please sit down   *Maupo ho kayo*
Please drive slowly   *Dahan-dahan po lang*
May I take a photo?
   *Maari po ba kayong kunan ng retrato?*
I cannot speak Tagalog
   *Hindi po ako nagsasalita ng Tagalog*
What do you call this in Tagalog?
   *Ano pong tawag dito sa Tagalog?*
Where do you live?   *Saan po kayo nakatira?*
where   *saan*

left   *kaliwa*
right   *kanan*
straight   *derecho*
Slow down   *Dahan-dahan*
Stop here   *Dito lanf*
Be careful   *Konting ingat lang*
entrance   *pasukan*
exit   *labasan*
enough   *tama na*
too much   *masyadong marami*
hot   *mainit*
cold   *malamig*
water   *tubig*
delicious   *masarap*
sweet   *matamis*
hungry   *nagugutom*
thirsty   *nauuhaw*
sleepy   *inaantok*
old   *matanda*
young   *bata*
big   *malaki*
small   *maliit*
to like   *magustuhan*
I want to go to …   *Gusto kong pumanta sa …*
Do you have?   *Meron ba kayong?*
I want more ...   *Gusto ko pa ng ...*
Bill, please   *Ang bil nga*

## WEB SITES

**www.philippine.org** is a great site for up-to-date information on transportation options and other practical information on most of the country's provinces.

**www.asiatravel.com** is a useful site to turn to for information on accommodations, particularly any promo rates that might be offered.

**www.sino.net/asean/philippn.html** provides practical tourist information, updates on visas, festivals, weather, accommodations, and more.

Dive Buddies Philippines, **www.divephil.com**, provides realms of information on diving in the Philippines' various provinces.

Asia Gateway, **www.asiagateway.com/Philippines/**, is the place for those interested in learning more about the Philippines business and financial markets.

**soar.berkeley.edu/recipes/ethnic/filipino/indexall.html** is a welcome source of Filipino recipes, just in case you are curious about cuisine before taking off, or craving the taste after your return.

# Recommended Reading

CREIGHTON MILLER, STUART. *Benevolent Assimilation: The American Conquest of the Philippines, 1942-1945.* University of Kentucky Press, 1996. An evaluation of America's influence in the Philippines during their occupation.

SAN JUAN, E., JR. *After Post-Colonialism.* Rowman and Littlefield, 2000. A tough analysis of modern Philippine history — its conficts, crisis, and struggle for identity.

FENTON, JAMES. *All the Wrong Places: Adrift in the Politics of the Pacific Rim.* Boston, Atlantic Monthly Press, 1988. A personal travel anthology through the Philippines and Southeast Asia, by a specialist in the politics of the region.

GELLE, GERRY. *Filipino Cuisine: Recipes from the Islands.* Red Crane, 1997. A close-up of the regional cooking styles of the archipelago.

HAGEDORN, JESSICA. *Dogeaters.* Penguin, 1991. A spirited novel about Manila by a Filipino-American author and poet.

HAMILTON-PATERSON, JAMES. *Ghosts of Manila.* New York, Vintage Press, 1988. A novel about the harshness of Manila and the struggle of its people.

HAMILTON-PATERSON, JAMES. *Playing With Water — Alone on a Philippine Island.* New York, Sceptre Books, 1987. This beautifully written book follows the author's inner and outer journey on a remote Philippine island.

IYER, PICO. *Video Night in Kathmandu: And Other Reports from the Not-So-Far East.* New York, Vintage Press, 1988. *Time* magazine writer Pico Iyer looks at today's Asia: Mohawk haircuts in Bali, yuppies in Hong Kong, and karaoke in Manila.

JUSTINIANI MCREYNOLDS, PATRICIA. *Almost American: A Quest for Dignity.* Red Crane Books, 1997. An autobiographical account of growing up half-Filipino in America.

KARNOW, STANLEY. *America's Empire in the Philippines.* New York, Random House, 1989. Putlitzer prize winning coverage of how America influenced its one true foreign colony — the Philippines.

LAPHAM, ROBERT and BERNARD NORLING. *Lapham's Raiders: Guerrillas in the Philippines, 1942-1945.* University of Kentucky Press, 1996. A true story of Lieutenant Lapham's influence over guerilla activity throughout the Pacific Rim during the Japanese occupation.

REID, ROBERT H. and EILEEN GUERRERO. *Corazon Aquino and the Brushfire Revolution.* Baton Rouge, Louisiana State University Press, 1995. An evocative look at the changes that took place under Aquino's administration.

WURFEL, DAVID. *Filipino Politics: Development and Decay.* Cornell University Press, 1991. An overview of the country's handling and mishandling of international relations and domestic issues through various administrations.

SMITH, D., M. WESTLAKE, and C. PORTFIRIO. *Diver's Guide to the Philippines.* Unicorn Books Limited, Hong Kong, 1982. Although a little outdated, this remains the most comprehensive guide to the Philippines' best dive locations.

# Photo Credits

Alain Evrard: title page, pages 3, 4, 7 (right), 14 (bottom), 21, 24, 26 (bottom), 41, 50, 51, 52, 53, 55, 64, 65, 66, 67, 68, 70, 75 (left and right), 84, 85, 89, 90, 100, 102, 105, 106, 125, 128, 135, 143, 150, 154, 161, 182, 183, 196, 197, 198, 199, 206, 209, 216, 233, 241, 252, 253, 254.

Robert Holmes: pages 5 (left and right), 6 (left), 10, 12 (top and bottom), 14 (top), 15, 19, 22, 25, 29, 31, 33, 34, 35, 38, 57, 61, 69, 82, 92, 103, 119, 129, 131, 132, 133, 136, 139, 140, 141, 142, 148, 151, 153, 195, 220, 221, 222, 225, 226, 229, 230, 232, 235, 237, 238, 240, 246, 249.

Fiona Nichols: pages 11, 27, 30, 42, 44, 45, 46, 58 (right), 159, 163, 176, 188 (top), 243.

Nik Wheeler: pages 6 (right), 7 (left), 16, 18, 23, 26 (top), 37, 39, 47, 48, 49, 54, 58 (left), 63, 71, 72, 74, 76, 78, 79, 83, 87, 93, 99, 104, 109, 111, 112, 116, 145, 147, 162, 164, 167, 168, 170, 174, 177, 179, 185, 186, 187 (left and right), 188 ( bottom), 202, 203, 205, 207 (left and right), 210, 211 (left and right), 213, 214, 217, 218 (left and right), 219, 245, 248, 255.

# Quick Reference A–Z Guide
## to Places and Topics of Interest with Listed Accommodation, Restaurants and Useful Telephone Numbers

The symbols Ⓕ FAX, Ⓣ TOLL-FREE, Ⓔ E-MAIL, Ⓦ WEB-SITE refer to additional contact information found in the chapter listings.